THE
EVERYTHING®
American Presidents Book

Dear Reader,

The forty-two men who have held the title of commander-in-chief of the United States are extraordinary individuals who all had the ambition to rise to the top. While not all of them have earned accolades from historians, each provides a fascinating story for us to tell.

We each got our love of American history from our parents. Reading the biographies of these great men was something that we learned to love from a young age. Their stories have at times surprised, inspired, saddened, and amused us as we researched and wrote this book. You can read this book in order to gain an understanding of how the presidency has evolved over time based on the individual personalities of the presidents, or you can choose to read it as a series of individual vignettes. Either way, we hope that you find the information here fascinating, entertaining, and enlightening as you learn about the men who have been elected chief executive of the United States of America.

Sincerely,

Martin Kelly   *Melissa Kelly*

The EVERYTHING® Series

Editorial

Publisher	Gary M. Krebs
Director of Product Development	Paula Munier
Managing Editor	Laura M. Daly
Associate Copy Chief	Sheila Zwiebel
Acquisitions Editor	Lisa Laing
Development Editor	Brett Palana-Shanahan
Associate Production Editor	Casey Ebert

Production

Director of Manufacturing	Susan Beale
Production Project Manager	Michelle Roy Kelly
Prepress	Erick DaCosta
	Matt LeBlanc
Interior Layout	Heather Barrett
	Brewster Brownville
	Colleen Cunningham
	Jennifer Oliveira
Cover Design	Erin Alexander
	Stephanie Chrusz
	Frank Rivera

Welcome to the EVERYTHING® Series!

These handy, accessible books give you all you need to tackle a difficult project, gain a new hobby, comprehend a fascinating topic, prepare for an exam, or even brush up on something you learned back in school but have since forgotten.

You can read an *EVERYTHING*® book from cover to cover or just pick out the information you want from our four useful boxes: presidential trivia, scandals and gossip, in their own words, and quirks and oddities. We literally give you everything you need to know on the subject, but throw in a lot of fun stuff along the way, too.

We now have well over 300 *EVERYTHING*® books in print, spanning such wide-ranging categories as weddings, pregnancy, cooking, music instruction, foreign language, crafts, pets, New Age, and so much more. When you're done reading them all, you can finally say you know *EVERYTHING*®!

SCANDALS & GOSSIP

Crimes, rumors, and bad decisions

PRESIDENTIAL TRIVIA

Presidential sound bytes

QUIRKS & ODDITIES

Personalities and eccentricities

IN THEIR OWN WORDS...

Presidential words of wisdom

THE
EVERYTHING®
AMERICAN PRESIDENTS BOOK

All you need to know about the leaders
who shaped U.S. history

Martin Kelly and Melissa Kelly

▲

Adams Media
Avon, Massachusetts

This book is dedicated to our beautiful and precious children,
Ty and Jess.

———————

An Everything® Series Book.
Everything® and everything.com® are registered trademarks of F+W Publications, Inc.

Published by Adams Media, an F+W Publications Company
57 Littlefield Street, Avon, MA 02322 U.S.A.
www.adamsmedia.com

ISBN 10: 1-59869-258-5
ISBN 13: 978-1-59869-258-7

Printed in the United States of America.

J   I   H   G   F   E   D   C   B   A

Library of Congress Cataloging-in-Publication Data
available from the publisher.

This book is available at quantity discounts for bulk purchases.
For information, please call 1-800-289-0963.

Contents

Acknowledgments

We would like to acknowledge the following people who helped make this work possible: Barb Doyen, our agent; Lisa Laing and Brett Palana-Shanahan at Adams Media; our amazing son Ty who, for a six year old, showed tremendous patience and made us laugh; our daughter Jessalyn, born while this book was being written, for being so beautiful and for actually taking naps; Mom and Dad Rawe, without whose help we would definitely not have been able to complete this work; Amy, Jimmy, and Teresa, Sonja and Jeff, and Tommy, for their love and support; Jenna for her infectious smile, Katie for her sense of humor, and Ali for her gentle ways; Jay for his magic tricks and Cara for her quiet intelligence.

We would like to recognize the staff at the Florida Virtual School who are truly leaders in the field of education. They bring passion to their job every day, inspiring with their commitment to excellence.

We would both like to thank all of the history teachers and professors we have had over the years who shared with us the amazing stories of the past, especially Dr. Lansing, Dr. Geary, Dr. McCord, and Dr. Jackie Young. Finally, we'd like to recognize our parents, Jon and Linda Kolb and Jim and Barbara Rawe for giving each of us a love of history and of learning.

Top Ten Things You Might Not Know about the Presidents

1. John Adams, patriot and founding father, actually defended the British soldiers involved in the Boston Massacre.

2. In 1796, Federalist candidate John Adams won the presidency while his opponent, Democratic-Republican Thomas Jefferson, was selected to be vice president. This was the only time that candidates from different parties held the two top positions in the executive branch.

3. John Tyler was the only president to join the Confederacy.

4. Grover Cleveland married a woman twenty-eight years his junior.

5. William Howard Taft's goal was actually not the White House but instead the Supreme Court. He got his wish when he became chief justice in 1921.

6. While living in the White House, President Hoover and his wife would sometimes speak in Mandarin Chinese, possibly to avoid eavesdroppers.

7. When Woodrow Wilson suffered a stroke during his presidency, his wife, Edith, took control and acted as the gatekeeper, deciding which issues were important enough to be brought before the president.

8. The press and pollsters had awarded the 1948 election to Republican candidate Thomas Dewey. However, Harry S. Truman actually won, forcing polling groups like the Gallup Organization to change their polling strategies.

9. Dwight D. Eisenhower never personally saw any field combat despite being in the military for thirty-five years and two world wars.

10. Gerald Ford was such a good football player that he was given offers to play professionally for both the Detroit Lions and the Green Bay Packers.

The Presidency: An Exclusive Club

The American presidency is an exclusive club to which only forty-two men have been invited. The presidency has evolved over time to become one of the most powerful executive offices in democratic society. While the president can personally earn respect both within the nation and on the world stage, it is the office of the president that conveys the full power and might of the United States. In our changing world, this power has affected and been impacted by world events.

The presidency of George Washington was as different from that of Abraham Lincoln as Lincoln's was from that of our current chief executive. This changing role is reflected in the amount of power that the executive has been given over time along with changes in the roles that the president must take on.

Roles of the President

The president of the United States must, in fact, take on at least seven different roles, five of which are constitutionally defined:

- **Chief of State**—The ceremonial head of the government.
- **Chief Executive**—The CEO of the United States, wielding power in both domestic and foreign affairs while leading one of the largest bureaucracies in the world, which currently has a budget exceeding two trillion dollars.
- **Chief Diplomat**—The individual who sets America's foreign policy and acts as the spokesperson for the United States with foreign powers.
- **Commander-in-Chief**—The head of the armed forces.
- **Chief Legislator**—The administrator who creates an agenda for public policy and endeavors to get it approved by Congress.
- **Chief of Party**—Though not listed in the Constitution, the head of their political party once they take office.
- **Chief Citizen**—The person who represents the people and their interests economically and otherwise.

Obviously, it can be extremely difficult for any one person to fulfill all of these roles effectively.

IN THEIR OWN WORDS...

Being president is a task that requires stamina and vision. It is not a job for the weakhearted. As John F. Kennedy said: "No easy problem ever comes to the president of the United States. If they are easy to solve, somebody else has solved them."

In fact, each president has had his own strengths and weaknesses. For example, some presidents, like Harry S. Truman, enjoyed the trappings of the presidency and reveled in their role as the ceremonial head of the government; others, like Thomas Jefferson, shunned this type of public attention and were often mistaken for common people. Richard Nixon spent much of his time in office building relationships with the Russians and the Chinese in his capacity as chief diplomat, while George Washington argued against foreign entanglements and in favor of neutrality.

Becoming the President

What does it take to be the president of the United States? A college degree? Good grades? A wealthy family? Actually, none of these is required. The United States has had presidents who came from poverty, who had little or no formal education, and who have not done well in school.

The Constitution only includes three formal requirements:

1. Must be a natural born citizen.
2. Must be at least thirty-five years old.
3. Must have resided in the United States for at least fourteen years. Those years do not have to have been consecutive or recent.

Of course, there are other qualifications not listed in the Constitution that have evolved over time. With the rise of mass media, the president has increasingly needed to appeal broadly to various groups in society. Before assuming the office, presidents typically have held some other public office or, in rarer cases, have had a stellar military career. There have been presidents who won in the past but who might not be elected today. For example, it would be hard to imagine electing a president today with a high, shrill voice (John Quincy Adams), or one who was the father of an illegitimate child that was kept in an orphanage before being adopted (Grover Cleveland), or one whose favorite hobby was cockfighting (Andrew Jackson). However, it would all depend on the media packaging and the charisma of the presidential candidate involved.

Richard Nixon seemed like a shoe-in going into his election against John F. Kennedy in 1960. However, once he met with Kennedy in a series of televised debates, his lead shrunk considerably. His haggard appearance and lack of makeup compared to Kennedy's tanned, all-American look made Nixon seem lackluster at best. Many credit the first debate with the beginning of the end for Nixon in the election.

The Nominating Process

Before running for the presidency, a person has to be nominated. In America, we have developed a two-party system. Even though third parties exist and their members have run in presidential elections throughout history, they are not considered major parties. These parties fulfill important roles like bringing up important issues and protesting certain policies. However, the true contenders for the presidency have typically come from two major parties, which today are the Democratic and the Republican parties.

At first, the individuals who were nominated to run for president were handpicked by small groups or caucuses. The congressional caucuses were used from 1800 to 1824. However, these were seen as corrupt and, by 1832, both parties had moved on to using national conventions. Conventions were at first controlled by a small group of individuals.

To combat this, the presidential primary was introduced, in which citizens (either intraparty or interparty) vote for the presidential nominee. Today, this system is complicated with some states holding all primary elections (Florida), some states holding just caucuses (Iowa), and some parties within states holding either a primary or a caucus (New Mexico, for example, has a caucus for the Democrats and a primary for the Republicans). The results of these primaries and caucuses are used to determine which delegates get sent to the national convention for each party where the nation's candidate is chosen.

Popular Versus Electoral Vote

Once the candidates are determined, they begin running against each other. In primaries candidates often run against members of their own party who will then become their supporters in the national election. The American governmental system is set up in such a way that the president is not actually chosen directly by popular vote. Instead, we have an electoral college system.

The founding fathers set up a system wherein the popular vote determines who becomes a member of the House of Representatives in Congress, the states determine who becomes a senator, and the elite decide who becomes president based on how the people vote for this position. Their goal was to keep the presidency from becoming a popularity contest and being subject to the "tyranny of the majority."

Thus, the electoral college system is based on the popular vote. Each state is given a number of electors equal to their membership in Congress. For example, small states who have only one representative are given three electoral college votes. According to the twenty-third amendment, Washington, D.C., is also given three votes.

Each state is allowed to determine who becomes an elector. All but two states use a winner-take-all system wherein whoever won the popular vote for the state—even if by only one vote—gets all the electors for the state. For example, George W. Bush received all twenty-five electors for the state of Florida even though it was eventually determined that he won by only 537 votes in the state. On the other hand, Maine and Nebraska use a proportional system wherein the electors are divided according to the results of the popular election.

QUIRKS & ODDITIES

Despite the method for determining electors for a state, electors themselves are not compelled to vote with the people. Faithless electors are those who do not vote for the candidate they were chosen to represent. Electors are meant to check the popular vote, so this leeway is central to their charge.

The electoral system has resulted in the election of presidents who did not win the popular vote. These include the Hayes/Tilden, Jackson/John Quincy Adams, and Bush/Gore races. In each of these cases, the person who won the plurality of the people's votes did not win the presidency. It is also common for someone to win the presidency without winning the majority of the popular vote (more than 51 percent).

Powers of the Presidency

The president of the United States is often regarded as the most powerful person in the world. However, the power of the president to get things done is often determined by the degree with which he won the presidency and his popularity among the people.

Constitutional Powers of the President

The president of the United States is given numerous constitutional powers. The framers of the Constitution, while seeing the need for a president who had broad powers, did not want to create a tyrant or a dictator. To combat this, each of the president's constitutional powers is checked by powers granted to the other two branches of government (the legislative and the judicial). The presidential powers include:

- The power to execute and administer the laws
- The power to appoint ambassadors, Supreme Court justices, and all other officers whose appointments are not specifically mentioned in the Constitution
- The power to receive ambassadors, thereby recognizing foreign governments
- The power to make treaties and executive agreements
- The power to control the military
- The power to recommend legislation
- The power to veto legislation
- The power to call Congress into special session and to adjourn Congress if they cannot agree on a date for adjournment
- The power to grant reprieves and pardons except in cases of impeachment

Over time, the powers of the president have expanded. Today there is a much stronger presidency than the one that was originally envisioned by the framers of the Constitution. The reasons for this are many and include the visibility of the office, the greater role the federal government plays in people's lives, and the powers various presidents have taken for themselves that have been upheld by the Supreme Court.

PRESIDENTIAL TRIVIA

During Abraham Lincoln's time in office, he enacted strict wartime measures that curtailed people's liberty. He suspended habeas corpus, which meant that he could hold suspected war criminals without bringing them to court to ensure that they were being legally held. The power to suspend habeas corpus has continued to be used in times of war, including during the modern-day War on Terror, with the broad powers granted to President George W. Bush.

Due to the system of checks and balances, a power struggle can sometimes erupt between the presidency and other branches of government. For example, even though the Constitution grants Congress the right to declare war, it makes the president the commander of the military. John Adams was the first president to command the navy to fight without getting a formal declaration of war. The Korean War and the Vietnam War were both undeclared wars. In 1973, Congress passed the War Powers Resolution, which made rules that the president must follow when moving troops into battle. The president must report to Congress within forty-eight hours of the action, and the combat must end within sixty days unless Congress authorizes a longer war. The constitutionality of this resolution has yet to be decided.

Ultimate Check on the President

As previously stated, there are many checks that exist to make sure the president does not overstep the bounds of the office. The ultimate check against the president is that of impeachment. Impeaching the president is a two-step process.

PRESIDENTIAL

TRIVIA

Two presidents have been impeached by the House: Andrew Johnson in 1868 and William Clinton in 1998. However, in neither of these cases was the president removed from office. Andrew Johnson came close, though, only being saved by one vote. Richard Nixon resigned from office in 1974 in the face of being impeached by Congress.

The House of Representatives is given the power to bring formal charges against the president. This is actually called the power to impeach. The power to remove a president from office is entrusted to the Senate.

The President's Cabinet and National Security Council

The president's cabinet is actually an informal group of advisers not even mentioned in the Constitution. In 1789, Congress created four offices tied to the executive branch to help administer the government: secretary of state, secretary of the treasury, secretary of war, and attorney general. The president appointed individuals to these posts and over time began seeking their advice. This group of individuals was called the cabinet and has expanded to include fifteen executive offices and departments.

Typically, the president meets with this group in cabinet meetings and asks for their advice on various issues. Each of these secretaries heads up a department that has become a huge bureaucracy over time, so it is often hard for new appointees to have much effect on day-to-day operations. The weight that presidents have given to their cabinets varies. Some, like Eisenhower's cabinet, played an important role in his administration. On the other hand, Kennedy and Jackson relied more on personal advisers than on their cabinets.

Another group of individuals important in advising the president is the National Security Council. Created in 1947 with the National Security Act, it typically consists of the President's top advisers including the vice president; the secretaries of state, treasury, and defense; the national security advisor; the chairman of the Joint Chiefs of Staff; and the director of national intelligence. Other secretaries and advisers are invited if their areas of responsibility are being discussed.

The White House

The White House holds a unique position in the United States. It is an important symbol of America, but at the same time it is a private residence. Each president is able to put their own stamp on the home and make changes. For example, President Grant added a billiards room, Theodore Roosevelt added tennis courts, and Franklin Roosevelt added an indoor, heated swimming pool. Rutherford B. Hayes installed the first telephone in 1876 with the phone number "1." Seventeen weddings have occurred at the White House, including the marriage of President Grover Cleveland in 1886.

The name "White House" was actually just a nickname in common use when referring to the president's home until 1901 when Theodore Roosevelt officially accepted the name. Construction on the White House began in 1792. The design of the White House was the result of a competition created by Thomas Jefferson and posted in newspapers. James Hoban won the $500 prize for his design. John and Abigail Adams were the first inhabitants of the house.

Survival Against the Odds

The house has survived being burned by the British during the War of 1812; the inauguration of Andrew Jackson where approximately 20,000 well-wishers traipsed through, only being enticed outside by tubs of whiskey; and Theodore Roosevelt's six rambunctious children. In fact, it was Roosevelt's large family that resulted in the creation of the West wing to separate the executive offices and the living quarters. In 1948, engineers realized that the White House was in danger of falling down. Truman moved out and the entire interior was gutted and recreated as an exact replica of the original.

Home Field Advantage

The White House gives the president a definite advantage when meeting with visiting dignitaries whether they be foreign or domestic.

SCANDALS & GOSSIP

Many scandals have arisen concerning how the White House has been used. Both Warren G. Harding and Bill Clinton were known to "entertain" women in or next to the Oval Office. Some presidents have used the White House as a reward for fundraising; most notably, Bill Clinton allowed his supporters to stay in the Lincoln Bedroom.

Designed to impress, it serves the purpose of overwhelming visitors with the pomp and circumstance of the office.

A Snapshot of the Presidents

The unique fraternity of presidents fascinates people from all walks of life. These men are scrutinized for the power that they wield and for their actions within their personal lives. Collectively, they have had thousands of books written about them and their actions. Before looking at each of the presidents individually, let's take a look at some of the facts surrounding the group as a whole.

Age

Most of the presidents were elected for the first time in their fifties. The youngest president to serve in office was Theodore Roosevelt, who was forty-two when he took over after William McKinley's assassination. The youngest elected president was John F. Kennedy at the age of forty-three. Ronald Reagan was the oldest president—he was elected at age sixty-nine and served until he was seventy-eight.

Religion

The two most common religions practiced by presidents are Episcopalian and Presbyterian. There have been two Quakers and one Roman Catholic president: Herbert Hoover and Richard Nixon, and John F. Kennedy, respectively. Here are the top six most common religious groups with percentages:

- Episcopalian—31 percent
- Presbyterian—24 percent
- Methodist—12 percent
- Baptist—9 percent
- Unitarian—9 percent
- Disciples of Christ—7 percent

Military Service

Thirty-one presidents (74 percent) have served in the military. The highest ranking military positions held were by George Washington as the general and commander-in-chief of the Continental Army; Dwight Eisenhower as five-star general of the Allied Forces during World War II; and Ulysses S. Grant as four-star general of the army during the Civil War. Six of the presidents served in the U.S. Navy. The presidents who saw no military service were:

- John Adams
- John Quincy Adams
- Martin Van Buren
- Grover Cleveland
- William Howard Taft
- Woodrow Wilson
- Warren G. Harding
- Calvin Coolidge
- Herbert Hoover
- Franklin D. Roosevelt
- William Jefferson Clinton

While military service is not a prerequisite for the presidency, it is seen as important due to the role the president will be assuming as commander-in-chief of the U.S. military.

Term of Office

There have been only twelve presidents in the history of the office who were elected to two terms. In the beginning, there was no official limit to the number of terms that a president could serve. George Washington set a precedent by leaving office after his second term that was upheld until Franklin D. Roosevelt. Roosevelt ran for and was elected to four terms. He died in office during his fourth stint and Harry S. Truman took over as president. The twenty-second amendment was passed to stop this from ever happening again. According to this amendment, a president is limited to two terms or ten years. A presidential term lasts only four years, but this rule allows for a person to succeed to the presidency for two years before actually running in the general elections.

If a president is unable to continue their duties due to death, resignation, or impeachment, then the Constitution states that the vice president will take over as president. In 1792, an act was passed to set up an order of succession in case the vice president isn't able to take over. However, it was not until the twenty-fifth amendment in 1967 that the order was constitutionally set or that any provision was made for filling the vice presidential office if a succession should occur. Following is the order of succession:

- Vice President
- Speaker of the House
- President Pro Tempore of the Senate
- Secretary of State
- Secretary of the Treasury
- Secretary of Defense
- Attorney General
- Secretary of the Interior
- Secretary of Agriculture
- Secretary of Commerce
- Secretary of Labor
- Secretary of Health and Human Services
- Secretary of Housing and Urban Development
- Secretary of Transportation
- Secretary of Energy
- Secretary of Education
- Secretary of Veteran's Affairs
- Secretary of Homeland Security

Future additions to the order of succession are made based on the order in which cabinet positions are created. Therefore, if a new cabinet post is created after homeland security, that office will become last in the line of presidential succession.

Education

Education has varied from president to president. Six presidents never attended college or studied for an advanced degree at all. They were:

- Andrew Jackson
- Zachary Taylor
- Millard Fillmore
- Abraham Lincoln (though he did become a lawyer by studying on his own and passing the bar)
- Andrew Johnson
- Grover Cleveland

The college from which the most presidents graduated was Harvard with five. Only one president, Woodrow Wilson, had a doctorate. William Henry Harrison attended medical school but dropped out before getting his medical degree. Bill Clinton was a Rhodes Scholar at Oxford University. The most common occupation before becoming president was lawyer. In fact, twenty-five of the forty-two individuals who became president practiced law.

Political Parties and Electoral Votes

The Republican party began around the time of Abraham Lincoln's first election as president. Including Lincoln, eighteen presidents have hailed from the Republican party. That means that 42 percent overall—or 64 percent of the possible elections in which they participated—have been won by Republicans. The political parties represented by the presidents over time are in order of percentage that won the vote:

- Republican—42 percent
- Democratic—33 percent

- Whig—9.5 percent
- Democratic-Republican—9.5 percent
- Union—2 percent (Lincoln ran under the Union party the second time)
- Federalist—2 percent
- No Party—2 percent

Presidents have won by very large and very narrow margins. The president who received the highest percentage of electoral votes was George Washington. He was the only one to be elected unanimously to both terms in office. Other presidents who received more than 90 percent of the electoral vote include James Monroe, Franklin Roosevelt, Ronald Reagan, and Richard Nixon.

The Evolving Presidency

The presidency has emerged over time from the head of a small nation that was not fully recognized by foreign powers for many years to become the head of one of the most powerful nations in the world. The president's currency lies in both his constitutional powers and his personal powers to persuade and effect change. Constitutional powers granted to the president are written very loosely, leaving them open to interpretation by those who hold the office. These interpretations have set up and continue to cause confrontations between the executive branch and the other branches of government. The introduction of mass media has served to increase the president's power.

In the end, the job of president is extremely difficult and calls for its owner to wear many different hats. A variety of individuals have taken on this challenge, some with greater success than others. These presidents have set America on its course domestically and internationally, for better or worse. Ultimately, each president brings a unique personality and perspective to the presidency.

George Washington: Father of Our Country

1

Born: February 22, 1732

Died: December 14, 1799

First Lady: Martha Dandridge Custis Washington

Political Party: None

Presidential Term: April 30, 1789 to March 3, 1797

Famous Quote: "I walk on untrodden ground. There is scarcely any part of my conduct which may not hereafter be drawn into precedent."

Timeline

1754 . . . . Built and then was forced to surrender Fort Necessity to the French

1754–1758 . . . . Fought in the French and Indian War

1759 . . . . Married Martha Dandridge Custis

1759–1769 . . . . Served in the Virginia House of Burgesses until it was dissolved

1774–1775 . . . . Member of the first and second Continental Congresses

1775–1783 . . . . Commander-in-chief of the Continental Army

1787 . . . . President of the constitutional convention

1789–1797 . . . . First president of the United States

1791 . . . . Bill of Rights ratified

1796 . . . . Published his farewell address

Fabled Childhood

Washington was born on February 22, 1732, in Westmoreland County, Virginia. His father, Augustine Washington, was a wealthy Virginia planter. Washington was born to Augustine's second wife, Mary Bell. He grew up in a relatively wealthy and comfortable environment.

Washington's mother was overprotective and demanding throughout his life. When his brother thought that service in the British Navy might suit Washington, his mother prohibited him from joining. She often demanded his attention for money and other comforts, even while he was in the midst of fighting during the Revolutionary War.

Growing Up with Lawrence

Washington's father died when he was only eleven, and his half brother, Lawrence, took over raising him. When Washington was sixteen, he went to live with Lawrence at Mount Vernon.

He did not study in Great Britain as was normal for wealthy young men during that time. Instead, he was taught in colonial Virginia, although it is not sure where or by whom. Washington was good at math, which suited his chosen profession of surveying, an important occupation as land was claimed and developed.

PRESIDENTIAL TRIVIA

Washington did not, in fact, cut down a cherry tree and then tell his father the truth. This story was an invention of author Mason Weems, who wrote a book called *The Life of Washington* shortly after Washington's death in which Weems glorified Washington and his life.

In 1749, Washington was appointed as surveyor for Culpepper County, Virginia, after a trek for Lord Fairfax into the Blue Ridge Mountains. He used the money he earned to buy land, eventually becoming one of the largest landholders in the country. He rented much of this land to tenant farmers.

In 1751, Washington traveled to Barbados with his half brother, Lawrence, in an attempt to find a cure for Lawrence's tuberculosis. While in Barbados, Washington contracted smallpox. Lawrence died in 1752.

When Lawrence's only daughter died in 1754, Washington inherited Mount Vernon. Washington loved working the land at Mount Vernon and tried new techniques in raising livestock and agriculture. He also enjoyed the social life that being a wealthy planter afforded him. He was an avid fox hunter and loved sports.

First Lady: Martha Dandridge Custis Washington

Washington got engaged to Martha Dandridge Custis in 1758. At the same time, it appears that he was in love with Sally Fairfax, his neighbor's wife, although there is no evidence that the affection was returned. However, he did marry Martha on January 6, 1759. She had two children from a previous marriage along with a great deal of money and land.

IN THEIR OWN WORDS...

Martha Washington had to deal with much hardship following her husband through his military command and presidency, but she always maintained high spirits. In her words: "I am still determined to be cheerful and happy, in whatever situation I may be; for I have also learned from experience that the greater part of our happiness or misery depends upon our dispositions, and not upon our circumstances."

While Martha did not receive a formal education, she knew how to efficiently run a household. She was a warm hostess much admired by all. She also loved her family and her privacy; unfortunately this need for privacy led her to burn the letters she had exchanged with her husband before her own death in 1802.

Military Hero and National Leader

Washington began his military career in 1752 as a part of the Virginia militia. In 1753, he volunteered as a messenger to the French at Fort le Boeuf on Lake Erie. The journey took two and a half months and was full of hardship. His message demanded that the French leave the Ohio Valley. However, the French refused, an action that led to the French and Indian War.

French and Indian War

Washington was promoted to colonel of the Virginia troops. He felt the French would attack and created Fort Necessity to stop them, but was forced to surrender Fort Necessity to the French on July 4, 1754. He resigned from the military in 1754, but then rejoined in 1755 as an aide-de-camp to General Edward Braddock. When Braddock was killed in battle during the French and Indian War (1754–1763), Washington managed to stay calm and keep the unit together as they retreated. As Washington wrote later, "I had four bullets through my coat, and two horses shot under me, yet escaped unhurt, altho' death was levelling my companions on every side!"

Commander-in-Chief

Washington served in the military from 1752 to 1758 before being elected to the Virginia House of Burgesses in 1759. While serving in the House, he spoke out against Britain's policies until the House of Burgesses was disbanded in 1769.

From 1774 to 1775, he represented Virginia in both Continental Congresses. He strongly believed in the need to use military action in response to British actions restricting liberty. He was unanimously named commander-in-chief of the Continental Army. He took the position without pay, accepting only reimbursement for his expenses, which actually resulted in him making more money in the end.

Revolutionary War

The Continental Army was no match for the British regulars and the German mercenaries, called Hessians. While Washington had an early victory over the British by forcing them to leave Boston, he was faced with desertions, inexperience, lack of discipline, and supply problems, and was forced to surrender New York City. He had significant victories at Trenton (1776) and Princeton (1777), but then lost Philadelphia. In October, Horatio Gates won a huge victory against the British at Saratoga.

Then came the winter at Valley Forge (1777–1778). The men survived mainly due to Washington's leadership. With the spring came news that France had recognized American independence and was going to send support. In addition, Baron von Steuben arrived and began training Washington's troops. Upon learning of the French involvement, the British consolidated their troops in New York City where Washington kept them from 1778 to 1781. When the French finally arrived in 1781, Washington worked with Count Rochambeau and the Marquis de Lafayette to win the surrender of the British under Cornwallis at Yorktown. However, it took two years for Congress to agree to peace. Officers under Washington's command considered overthrowing Congress but Washington talked them out of it. Once the British left, Washington turned in his command saying, "I here offer my commission, and take my leave of all the employment of public life."

Constitutional Convention

In 1781, Congress created the Articles of Confederation as the foundation for the new American government. The articles united the thirteen states in a loose confederation capable of declaring war and making diplomatic treaties but little else. Washington felt that the national government needed to be much stronger, especially after the events of Shay's Rebellion, an armed uprising in Massachusetts by farmers who were angered by debt and taxes. The lack of response by the government and inability to address the problem became a cause of concern for Washington. He was first a delegate and then named the president of the constitutional convention in 1787.

Unanimously Supported President

Washington was immensely popular as a war hero and was an obvious choice as the first president for both Federalists (those who argued for the Constitution) and anti-Federalists (those who argued against a new constitution because they feared that it gave too much power to the national government). He was unanimously elected by the sixty-nine electors. John Adams became his vice president with thirty-four votes.

QUIRKS & ODDITIES

George Washington often looks very stern in his portraits. This had more to do with his dentures than his outlook on life. His dentures were not in fact carved out of wood but were actually made of ivory and gold. They were also made in such a way that Washington's mouth would remain open at rest unless he actively closed his jaws.

In 1793, Washington was again unanimously elected to the presidency. He had decided to retire after one term but was urged to stay on in the hopes of keeping the nation unified. John Adams was again chosen to be his vice president.

Presidential Administration

Washington's administration set many precedents and created many traditions. Washington's actions set up numerous standards that are still followed today. He appointed his cabinet unchallenged by Congress and began to rely on them for advice. He chose John Jay's successor as chief justice from outside the bench instead of based on seniority. Further, he chose to serve only two terms, setting a precedent that lasted until Franklin Roosevelt.

Domestically, Washington relied on his secretary of the treasury, Alexander Hamilton, to help him fix monetary issues in the nation. He had the national government assume all state debts and borrow money from foreign governments to pay them. Further, the Bill of Rights was approved, which led to the last two holdouts, North Carolina and Rhode Island, joining the Union.

Washington feared any actions that divided the nation. He fought against the rise of factions, especially within his own cabinet between his secretary of state, Thomas Jefferson, and his secretary of the treasury, Alexander Hamilton. To Washington's dismay, they both resigned during his second term.

Whiskey Rebellion

During his second term, Washington was able to stop the first real challenge to federal authority with the suppression of the Whiskey Rebellion in 1794. Pennsylvania farmers refused to pay a tax on whiskey because they felt that the federal government did not have the right to collect taxes. He sent troops to ensure compliance, which effectively ended the rebellion.

Neutrality

In foreign affairs, Washington declared the Proclamation of Neutrality in 1793, which stated that the United States would be impartial toward belligerent powers currently in a war. This upset some who felt that the United States owed a greater allegiance to France, which had helped to defeat the British in the Revolutionary War. At the same time, Washington tried to normalize relations with the British by agreeing to Jay's Treaty, which established trade relations and led to the British withdrawal from the Northwest Territory in exchange for allowing the British to search and seize anything found on American ships traveling into the ports of Britain's enemies. This forestalled conflict with the British until the War of 1812.

In 1795, Pinckney's Treaty created a boundary between the United States and the Spanish-held Florida. Further, the United States was allowed to travel the entire Mississippi for purpose of trade.

Washington's belief in neutrality was reiterated during his farewell address in 1796, in which he warned against foreign entanglements. This warning became part of the American political landscape as seen in the issues that arose around joining World War I and World War II.

Retirement to Mount Vernon

Washington retired at the end of his second term to Mount Vernon, where he hoped to find peace. However, he was again asked to be the commander of the American forces if the United States went to war with France over the XYZ affair. He helped formulate plans with the secretary of war and other officials, but since fighting never occurred on land, he did not have to serve. Washington died on December 14, 1799, possibly from a streptococcal infection of his throat made worse by being bled four times. He was buried at Mount Vernon, and his life was commemorated throughout the nation with memorial services.

PRESIDENTIAL TRIVIA

Over the years, Washington grew to believe that slavery was immoral. In his last will and testament, he freed all 123 slaves that he personally owned. He was the only founding father to free all of his slaves upon his death.

Washington's importance to the founding of the new nation cannot be understated. Only a figure removed from politics like Washington could have helped stabilize the country as it began a new experiment in government. As Thomas Jefferson said in a letter after Washington's death, "His integrity was most pure, . . . no motives of interest or consanguinity, of friendship or hatred, [were] able to bias his decision. He was indeed . . . a wise, a good and a great man."

John Adams:
Man Behind the Scenes

Born:	October 30, 1735, in Braintree (Quincy), Massachusetts
Died:	July 4, 1826, in Quincy, Massachusetts
First Lady:	Abigail Smith Adams
Political Party:	Federalist
Presidential Term:	April 4, 1797 to March 3, 1801
Famous Quote:	"I must study politics and war that my sons may have liberty to study mathematics and philosophy."

Timeline

1755 . . . . Graduated from Harvard

1764 . . . . Married Abigail Smith

1774–1776 . . . . Massachusetts delegate to the first and second Continental Congresses

1779 . . . . Primary author of the Massachusetts constitution

1780–1788 . . . . Diplomat in France, the Netherlands, and Great Britain

1789–1797 . . . . First vice president of the United States under President Washington

1797–1801 . . . . Second president of the United States

1824 . . . . Son John Quincy Adams elected sixth president of the United States

Growing Up in Braintree

John Adams grew up on a farm in Braintree, Massachusetts. His father, who was also named John Adams, had gone to Harvard and believed in a solid education. John Adams Sr. taught his son personally before sending him off to Harvard to follow in his father's footsteps. Although Adams would become a revolutionary figure, schooled in the art of political theory, he was first and foremost a farmer at heart.

Childhood

Adams came from a family who had been in America for five generations. He grew up helping on his father's farm and learning at his father's knee. The elder John Adams held various public offices. He taught his son how to read before he entered his first school, which was taught by a woman named Mrs. Belcher. Little is known of Adams's mother, Susanna Boylston, other than that she was a religious woman. Adams had two brothers: Peter Boylston and Elihu.

Harvard

Adams finished his lower school and moved into Joseph Cleverly's Latin School before becoming a student of Joseph Marsh to pass the Harvard entrance exam. In 1751, he became a student at Harvard. When Adams graduated he was unsure of what he wanted to do and tried teaching for a short time before deciding on law.

PRESIDENTIAL TRIVIA

When John Adams graduated from Harvard in 1755, he was ranked fourteenth in his class. However, at that time, class ranking was based more on social class than on grades and knowledge. He was actually a much better student than his rank showed.

He was admitted to the Massachusetts bar in 1758. He proved himself to be an independent thinker who believed in the rule of law—the idea that government can only act according to written, valid laws and enforce these laws in established ways. This would stop the government from acting in an arbitrary manner, differing from the experiences of many colonists under monarchical rule.

First Lady: Abigail Smith Adams

Abigail Adams, though she received no formal education, was extremely well read. Born on November 11, 1744, she grew up in a prestigious family. She married Adams in 1764 and they had four children who lived to maturity: Abigail, John Quincy (the future sixth president of the United States), Charles, and Thomas Boylston. She was an extremely important figure in the history of the American Revolution and the foundation of the American presidency.

Abigail's impact on the Revolution and more can be judged by the many letters that she exchanged with her husband. Most of these provided commentary on the Revolution from her point of view and shared her views on government and politics with her husband. One of her most well-known quotes deals with how women should be treated by the newly created government: "[R]emember the ladies, and be more generous and favorable to them than your ancestors. Do not put such unlimited power into the hands of the Husbands. . . . If particular care and attention is not paid to the Ladies we are determined to foment a Rebellion."

Revolutionary and Diplomat

John Adams was a true revolutionary. While not as charismatic as his cousin, Samuel Adams, he was involved in pre–Revolutionary War activities from the beginning. In 1765, he wrote anonymous letters to the *Boston Gazette* denouncing the Stamp Act and gave a speech before the governor about the fact that the tax was passed without representation in Congress. He was an independent thinker, not always doing what was politically expedient but rather what he felt was right.

The Boston Massacre

In 1770, Adams decided to defend the British soldiers involved in the Boston Massacre, causing many to speak out against him. These soldiers were being tried for the deaths of five colonists that occurred on Boston Green.

PRESIDENTIAL TRIVIA

Paul Revere created a famous engraving depicting what he titled, "The Bloody Massacre." The image was used to fan the flames of rebellion. The depiction was not entirely accurate and the use of the word massacre lived on as a descriptor of the event even though the facts surrounding the incident are unclear, including who was actually at fault.

His decision was based on his belief that the event was more the fault of British policies than the actions of the soldiers themselves. It was important to ensure these men were given a fair trial. Due to his defense, only two of the eight soldiers were found guilty of manslaughter and the rest were acquitted.

The First and Second Continental Congresses

Adams served in the Massachusetts legislature before attending the first and second Continental Congresses in 1774 and 1775, respectively. Noticing that the North and South were disagreeing about how America should deal with Great Britain, he decided to take action and unify the two. Adams believed that only through unification could they hope for success. To this end, Adams nominated George Washington, a southerner from Virginia, to be commander-in-chief. Adams was also part of the committee that wrote the Declaration of Independence, deferring to Jefferson—another southerner—to write the first draft.

Diplomatic Endeavors

John Adams was a diplomat to France with Benjamin Franklin and Arthur Lee in 1778, but soon returned to the United States to serve as the primary author of the Massachusetts state constitution. He then traveled as a diplomat to the Netherlands in 1780. He returned to France in 1782 and, with Franklin and John Jay, created the Treaty of Paris, officially ending the American Revolution.

From 1785 to 1788, Adams served as the first American minister to Great Britain where he hoped to rebuild a relationship and create a trade treaty. However, he was unsuccessful and returned to America where he served as George Washington's vice president for two terms.

Washington's Successor

John Adams was the next logical Federalist candidate for president, having served two terms as Washington's vice president. He had found his role as vice president to be undesirable, but he looked forward to becoming president. In the election, he was opposed by Thomas Jefferson, a Democratic-Republican who fought against the idea of a strong, national government.

IN THEIR OWN WORDS...

John Adams did not relish his position as second-in-command as can be told from his words on the vice presidency: "My country has in its wisdom contrived for me the most insignificant office that ever the invention of man contrived or his imagination conceived."

Campaign

The campaign between Adams and Jefferson was fierce. While both of them remained above the fray, their campaigns focused on personal attacks. The Democratic-Republicans were unhappy with Washington's policies but could not attack such a popular leader directly, so they instead heaped their attacks on Adams. Adams's camp shot back that Jefferson wanted to overthrow the Constitution. Further, Adams believed that France was the greater concern to national security while Jefferson felt that it was Great Britain. This campaign would cause a rift between the two friends for years.

Election of 1796

According to the Constitution, whoever received the most votes became president and whoever had the second most votes became vice president. Thomas Pinckney had been Adams's running mate for vice president. Alexander Hamilton tried to get Pinckney elected over Adams. However, his plan backfired and the presidency almost went to Thomas Jefferson who lost by only three votes. Therefore, Adams and Jefferson, political adversaries representing different parties, were elected as president and vice president, respectively.

Presidential Administration

Adams's major accomplishment while in office was keeping America out of war with France. However, his policies on this matter also led to his downfall. His use of the Alien and Sedition Acts against his political opposition pushed the Republicans over the edge and was a huge part of the campaign against him in 1800.

XYZ Affair

When Adams became president, the French were regularly raiding American ships in the Atlantic. Adams sent ministers to try and stop this, but his ministers were rebuffed and three diplomats from France instead sent a letter asking for tribute of $250,000 in exchange for the meeting. Fearing that this posturing would eventually lead to war with France, Adams decided that the best course of action was to ask Congress to begin building up the military. The Democratic-Republicans balked against Adams's request. In response, Adams released the letter to the public replacing the names of the three French diplomats with the initials X, Y, and Z. A public uproar resulted forcing the Democratic-Republicans to change their stance. Trying to avert war, Adams quickly sent diplomats back to France who were able to come to an agreement and preserve the peace.

Alien and Sedition Acts

While America was preparing for a possible war with France, Congress passed the Alien and Sedition Acts. These measures were designed to limit immigration and free speech. Unfortunately, the acts were then used to suppress the political opponents of the Federalists, who were speaking out against the government's policies. Many were arrested and some newspapers were closed down. Jefferson and James Madison crafted the Kentucky and Virginia Resolutions in protest. While they did not really change the situation, they were used to sway public opinion against Adams.

No Second Term

Adams did not win a second term in office, most likely because he was opposed not only by Thomas Jefferson and the Democratic-Republicans but also by members of his own party including Alexander Hamilton. Thomas Pinckney again ran for vice president and Hamilton campaigned for him. Jefferson won the election.

Midnight Appointments

Adams spent his last hours in office appointing Federalist judges and office holders based on the Judiciary Act of 1801. His goal was to fill posts with those he felt shared his views on the role of the national government. These were collectively given the title, "midnight appointments." When Jefferson took over, he removed many of these people from office.

Life After the Presidency

John Adams retired from public life to his farm. He spent his time reading and corresponding with old friends. In 1812, Adams and Jefferson reconciled when Adams wrote, "You and I ought not to die before we have explained ourselves to each other." They continued their letter writing until their deaths.

**QUIRKS &
ODDITIES**

Due to illnesses including a light case of smallpox, which was treated with a milk diet and daily doses of mercury, Adams eventually lost most of his teeth and spent his later years with a pronounced lisp.

Adams was able to live long enough to see his son John Quincy Adams become the sixth president in 1825. John Quincy Adams had won a narrow victory over Andrew Jackson. Thankfully, Adams did not live to see his son lose to Jackson in 1828 after a fierce campaign full of bitterness.

John Adams died on July 4, 1826, the fiftieth anniversary of the ratification of the Declaration of Independence. Ironically, this was the same day as Jefferson's death. Adams last words were, "Thomas Jefferson still survives." He was ninety years old when he died.

Thomas Jefferson: America's Renaissance Man

3

Born: April 13, 1743, in Albemarle County, Virginia

Died: July 4, 1826, at Monticello, Albemarle County, Virginia

First Lady: None. His wife, Martha Wayles Skelton Jefferson, died before he took office

Political Party: Democratic-Republican

Presidential Term: March 4, 1801 to March 3, 1809

Famous Quote: "The tree of liberty must be refreshed from time to time with the blood of patriots and tyrants."

Timeline

1762 . . . . .Graduated from the College of William and Mary

1769–1779 . . . . . .Served in the Virginia legislature

1772 . . . . .Married Martha Wayles Skelton

1775–1776 . . . . . . .Virginia delegate to the second Continental Congress

1776 . . . . .Primary author of the Declaration of Independence

1779–1781 . . . . . . .Governor of Virginia

1785–1789 . . . . . . .U.S. minister to France

1789–1793 . . . . . .Secretary of state under George Washington

1797–1801 . . . . . . .Vice president under President John Adams

1801–1809 . . . . . . Third president of the United States

1803 . . . . .Ohio admitted to the Union

1816–1825 . . . . . .Founder and chief architect of the University of Virginia

Educating a Statesman

Thomas Jefferson's father, Colonel Peter Jefferson, was a planter and public official. Colonel Jefferson died when Thomas was just fourteen, leaving him to be the head of the family. Thomas Jefferson's mother, Jane Randolph, was a member of one of the most distinguished families in Virginia. Jefferson was a quick learner and excelled at college. His years at school and studying law prepared him for the many tasks that would be asked of him.

PRESIDENTIAL TRIVIA

Thomas Jefferson's father was self-taught but according to his son was so well respected that he was chosen with Joshua Fry, professor of mathematics at William and Mary, to create the first map of Virginia.

Childhood

When Jefferson was three, his father took on the responsibility of raising the orphaned children of his friend and wife's relative, William Randolph. Jefferson grew up with the Randolph children and his own seven siblings. He was tutored at home by a clergyman named William Douglas. After attending Reverend James Maury's school for two years, he gained entrance to the College of William and Mary. Jefferson enjoyed dancing and playing the violin along with fox hunting and shooting.

College and Beyond

Jefferson thrived at college. He became close friends with three older men: Governor Francis Fauquier, William Small, and George Wythe, the first American law professor. He spent many evenings with these men in political and philosophical discussions. After graduating, he studied law for five years with George Wythe and was admitted to the Virginia bar in 1767.

Personal Relationships

Jefferson did not marry until he was twenty-nine. He had previously stated that he was not interested in marriage because, "[m]any and great are the comforts of a single state." He was known for numerous romances throughout his youth. However, he did eventually settle down with Martha Wayles Skelton.

Martha Wayles Skelton

Martha was an extremely wealthy widow who doubled Jefferson's holdings. They moved into Monticello, a home that was built on land that he had inherited from his father. Unfortunately, only two of their six children lived to maturity: Martha "Patsy" and Mary "Polly." Jefferson's wife, Martha, died in 1782 after only ten years of marriage. He was distraught and never remarried.

Bachelor President

When Jefferson became president, he did not have a first lady. Instead, his two daughters, along with Dolley Madison, filled the role of first lady. The function of the first lady is to act as official hostess at state functions, organize events, and meet with the wives of visiting dignitaries. Dolley Madison was the wife of one of Jefferson's good friends, the future president James Madison. She was known as a fabulous hostess and, in fact, often accompanied Jefferson to the more formal affairs of his presidency. Jefferson also helped out by choosing food and entertainment for dinner parties.

Sally Hemings

Over the years, many have claimed that Thomas Jefferson had a long-standing relationship with Sally Hemings, one of his slaves. Sally was the child of a slave, Elizabeth Hemings, and Jefferson's father-in-law, John Wayles. In 1787, Sally accompanied Jefferson's daughter Mary when Mary went to Paris to join her father. Some claim this is when the relationship between Hemings and Jefferson began.

Sally had six children, and it has been proven that there was a window of opportunity for Jefferson to have been the father of each of them. Further, DNA tests have shown that Jefferson could have been the father of the children.

SCANDALS & GOSSIP

In 1802, a journalist named James Callender wrote that Jefferson kept Hemings as his "concubine." This rumor continued to be discussed throughout the nineteenth century. One interesting side note to the story is that when Jefferson died, he freed five of his slaves including both of Sally's sons, Madison and Eston Hemings. Hers was the only family to be freed in its entirety.

Revolutionary Leader

From the time that Jefferson joined the Virginia House of Burgesses, the legislative branch of the Virginia colony, in 1769, he opposed British domination in the colonies. He was part of the Committees of Correspondence in Virginia, a group that linked patriotic leaders in the different colonies. He truly believed in the rights of individuals and the colonies to choose their own course.

Second Continental Congress

In 1775, Jefferson represented Virginia at the second Continental Congress. When they decided to officially declare independence, they appointed a five-man committee including John Adams, Benjamin Franklin, Thomas Jefferson, Robert Livingston, and Roger Sherman to draft the resolution. Jefferson was chosen to write the first draft of the Declaration of Independence. He was well-known for his eloquence, and it did not hurt that he was a southerner, which helped to ensure Southern support. After revisions from the entire group, the Declaration was ratified on July 4, 1776.

Minister to France

After the Revolutionary War, Jefferson was sent to France as minister (1785–1789). He found France to be fascinating, especially since he was there when the revolutionary spirit was taking over. He returned home in 1789, after the storming of the Bastille and the beginnings of the French Revolution.

Jefferson the Free Thinker

When Jefferson returned from France, he was appointed as George Washington's first secretary of state. He spent much of his time trying to help maintain peace with Europe and the Native Americans. He led the charge for America to recognize the new French Republic. However, he disagreed with Washington's decision to remain neutral when other European countries declared war on France.

PRESIDENTIAL TRIVIA

Thomas Jefferson regretted being asked to become Washington's secretary of state because he wished to return to France to witness the French Revolution. He believed the Revolution would be "certainly and happily closed in less than a year."

Clash with Hamilton

Shortly after becoming secretary of state, Jefferson began to have problems with Alexander Hamilton, secretary of the treasury. He thought Hamilton's creation of the Bank of the United States was unconstitutional because this power was not specifically granted in the Constitution. They clashed over other issues, including neutrality toward France. Jefferson eventually felt that Washington was listening more to Hamilton than to him and resigned from his post in 1793.

Leader of the Democratic-Republicans

After Jefferson's resignation, he spent time at Monticello. However, this did not keep him from becoming involved with public policy again. When Jay's Treaty was ratified, he openly expressed disgust at its neutrality. He felt that America should be spending more time supporting the French.

He was nominated and ran for president against Federalist John Adams in 1796. He only lost to Adams by three votes. Because of the way the Constitution was written, whoever received the second most votes became vice president. Therefore, he served as John Adams's vice president from 1797 to 1801, the only time in American history that members of opposing parties served in the two top positions.

Road to the Presidency

In 1800, Jefferson was again the candidate for the Democratic-Republicans with Aaron Burr as the candidate for vice president. This campaign was particularly fierce. The main issue against Jefferson's opponent, John Adams, was the use of the Alien and Sedition Acts against Federalist opponents. The Federalists shot back that Jefferson was an atheist who wanted to destroy the Constitution.

Burr Controversy

Ironically, Jefferson and Burr actually tied in the electoral votes. Even though Jefferson had run as the presidential candidate, whoever received the most votes would be elected president. The twelfth amendment was ratified in 1804 to correct this problem by ensuring that each elector cast distinct votes for president and vice president. The outcome of the election had to be determined by the House of Representatives because Burr refused to concede. In the House, each state was allowed to cast one vote. Jefferson won on the thirty-sixth ballot. The strength of the American republic was proven by the peaceful transfer of power from Federalists to Democratic-Republicans.

Election of 1804

Jefferson was again nominated in 1804 with George Clinton as his vice presidential running mate. He was opposed by Charles Cotesworth Pinckney, an influential South Carolinian. Jefferson won easily, receiving 162 out of 176 electoral votes. This victory led to the downfall of the Federalist party.

Presidential Administration

Thomas Jefferson served two terms as president. He spent much of his time fighting the Federalist agenda from the two previous administrations. He also found that even though he was a proponent of states's rights at heart, there were times when the federal government needed to stretch the bounds of the Constitution.

In 1807, Jefferson ended the foreign slave trade beginning January 1, 1808. He also established the precedent of executive privilege when he refused to testify in the Aaron Burr treason trial. Burr had been accused of trying to create an independent country within the United States that hinged on the taking of New Orleans. When Jefferson was subpoenaed by Burr's defense attorneys to provide documents, he refused on the premise that the executive branch was independent and that this action would go too far in usurping his power.

Fighting the Federalist Agenda

When Jefferson first took office, he had to deal with the midnight appointments from Adams's last hours in office. He immediately removed many of these officials from office. In the end, this led to the landmark Supreme Court Case, *Marbury v. Madison* (1803) in which the Judiciary Act, which allowed for Adams's last minute appointments, was ruled unconstitutional. This created the rule of judicial review that allowed the Supreme Court to rule laws unconstitutional.

Jefferson let the Alien and Sedition Acts expire. He also removed the tax on liquor that had caused the Whiskey Rebellion during Washington's presidency. The reduced revenue meant that Jefferson had to cut costs, including reducing the military, relying instead on state militias.

Fighting the Pirates

From 1801 to 1805, America engaged in a war with Tripoli. The United States had been paying money to pirates in the Barbary States, a group of North African states including Tripolitania and Morocco, to keep them from attacking American ships. Jefferson refused their demands for more money, and Tripoli declared war. The United States was able to defeat

Tripoli but did have to continue paying tribute to pirates from other Barbary States.

Louisiana Purchase

Jefferson had a difficult decision to make in 1803 when he was offered the Louisiana Territory, an area comprising more than 529 million acres of land including parts or all of fifteen present day states. Napoleon offered it for the price of $15 million. Jefferson felt it important to possess this area, but at the same time he did not believe that the Constitution allowed him to take this action.

IN THEIR OWN WORDS...

Jefferson's thoughts on the Louisiana Purchase: "I know that the acquisition of Louisiana has been disapproved by some . . . that the enlargement of our territory would endanger its union. . . . Is it not better that the opposite bank of the Mississippi should be settled by our own brethren and children than by strangers of another family?"

Not wanting to lose the deal, he went ahead and got Congress to authorize the expenditure. He then sent Meriwether Lewis and William Clark to explore the area.

Chesapeake *and the Embargo Act*

During Jefferson's second term, American trade ships were caught in the crossfire between warring France and Britain. The British practice of impressment—forcing sailors to work on their vessels—caused much contention. This came to a head when the British boarded the *Chesapeake*, impressing three sailors and killing one. In response, Jefferson signed the Embargo Act of 1807, which stopped all imports and exports of foreign goods. Jefferson hoped this would hurt France and Great Britain economically but instead it ended up hurting American trade. However, the fallout from this act would not be felt until the next president,

James Madison, was in office, and would eventually be one of the causes of the War of 1812.

Life After the Presidency

Jefferson decided not to seek a third term. He saw his retirement as a source of relief. He never reentered public service again, but instead spent much of his time at his beloved Monticello. In 1815, he sold his library to the U.S. government to pay off debts. It formed the basis of the Library of Congress.

Jefferson's great passion in retirement was creating the University of Virginia. He designed the campus, hired the professors, and created the curriculum. When it opened, he became the university's first rector. He saw this as one of his greatest accomplishments.

Death

In retirement, Jefferson became close once again to John Adams through their letters. This correspondence provides insight into the minds of these great men and the times they endured. Ironically, Jefferson died on the same day as Adams—July 4, 1826—which also happened to be the fiftieth anniversary of the Declaration of Independence.

Thomas Jefferson truly embodied the spirit of a Renaissance Man. He was a politician, philosopher, architect, author, lawyer, inventor, and educator. His tombstone mentions nothing about his time as president. Instead it reads, "Here was buried Thomas Jefferson, Author of the Declaration of Independence, Of the Statute of Virginia for Religious Freedom, And Father of the University of Virginia."

4

James Madison:
Father of the Constitution

Born: March 16, 1751, at Port Conway, Virginia
Died: June 28, 1836, at Montpelier, Orange County, Virginia
First Lady: Dolley Payne Todd Madison
Political Party: Democratic-Republican
Presidential Term: March 4, 1809 to March 3, 1817
Famous Quote: "Every word [of the Constitution] decides a question between power and liberty."

Timeline

1771 . . . . Graduated from the College of New Jersey at Princeton
1776–1777 . . . . Member of the Virginia House of Delegates
1780–1783 . . . . . . Member of the Continental Congress
1784–1786 . . . . . . Member of the Virginia House of Delegates
1787 . . . . Primary author of the U.S. Constitution at the Constitutional Convention
1789–1797 . . . . . . U.S. representative
1798 . . . . Author of the Virginia Resolutions
1799–1800 . . . . . . Member of the Virginia House of Delegates
1801–1809 . . . . . . Secretary of state under President Thomas Jefferson
1809–1817 . . . . . . Fourth president of the United States
1812 . . . . Louisiana admitted to the Union
1816 . . . . Indiana admitted to the Union
1819 . . . . Helped create the American Colonization Society
1829 . . . . Chairman with James Monroe of the Virginia state Constitutional Convention

Childhood and Education

James Madison was born on March 16, 1751, the eldest of seven children. Both of his parents were wealthy and he grew up on a plantation in Virginia called Montpelier, which Madison would eventually inherit. His father, James Madison Sr., served in various public offices in Orange County, Virginia, including county lieutenant and sheriff. His mother, Eleanor Rose Conway, lived to be ninety-eight years old and to see her son become president.

Madison studied under two tutors—Donald Robertson and Reverend Thomas Martin—before attending the College of New Jersey, which would later become Princeton. He was an excellent student and graduated in two years.

First Lady: Dolley Payne Todd Madison

On September 15, 1794, James Madison married Dolley Payne Todd, a woman seventeen years his junior. She was the daughter of a devout Quaker and a widow when she married Madison.

SCANDALS & GOSSIP

Because Dolley Todd married James Madison, who was Episcopalian and not a Quaker, she was disowned from the Society of Friends. This was a common practice at the time. Typically, a Quaker was visited by a committee and asked to acknowledge their misdeeds. If they were unwilling to do so, they were disowned by the community.

Her first husband had died of yellow fever and she was left with a son, John Payne Todd. However, she and James Madison had no children together.

Well-Loved Hostess

Dolley Madison is remembered as one of the most well loved first ladies. She helped Thomas Jefferson when he was in office since his wife had died before he became president. As first lady, she created weekly social events and entertained Washington society and dignitaries. For many years after her time in the White House, other first ladies were measured against her.

Saving National Treasures

In 1814, the British were advancing on Washington. Dolley Madison had to leave the White House because it appeared that there was no stopping the enemy. However, she refused to leave without packing up as many national treasures as she could, including the full-length portrait of George Washington by Gilbert Stuart. Without her determination, much would have been lost when the White House was ransacked and burned by the British.

Influential Political Thinker

James Madison was foremost a political thinker. His influence extended from championing a stronger national confederacy to fighting for the separation of church and state in Virginia. In the end, he had an immeasurable impact on the U.S. government.

Early Career

In 1776, James Madison was a delegate to the Virginia Convention before becoming a member of the Virginia House of Delegates. He fought for the passage of a statute promising religious freedom. Again, from 1784 to 1786, he would serve in the House of Delegates and create a bill that disallowed religious tests as a requirement for holding public office.

Madison served as the youngest member of the Continental Congress from 1780 to 1783. He was one of the key members in calling for a constitutional convention.

Father of the Constitution

The effect that James Madison had on the United States cannot be underestimated. As the author of the U.S. Constitution, his words and ideas still affect each of us today. James Madison was responsible for drafting most of the Constitution, a document that created a very strong central government.

However, his real struggle began after the creation of the document with the fight for ratification.

Nine of the thirteen states had to ratify the Constitution for it to go into effect. However, not every state was immediately on board. James Madison, Alexander Hamilton, and John Jay authored the "anonymous" Federalist Papers to argue for ratification in New York.

IN THEIR OWN WORDS...

James Madison in Federalist #51: "If men were angels, no government would be necessary. If angels were to govern men, neither external nor internal controls on government would be necessary. In framing a government which is to be administered by men over men, the great difficulty lies in this: you must first enable the government to control the governed; and in the next place oblige it to control itself."

Leaders of other states took up these arguments as they worked to convince their own state leaders to ratify the Constitution.

Bill of Rights and Virginia Resolutions

As a U.S. representative from 1789 to 1797, Madison was instrumental in getting the first ten amendments through the House. They would be ratified in 1791. Despite his belief in the need for a strong, central government, Madison sided politically with Thomas Jefferson over Alexander Hamilton. In 1798, Madison and Jefferson created the Virginia and Kentucky resolutions, respectively, to fight against the Alien and Sedition Acts passed during John Adams's administration.

Road to the Presidency

Because of Madison's loyalty to Jefferson and his experience in politics, he was easily nominated by the Democratic-Republicans as Jefferson's pick to run for president in 1808. George Clinton was his vice president. He ran against Charles Cotesworth Pinckney. Pinckney and the Federalists attacked Madison throughout the campaign for his support of the Embargo Act, which was passed at the end of Jefferson's second term. Madison had been a strong proponent of the unpopular measure. However, he was able to handily defeat Pinckney, winning 122 out of 175 electoral votes to become the president of the United States.

Madison was quickly nominated to run again in the election of 1812. America had just entered the War of 1812 during the election, and that was the main issue of the campaign. His opponent, DeWitt Clinton, mistakenly tried to appeal to both those who agreed with the war and those who were opposed to it. Thus, Madison was able to easily win with 128 out of 217 electoral votes.

QUIRKS & ODDITIES

Both of James Madison's vice presidents, George Clinton and Elbridge Gerry, died while he was president. Elbridge Gerry's name lives on with the word Gerrymandering, which is a combination of Gerry's name and the word salamander. This term refers to the redrawing of districts into odd shapes to favor one political party over another. This infamous behavior happened in Massachusetts when Gerry was governor.

Presidential Administration

Much of President Madison's time in office was spent on foreign affairs. Jefferson had left the presidency with an unsolved situation between the United States, France, and Great Britain, which led America into war against Britain in 1812. In the end, however, Madison's goal was to follow the strictures of the Constitution. It is fascinating to look at how he dealt with constitutional issues since he was the primary author of the document.

Foreign Relations

The Embargo Act passed during Jefferson's administration to fight French and British shipping abuses was in effect until it was replaced by the Non-Intercourse Act of 1809. Madison attempted to enforce this act, which allowed the United States to trade with all nations except France and Great Britain. Madison extended the offer to either nation that if they would protect America's shipping rights then they would be allowed to trade. This did not have much effect.

In 1810, Macon's Bill No. 2 repealed the Non-Intercourse Act. This bill provided that whichever nation would stop attacking American ships would be favored. The United States, in turn, would agree to stop trading with the other nation. France agreed and Britain continued its practice of impressment.

War of 1812

When Great Britain failed to stop harassing American ships and impressing soldiers, Madison went to Congress to ask for a declaration of war. Even though support for the war was not unanimous, there were enough votes to agree and thus began the War of 1812. America struggled at the beginning of the war. General William Hull attempted to invade Canada but instead ended up surrendering Detroit without a fight. However, the U.S. Navy had much more success and began defeating British ships. On September 13, 1813, Commodore Perry led the defeat of the British Navy on Lake Erie and delivered his ringing message, "We have met the enemy and they are ours." The British, however, were able to march on Washington and burn the White House. American troops stopped them later on their way to Baltimore.

By 1814, the United States and Great Britain decided to end the war with the Treaty of Ghent. This treaty essentially ended the war in a stalemate with no changes to previous policies, and with none of the prewar issues resolved. However, the war is often called the "Second War of Independence" because it marked the end of economic dependence on Great Britain.

PRESIDENTIAL TRIVIA

The South was not the first group to call for secession from the Union. At the Hartford Convention, which met to discuss what actions should be taken in protest to "Mr. Madison's War," there was talk of secession. Cooler heads prevailed and they demanded greater states' rights. The convention's demands arrived after the war had ended, and the members were disgraced.

Life After the Presidency

Upon the end of James Madison's second term as president, he returned to his plantation in Virginia. However, he stayed politically active throughout the rest of his life. He attended the Virginia constitutional convention in 1829. Further, he spoke against the misuse of his Virginia Resolutions that were being cited as grounds for the idea of nullification, or the ability of a state to proclaim a federal law as unconstitutional.

American Colonization Society

In 1833, James Madison became the president of the American Colonization Society. He had been a founding member of this group in 1816 that was created to help repatriate freed black slaves back to Africa. Over time, both the proslavery forces and the radical abolitionists fought against the society. It continued to exist after Madison's death until it was dissolved in 1913.

Death

James Madison died on June 28, 1836, at his estate, Montpelier, in Virginia. Madison was truly an influential man in America's founding and early years. As Albert Gallatin said upon Madison's retirement from the presidency, "Never was a country left in a more flourishing situation than the United States at the end of [his] administration; and they are more united at home and respected abroad than at any period since the war of . . . independence."

James Monroe: Author of the Monroe Doctrine

5

Born: April 28, 1758, in Westmoreland County, Virginia
Died: July 4, 1831, in New York City
First Lady: Elizabeth Kortright Monroe
Political Party: Democratic-Republican
Presidential Term: March 4, 1817 to March 3, 1825
Famous Quote: "The American continents . . . are henceforth not to be considered as subjects for future colonization by any European powers."

Timeline

1776–1780 . . . . . . Fought in the Revolution, rising to the rank of lieutenant colonel
1780 . . . . Named military commissioner of Virginia by Thomas Jefferson
1782–1783 . . . . . . Served in the Virginia Assembly
1783–1786 . . . . . . Member of the Continental Congress
1786–1790 . . . . . . Served in the Virginia Assembly
1786 . . . . Married Elizabeth Kortright
1790–1794 . . . . . . U.S. senator from Virginia
1794–1796 . . . . . . U.S. minister to France
1799–1802 . . . . . . Governor of Virginia
1803 . . . . Negotiated the Louisiana Purchase

1803–1807 . . . . . . U.S. minister to Great Britain
1811–1817 . . . . . . Secretary of state under President Madison
1814–1815 . . . . . . Secretary of war
1817–1825 . . . . . . Fifth president of the United States
1817 . . . . Mississippi admitted to the Union
1818 . . . . Illinois admitted to the Union
1819 . . . . Alabama admitted to the Union
1820 . . . . Maine admitted to the Union
1821 . . . . Missouri admitted to the Union
1829 . . . . Chairman, with James Madison, of the Virginia state constitutional convention

Becoming a Patriot

James Monroe was born into relative wealth in Virginia. His father, Spence Monroe, was a planter and a carpenter who had joined the patriots in their fight against British colonial policy. Little is known of his mother, Elizabeth Jones. However, he did grow up with one sister, Elizabeth Buckner, and three brothers: Spence, Andrew, and Joseph.

Early Life

From ages eleven to sixteen, Monroe studied at the Campbelltown Academy. He was an apt pupil, studying varying topics including Latin and math. He actually had John Marshall, future chief justice of the Supreme Court, as one of his classmates.

When Monroe was sixteen his father died, leaving Monroe to inherit his father's estate and become responsible for his younger brothers. His uncle, Joseph Jones, was made his guardian. Jones was a member of the Continental Congress.

SCANDALS & GOSSIP

When James Monroe was at William and Mary, numerous students were clamoring to join the ranks and fight against the British. In 1775, Monroe and twenty-three students stormed the governor's palace in Williamsburg and seized weapons to be used in the Revolution.

Also when Monroe turned sixteen, he went to the College of William and Mary. However, he did not stay there long, dropping out in 1776 to join the Continental Army. He did not return to college. Instead, he spent some time from 1780 to 1783 studying law with his friend and mentor, Thomas Jefferson.

First Lady: Elizabeth Kortright Monroe

James Monroe married Elizabeth Kortright, a woman ten years his junior, on February 16, 1786. She was from New York City and was considered to be extremely beautiful. However, she did suffer from ailments that kept her in later years from consistently acting the part of first lady. She and President Monroe had two daughters, Eliza and Maria Hester.

Background

Elizabeth was the daughter of a businessman, Laurence Kortright, who had also been an officer in the British Army. James Monroe married her and actually lived with her father while Monroe was serving in the Continental Congress. When she went to France with her husband, she played an important role in saving the Marquis de Lafayette's wife from the guillotine. She was very popular in France and received the nickname *la belle Americaine.*

Unpopular First Lady

Unfortunately, she was not as well loved at home once she became first lady. She was often not able to attend official functions due to chronic ailments and her daughters took over at these times. She was not one to entertain the Washington socialites as Dolley Madison had before her, and this caused many to dislike her. Further, she kept her daughter Maria's White House wedding private, which was seen as rude. Elizabeth died in 1830 at the Monroe's Oak Hill estate.

War Hero

James Monroe was involved in many of the American Revolution's major events before leaving the military in 1780. He joined the army as a lieutenant in 1776 and over time rose to the rank of lieutenant colonel. Further, he earned the respect of his fellow soldiers, especially George Washington who called him "brave, active, and sensible."

Crossing the Delaware and More

James Monroe crossed the Delaware with George Washington to fight at the Battle of Trenton where he was wounded and received a commendation for his bravery. He was aide-de-camp to Lord Stirling during the winter at Valley Forge. He fought at Brandywine, Germantown, and Monmouth, including serving as a scout for Washington during the latter battle.

Restless Under Lord Stirling

In 1778, James Monroe decided to leave Lord Stirling's service to try and create his own command out of volunteers from Virginia.

Lord Stirling was actually a man named William Alexander who had claimed the title of his ancestors in Scotland though his claim was never fully accepted by the British government. He was extremely heroic and well respected by Washington. In fact, he was given command of the Northern armies in 1781. He died before the end of the war.

On this front he was not successful. In 1780, Governor Thomas Jefferson made him military commissioner of Virginia. He would never again enter active duty, instead devoting his life to public service.

Advocate of States' Rights

James Monroe was first and foremost an advocate for states' rights. In fact, he would not agree to the ratification of the Constitution until the Bill of Rights was officially added in 1791. He served in the Virginia Assembly and the Continental Congress before becoming a U.S. senator for Virginia (1790–1804).

Diplomat

In 1794, James Monroe was made the U.S. minister to France by President Washington. He was important in gaining Thomas Paine's release from prison. However, in 1796 he was recalled by Washington for failing to fully support Jay's Treaty with Great Britain. Like Thomas Jefferson, he felt that the United States should be more supportive of France and its bid for democracy.

Monroe served as the governor of Virginia from 1799 until 1802. When Jefferson became president, he made Monroe a special envoy to France to help negotiate the terms of the Louisiana Purchase. Monroe was then sent to Great Britain and served as U.S. minister there from 1803 to 1807. He was unable to make any progress with the British as conditions continued to deteriorate between the two countries.

Secretary of State and War

President James Madison appointed Monroe to be secretary of state in 1811. Monroe quickly realized that war was inevitable with Britain. The War of 1812 began in June 1812 when the United States declared war. After the British marched on Washington in 1814, Monroe was named secretary of war by Madison and was the only person ever to hold both posts concurrently. He earned great acclaim for his role in strengthening the military and for his service to his country.

Virtually Uncontested

James Monroe was extremely popular at the end of Madison's term in office. He was the choice for president of both Thomas Jefferson and James Madison. Therefore, he easily won the nomination of the Democratic-Republicans.

Election of 1816

The Federalist party was defunct at the end of the War of 1812. However, Rufus King stepped forward to run against Monroe and his vice presidential candidate, Daniel D. Tompkins. King was supported by the remnants of the Federalist party. The campaign itself was not fierce, with little campaigning actually taking place, and Monroe won easily with 183 out of 217 electoral votes.

Election of 1820

The election of 1820 was truly unique. No candidate was named to run against President Monroe. He was the obvious choice and when the time for counting votes occurred, he received all of the electoral votes except one. This is when the term "Era of Good Feelings" arose due to the lack of partisanship.

SCANDALS & GOSSIP

Tradition had it that William Plumer did not cast his electoral vote for Monroe in the 1820 election so that Washington would be the only unanimously elected president. However, in *Life of William Plumer* by William Plumer Jr. (1857), his son stated that he actually did not like Monroe and voted instead for John Quincy Adams.

Presidential Administration

While Monroe's time in office was called the "Era of Good Feelings," there were actually problems brewing. America entered its first depression (1819–1821), which at that time was called a panic. Sectionalism would continue to rear its ugly head until it was decisively cut off with the Civil War. Finally, America needed to find its place in the world. Monroe stepped up and delivered the Monroe Doctrine to this end.

First Seminole War

One of the first things that President Monroe had to contend with was the First Seminole War (1817–1818). Seminole Indians were raiding Georgia from across the border in Spanish-held Florida. Monroe sent General Andrew Jackson to the region to try to contain the situation. However, Jackson disobeyed orders against invading Florida and instead moved against it and deposed the military governor.

While many called for Jackson to be reprimanded for his actions, no such statement was made. The move against Florida most probably helped speed up the Adams-Onis Treaty, which occurred in 1819 and by which Spain gave Florida to the United States while keeping control of Texas.

Missouri Compromise

The issue of slave states versus free states was heading toward direct confrontation with each new state entering the Union. The Missouri Compromise (1820) was an effort to maintain the balance between the two, thereby alleviating any problems. In this compromise, Missouri was admitted as a slave state while Maine became a free state. Further, any future states created out of the land of the Louisiana Purchase above latitude 36 degrees 30 minutes were to be free. This compromise helped stave off the Civil War for a few more decades.

Monroe Doctrine

The most enduring event that occurred during Monroe's presidency was the delivery of the Monroe Doctrine in 1823. In a speech before Congress, Monroe made a pronouncement that would guide American foreign policy throughout the nineteenth century. He stated that America would not allow European powers to expand into or intervene in the Western Hemisphere.

This, along with Theodore Roosevelt's Roosevelt Corollary and Franklin Roosevelt's Good Neighbor policy, is still a central part of U.S. foreign policy.

Life After the Presidency

James Monroe did not seek a third term in office and instead retired with his wife to his estate, Oak Hill, in Virginia. In 1829, he and James Madison were named chairmen of the Virginia constitutional convention. Unfortunately, he was deeply in debt and sold Oak Hill upon his wife's death in 1830. He then moved to New York City and lived with his daughter until his death at age seventy-three on July 4, 1831.

6

John Quincy Adams: World Traveler

Born:	July 11, 1767
Died:	February 23, 1848
First Lady:	Louisa Catherine Johnson Adams
Political Party:	Democratic-Republican
Presidential Term:	March 4, 1825 to March 3, 1829
Famous Quote:	"America does not go abroad in search of monsters to destroy. She is the well-wisher to freedom and independence of all. She is the champion and vindicator only of her own."

Timeline

1787 . . . . .Graduated from Harvard
1794–1797 . . . . . . .U.S. minister to the Netherlands
1797 . . . . .Married Louisa Catherine Johnson
1797–1801 . . . . . . .U.S. minister to Prussia
1803–1808 . . . . . .U.S. senator from Massachusetts
1809–1814 . . . . . .U.S. minister to Russia
1814 . . . . .Chief negotiator for Treaty of Ghent
1815–1817 . . . . . . .U.S. minister to Great Britain
1817–1825 . . . . . . .Secretary of state
1825–1829 . . . . . .Sixth president of the United States
1830–1848 . . . . . .U.S. representative from Massachusetts

Son of a President

John Quincy Adams was born on July 11, 1767, in Braintree, Massachusetts. As the son of the John Adams, second president of the United States, and Abigail Adams, one of the most erudite of America's first ladies, John Quincy Adams had a fascinating childhood. He was almost nine when independence was declared, and he personally witnessed the Battle of Bunker Hill with his mother. Obviously this upbringing had a huge impact on his future life.

Traveling in His Youth

When Adams was ten years old, he moved to Europe with his father who was sent there on various diplomatic missions. He received his first formal education near Paris and attended Leyden University in Amsterdam. In 1781, Adams became the secretary to Francis Dana who was on a mission to Russia. The mission was not a success, as Catherine II would not receive them. Adams then spent five months traveling through Europe on his way to meet his father at the Hague.

IN THEIR OWN WORDS...

John Quincy Adams on the importance of liberty: "Individual liberty is individual power, and as the power of a community is a mass compounded of individual powers, the nation which enjoys the most freedom must necessarily be in proportion to its numbers the most powerful nation."

Adams returned to America at the age of seventeen, having seen more of Europe than many of his time. This would have a huge effect on his future life as a diplomat.

Harvard and Law

After returning from Europe, Adams entered Harvard as a junior. He graduated second in his class and was chosen to deliver the senior English oration. He then studied law with Theophilus Parsons in Massachusetts. He was admitted to the Massachusetts bar in 1790.

First Lady: Louisa Catherine Johnson Adams

John Quincy Adams's wife was the only foreign-born first lady America has had. She was the daughter of an American merchant and an Englishwoman and grew up in London and France. She was often sick with migraine headaches and also suffered from depression. Their marriage was not marked by much happiness. Louisa herself felt that the Adams men were cold and often unapproachable. Louisa and John had three sons: George Washington, John, and Charles Francis. Their youngest, Charles, followed in his father's footsteps and became an influential diplomat. Louisa Adams died on May 15, 1852.

Career Before the Presidency

After being admitted to the bar, Adams began a short-lived law career in Boston from 1790 until 1794. During this time, his father was serving as vice president of the United States. John Quincy Adams was a huge supporter of the Washington administration and published articles in support of its policies. Due to this and the fact that he could speak Dutch, Washington appointed him as diplomat to the Netherlands in 1794. Thus began his illustrious career as a diplomat.

The Diplomat

From 1794 to 1801 and then again from 1809 until 1817, Adams served as a minister to various European countries. He ensured that America paid its debts to the Dutch for money lent during the American Revolution. In 1797, he was sent to Prussia by his father who had recently been inaugurated as president. He completed an important commercial treaty there before returning home in 1801.

From 1802 until 1808, Adams was in the United States serving first as a Massachusetts state senator and then as a U.S. senator. Despite his experience as a diplomat, Adams was not known for his tact or interpersonal skills in Congress. Even though he was elected as a Federalist, he actually supported Thomas Jefferson as president. Because he did not support Federalist policies during his time as representative, he was forced to resign in 1808.

From 1809 until 1814, President James Madison appointed Adams to be the minister to Russia. He was able to establish a good relationship with Tsar Alexander and witnessed Napoleon's failed attempt to invade Russia.

As a sign of the faith placed in Adams's diplomatic skills, Madison chose Adams to be the chief negotiator of the peace treaty between America and Great Britain that officially ended the War of 1812. After completing his work on the Treaty of Ghent, he was assigned to be the U.S. minister to Great Britain until 1817.

Secretary of State

In 1817, Adams was recalled to the United States when President James Monroe appointed him to be his secretary of state. This was a job that was particularly suited for him and in which he proved to be one of the best who ever held that position. During his time as secretary, he was able to establish fishing rights with Canada, formalize the western U.S.-Canadian border, and negotiate the Adams-Onis Treaty, which gave Florida to the United States. He helped craft the Monroe Doctrine that warned European powers against interfering in the Western Hemisphere and insisted that America present this as a unilateral declaration instead of a joint declaration with Great Britain. He left the office better organized and able to manage future diplomatic duties.

Election of 1824

Despite his successes as a diplomat and as secretary of state, John Quincy Adams did not enter the presidency with resounding support. The election of 1824 was unique because none of the candidates declared a party. In fact, no major caucuses or national conventions existed to nominate candidates. John Quincy Adams had three major opponents: Andrew Jackson, William Crawford, and Henry Clay. The campaign was full of sectional strife. Jackson was much more a "man of the people" than Adams and had widespread support. He won 42 percent of the popular vote versus Adams's 32 percent. However, Jackson received 37 percent of the electoral vote and Adams got only 32 percent. Since no one received a majority, the election was sent to the House of Representatives as required by the U.S. Constitution.

With the election to be decided in the House, each state could cast one vote for president. Henry Clay dropped out of the race and his supporters backed John Quincy Adams. Adams was elected to be president on the first vote. He was the only president to be elected with both less popular votes and less electoral votes than his opponent.

SCANDALS & GOSSIP

Opponents of John Quincy Adams claimed that he and Henry Clay had made a "corrupt bargain." After a private meeting between Clay and Adams, Clay's supporters switched their votes to Adams. When Adams became president, one of his first actions was to name Clay his secretary of state. Both Adams and Clay denied any wrongdoing.

Presidential Administration

President Adams fully realized when he took office that he did not start with the support of the majority, nor even with most of the popular votes. As he said in his inaugural speech, "Fellow-citizens, you are acquainted with the peculiar circumstances of the recent election. . . . Less possessed of your confidence in advance than any of my predecessors, I am deeply conscious of the prospect that I shall stand more and oftener in need of your indulgence. Intentions upright and pure, a heart devoted to the welfare of our country, and the unceasing application of all the faculties allotted to me to her service are all the pledges that I can give for the faithful performance of the arduous duties I am to undertake."

Throughout his presidency he did not have the support of Congress or the people, and therefore he did not accomplish much during his one term as president. He asked for extensive internal improvements, but very few were passed.

QUIRKS & ODDITIES

John Quincy Adams swam nude almost daily in the Potomac River and was known for denying interviews to reporters. Anne Royall, a very outspoken female reporter, became the first woman to interview a president when one day she went to the Potomac, sat on his clothes, and would not get up until he granted her an interview.

Tariff of Abominations

In 1828, a tariff called the Tariff of Abominations by its adversaries was passed. This bill placed a high tax on imported manufactured goods. Its goal was to protect American manufacturing. It was strongly opposed—mainly in the South—because the British would require less cotton from that region to make their manufactured goods.

Adams's own vice president, John C. Calhoun of South Carolina, argued against the law. He claimed that South Carolina should have the right of nullification, or the right to rule the tariff unconstitutional and therefore ignore it in the state. He even went so far as to threaten that, if the tariff was not repealed, the state of South Carolina would secede from the Union. The South Carolina legislature did not accept his proposal. However, the idea of nullification would surface again when Andrew Jackson was president.

Life After the Presidency

In 1828, John Quincy Adams was chosen by his party, now called the National Republicans, to run for reelection against Andrew Jackson. The campaign was more about mudslinging and less about the issues. The "corrupt bargain" charge resurfaced and dogged Adams throughout the campaign. In the end, Jackson won the election and Adams left to go back home to Massachusetts.

U.S. Representative

Adams's retirement from politics did not last long. He was elected to represent his district in the U.S. House of Representatives in 1830. He was the only president to serve in Congress after being a president. He played an important role in the House for seventeen years. He was always true to his own beliefs, even when he was in the minority, as he was when he opposed the annexation of Texas.

Amistad Case

In 1841, Adams was part of the defense team for the slave mutineers in the Amistad case. In 1839, forty-nine Africans seized the Spanish ship *Amistad* off the coast of Cuba and tried to get two Cuban survivors to sail them back to Africa. However, they ended up in America where they were immediately seized. The Spanish demanded that the Americans deliver them to Cuba to stand trial. However, the mutineers's fates were eventually decided by the U.S. Supreme Court. Adams threw himself into the defense and helped fellow attorney Roger Baldwin gain their freedom.

Death

On February 21, 1848, John Quincy Adams collapsed on the floor of the U.S House of Representatives. He had suffered a cerebral hemorrhage. He was taken to the Speaker of the House's private chamber where he died two days later on February 23. His last words are thought to have been, "This is the end of earth, I am content."

Andrew Jackson: Man of the People

Born:	March 15, 1767
Died:	June 8, 1845
Marriage:	None. His wife, Rachel Donelson Robards Jackson, died in 1828 before he took office.
Political Party:	Democratic
Presidential Term:	March 4, 1829 to March 3, 1837
Famous Quote:	"One man with courage makes a majority."

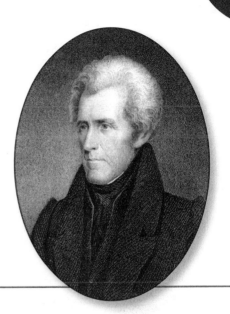

Timeline

Child of the American Revolution

Andrew Jackson was born on March 15, 1767, near the border between North and South Carolina. His father, also named Andrew Jackson, died the year he was born. He was raised against the backdrop of the American Revolution. In fact, it robbed him of his mother, Elizabeth Hutchinson, who died of cholera contracted while nursing injured soldiers, and his two brothers, Hugh, who died in battle, and Robert, who died from smallpox that he contracted while a prisoner of war. Jackson was only fourteen years old when he was left on his own to be raised by two different uncles.

IN THEIR OWN WORDS...

Growing up as Jackson did led to strongly held beliefs concerning courage, union, and morality. As he said: "The individual who refuses to defend his rights when called by his Government, deserves to be a slave, and must be punished as an enemy of his country and friend to her foe."

Jackson learned to read at a very young age and received a fairly good education. However, when he inherited a large sum of money upon the death of his grandfather in Ireland, he quickly wasted it on gambling and alcohol. Broke at fifteen, he chose to go back to school and became a lawyer in 1787.

Marriage: Rachel Donelson Robards Jackson

Rachel Donelson was born in 1767 and grew up on the frontier. She began life in Virginia but moved with her parents to Tennessee and then Kentucky. At the age of seventeen, she married Lewis Robards of Mercer County. However, they separated by 1790, and she heard that he was filing a petition for divorce.

Honest Mistake

In 1791, Rachel married Andrew Jackson. They were very much in love. Once married, however, they were horrified to discover that while Robards did in fact file a petition for divorce, he did not actually proceed with the divorce. Robards brought a suit against Rachel for adultery. Jackson and Rachel were not able to remarry legally until 1794. This would later be used against Jackson during the campaign of 1828. While Jackson and Rachel did not have any natural children, they did adopt one son who they named Andrew Jr.

Untimely Death

Rachel Jackson died two months before her husband took office in 1829. The cause of her death is unknown but Jackson blamed John Quincy Adams and other political enemies because of the personal attacks made against her character over questions of adultery and bigotry from their marriage. Rachel's niece Emily Donelson acted as Jackson's unofficial first lady until his daughter-in-law, Sarah Yorke Jackson, joined Emily in acting as a hostess for the White House.

Military Service

Although Jackson served for a brief time in the Revolutionary Army when he was thirteen, his first real military service came as major general of the Tennessee Volunteers from 1813 to 1814. He led a campaign against the Creek Indians who had attacked American settlers north of Mobile, Alabama. He defeated the Creeks decisively at the Battle of Horseshoe Bend in March 1814. On August 9, 1814, Jackson signed the Treaty of Fort Jackson, officially ending the Creek War and causing the Indians to surrender their lands in Georgia and Alabama.

PRESIDENTIAL TRIVIA

Andrew Jackson was the only president to have also been a prisoner of war. He and his brother Robert were captured during the Revolutionary War. Both were released in a matter of weeks. They both contracted smallpox during the ordeal. Robert died a few days after release while Jackson was able to recover.

Battle of New Orleans

In 1814, Jackson became a major general in the regular army to fight in the War of 1812. His huge victory came on January 8, 1815, when he defeated the British at the Battle of New Orleans. Ironically, unbeknownst to Jackson or the British, his victory came after the Treaty of Ghent had been signed, officially ending the war. Nonetheless, this battle was a huge popularity boost for Jackson, who became a national hero.

Jackson Disobeys Orders

Jackson left military service until he was recalled to fight in the First Seminole War in December 1817. Seminole Indians and runaway slaves were attacking Georgia from Spanish-held Florida. He was ordered to repel the attackers but instead invaded Spanish Florida—without President James Monroe's authorization.

Jackson's invasion initially caused international censure of the United States and many claimed that Jackson should be disciplined. However, Secretary of State John Quincy Adams was able to spin this so that the United States could blame it on Spanish negligence in protecting their borders. Adams actually used this affair to get the Adams-Onis Treaty signed whereby Spain ceded Florida to the United States.

Representing the Democratic Spirit

In 1796, Tennessee was admitted as the sixteenth state in the Union. Andrew Jackson was a delegate to the convention that framed Tennessee's constitution and was then elected as that state's first U.S. representative. He was quickly elected to the U.S. Senate in 1797 but resigned after only five months, feeling that the Senate did not move fast enough to pass required legislation.

Despite his limited experience practicing law, Jackson was appointed as a justice on the Tennessee Supreme Court from 1798 until 1804. He was known for his fair and swift judgments.

Triumph of the Common Man in 1828

After becoming a war hero and having served as the military governor of Florida, Andrew Jackson again became a U.S. senator. It was during this time that he ran for president against John Quincy Adams in 1824.

Jackson won the popular vote but lacked an electoral majority. Therefore, when the election was decided by the House of Representatives, as required by the Constitution, it went to John Quincy Adams. Proponents for Jackson claimed a corrupt bargain had been made for it was believed that Adams was given the presidency in exchange for Henry Clay's appointment as secretary of state. The backlash from this helped Jackson gain popular support for nomination to run again in 1828 and caused the Democratic-Republican party to split into two camps.

Jackson became the Democratic nominee for president in 1825 and began his opposition while Adams was in his first year in office. John C. Calhoun of South Carolina was his running mate. The presidential campaign centered around the candidates themselves. Jackson was seen as representing the common man and his interests. In the end, Jackson won 54 percent of the popular vote and 68 percent of the electoral vote.

King Andrew I Wins in 1832

Prior to the election of 1832, parties typically decided their candidates through small groups of insiders called caucuses. In 1832, this changed when the two major parties first used national party conventions, which allowed for much greater participation by the electorate. Jackson ran as the incumbent against Henry Clay. Jackson's opponents had given him the nickname King Andrew I during his first term in office due to his extensive use of the presidential veto, his belief in rewarding loyal followers with offices through the spoils system, and his opposition to the Bank of the United States. In spite of this, Jackson was able to easily win with 76 percent of the electoral vote.

Presidential Administration

Andrew Jackson was not known for his tact or his willingness to back down. In fact, during his presidential administration, he vetoed more bills than all previous presidents combined. He believed in using the full force of his position to set policy and to reward loyalty. Instead of relying on his official cabinet, as previous presidents had, he gathered together an informal group of advisers that was called the "kitchen cabinet."

An example of Jackson's willingness to fight for his beliefs came with his veto of the second Bank of the United States. He felt that the federal government had no right to create such a bank that did not have any safeguards in place to provide oversight. He saw that the bank had the potential to wield great political power by using its financial influence. This veto was unpopular with many, including many of the members of his formal cabinet. However, he did not back down and despite final efforts by the bank to retain power, it was ultimately finished.

Peggy Eaton was the wife of Jackson's secretary of war, John Eaton. Because of rumors that Peggy's first husband had committed suicide due to her infidelities, she was shunned by Washington society. Jackson abhorred this conduct, possibly because he blamed the death of his own wife on the treatment she endured during his campaign. His cabinet spent more time dealing with this scandal than doing the work of the nation.

Sectional Strife

As time progressed, divisions between the Northern and Southern states were growing worse. Part of this was due to the different ways that the North and the South viewed the powers of the national government. Many of the Southern states fought hard to preserve states's rights and saw actions that they perceived as impeding these rights as unconstitutional.

Many southerners did not believe that the national government had the right to impose direct taxes or tariffs on them. When Jackson signed a tariff into law in 1832, South Carolina felt that it had the right to ignore it on the premise of nullification—the belief that a state could rule a federal act unconstitutional. Jackson, a southerner himself, took a strong stance and showed that he was ready to use the military to make sure that South

Carolina paid the tariff. In 1833, a compromise was reached to help mollify the South for a time, but tempers continued to rise until the United States reached a breaking point and the Civil War broke out.

Trail of Tears

The state of Georgia appealed to Andrew Jackson about removing Cherokees from the state to reservations in the West. The Supreme Court had decided in *Worcester v. Georgia* (1832) that the state had no right to expel the Cherokees. However, Jackson ignored the ruling and, using the Indian Removal Act of 1830, had his commissioner create a treaty with the Cherokees in which they agreed to exchange their lands for those out West. The treaty was ratified in 1836 and the Cherokees had two years to leave Georgia. President Martin Van Buren, Jackson's successor, ended up having to forcibly remove more than 15,000 Cherokees from Georgia to the West along the Trail of Tears. The journey was so poorly planned and managed that nearly 4,000 Cherokees died on the trip.

PRESIDENTIAL TRIVIA

Jackson survived an assassination attempt in 1835. Richard Lawrence blamed Jackson for keeping him out of work. He fired a derringer at the president but it misfired. A second gun was tried and also didn't fire. The guns were later tested and shown to work correctly. Lawrence was the first person to attempt to assassinate a president. He was arrested and found not guilty by reason of insanity.

Life After the Presidency

Andrew Jackson retired from the presidency in 1837. He returned to his home, the Hermitage, near Nashville, Tennessee. Jackson stayed politically active, campaigning for his successor Martin Van Buren in the 1840 election and actively supporting the annexation of Texas and the election of James K. Polk. Despite owning slaves and being from the South, Jackson never gave any support to those who talked of seceding from the Union. He died at the age of seventy-eight on June 8, 1845.

8

Martin Van Buren: The Little Magician

Born:	December 5, 1782
Died:	July 24, 1862
First Lady:	None. His wife, Hannah Hoes Van Buren, died in 1819 before he took office.
Political Party:	Democratic
Presidential Term:	March 4, 1837 to March 3, 1841
Famous Quote:	"For myself, therefore, I desire to declare that the principle that will govern me in the high duty to which my country calls me is a strict adherence to the letter and spirit of the Constitution as it was designed by those who framed it."

Timeline

1803 . . . . .Admitted to the bar

1807 . . . . .Married Hannah Hoes

1812–1820 . . . . . . .New York state senator

1821–1828 . . . . . . .U.S. senator from New York

1829 . . . . .Governor of New York

1829–1831 . . . . . . .U.S. secretary of state

1833–1837 . . . . . . .Vice president of the United States under President Jackson

1837–1841 . . . . . . .Eighth president of the United States

Childhood and Education

Martin Van Buren was born in Kinderhook, New York, to Abraham and Maria Van Buren. He was of Dutch descent, although his ancestors had been in America for more than one hundred years. His father was a farmer and tavern keeper, and Martin worked in the tavern during his youth while attending a local school. The tavern was frequented by lawyers and politicians including Aaron Burr and Alexander Hamilton. In this environment, Van Buren kindled his love of politics. His father maintained a neutral stance in public on divisive issues but privately was an anti-Federalist. Van Buren finished his formal education by the age of fourteen and then went on to study law. He was admitted to the New York bar in 1803 at the age of twenty-one.

On February 21, 1807, Van Buren married Hannah Hoes, a distant relative of his mother. Not much is known about Hannah outside of accounts that said she was kind, social, and deeply involved in her religion, which was Dutch Reformed. She bore five sons and four of them lived to maturity: Abraham, John, Martin Jr., and Smith Thompson. John was the most famous of their children and grew up to become a member of the U.S. House of Representatives in 1841. He was also an important abolitionist leading up to the Civil War. Hannah died in 1819 at the age of thirty-five, probably from tuberculosis, and Van Buren never remarried.

While Van Buren was president, his son Abraham met one of Dolley Madison's relatives, Angelica Singleton. They married in 1838 and while Abraham served as his father's private secretary, Angelica performed the traditional first lady duties from 1838 until 1840.

Old Kinderhook's Early Career

After Van Buren was admitted to the bar, he began to practice law in New York. In 1812, he was elected to the New York State Senate, where he served until 1820. He became an important figure in the Democratic party during this time. In fact, he held the post of state attorney general while still serving in the Senate from 1815 until 1819.

Van Buren also created one of the first political machines in the form of the Albany Regency. His group of democratic allies was active on both the state and national levels and was very effective in maintaining party discipline and using patronage positions to influence people.

QUIRKS & ODDITIES

The term "OK" probably had its origins with Martin Van Buren. The oldest written reference to the term in fact was during the election of 1840. His nickname was "Old Kinderhook" after his birthplace in New York, and his supporters formed the "OK Club." "OK" later came to mean "all correct."

U.S. Senate

Van Buren was elected to serve in the U.S. Senate beginning in 1821. He did not always follow a consistent voting record in the Senate—for example, he supported the national government's right to impose tariffs but did not always agree that it had the right to make internal improvements like interstate roads. However, he strongly supported Andrew Jackson in 1828 and worked hard to get him elected. In fact, he ran for governor in the state of New York as a means to garner support for Jackson in 1828.

Serving Under Andrew Jackson

When Jackson took office in 1828, he appointed Van Buren to be his secretary of state. Van Buren, who had served as governor of New York for three months, resigned this elected position to take the appointment. Van Buren was a very influential member of Jackson's cabinet and a prominent figure in his "kitchen cabinet." He held this position until he resigned in 1831 over the Peggy Eaton affair. He felt that the scandal was overtaking national concerns within the cabinet. The effect of his move was that other cabinet members also resigned, allowing Jackson to appoint new members who he felt would be more in line with his policies. In 1832, Van Buren ran and won as Jackson's vice president.

PRESIDENTIAL TRIVIA

Only four vice presidents have succeeded the president under whom they served. Three of these, John Adams, Thomas Jefferson, and Martin Van Buren, happened within the first forty years of the presidency. This did not occur again until 1988 when George H. W. Bush succeeded Ronald Reagan to become the forty-first president of the United States.

Election of 1836

Jackson rewarded Van Buren's loyalty by supporting him for the Democratic nomination of 1836. The opposing party, the Whigs, was created in 1834 for the sole purpose of opposing Andrew Jackson. This election was unique in that the Whig party did not oppose Van Buren with a single candidate but instead chose three separate candidates who could do well in particular regions of the country. They felt that if they could deny Van Buren a majority, then this would send the vote into the House of Representatives to decide who would be president, thus giving them a better chance of winning. However, the Whig party's plan backfired and Van Buren was able to carry the majority and win the presidency with 58 percent of the electoral vote.

Presidential Administration

Martin Van Buren's term in office was not marked by major events like the terms of many other presidents. One important event that did occur was an economic depression that began in 1837 and lasted until 1845 and was called the Panic of 1837. Because of restrictions placed on state banks during Jackson's time in office, they severely restricted credit and called for the repayment of loans. There was a run on the banks by many depositors wanting to withdraw their money. In the end, more than 900 banks closed and many people lost their jobs and their money. Van Buren blamed the banks for the panic and did not feel that the government should play a huge part in alleviating the problems. However, he did fight for an independent treasury to ensure that funds could be safely deposited.

In 1836, Texas applied for statehood. If admitted, however, then it would add another slave state to the Union. Van Buren did not want to increase sectional problems so he agreed with the North and helped block admission. His decision to maintain sectional balance delayed Texas's admission to the Union until 1845.

Some presidents have relished their position, but Martin Van Buren was not one of them. According to him: "As to the Presidency, the two happiest days of my life were those of my entrance upon the office and my surrender of it."

One problem that Van Buren had to deal with in 1839 was a boundary dispute with Canada termed the "Aroostook War." Although it was called a war, no fighting actually occurred. There were more than 12,000 square miles between Maine and Canada along the Aroostook River that had no defined boundary. When a Maine official attempted to send Canadians out of the region and was met with resistance, both sides sent militias to the region. However, Van Buren was able to resolve the issue quickly by sending General Winfield Scott to make peace.

Van Buren was heavily criticized for his lifestyle while the nation was experiencing a depression. He enjoyed fine wines and held lavish private parties. False stories began to circulate about his excesses. In the end, this helped bring about his defeat by William Henry Harrison.

Life After the Presidency

In 1840, Van Buren lost his bid for reelection to war hero William Henry Harrison. He tried again in 1844 and 1848 but was denied the presidency each time. At that point, he decided to retire from public life. He did come back to serve as a presidential elector for both Franklin Pierce and James Buchanan. He lived to see the beginning of the Civil War but died on July 2, 1862, of heart failure.

William Henry Harrison: Old Tippecanoe

Born:	February 9, 1773
Died:	April 4, 1841
First Lady:	Anna Tuthill Symmes Harrison
Political Party:	Whig
Presidential Term:	March 4, 1841 to April 4, 1841
Famous Quote:	"But I contend that the strongest of all governments is that which is most free."

Timeline

1791 . . . . .Left medical school to join the army

1795 . . . . .Married Anna Tuthill Symmes

1798–1799 . . . . . .Secretary of the Northwest Territory

1800–1812 . . . . . .Governor of Indiana Territory

1812 . . . . .Served as a major general during the War of 1812

1816–1819 . . . . . . .U.S. representative for Cincinnati, Ohio

1819–1821 . . . . . . .Ohio state senator

1825–1828 . . . . . . U.S. senator representing Ohio

1828–1829 . . . . . .Minister to Colombia

1841 . . . . .Ninth president of the United States

Political Legacy

William Henry Harrison was born in Virginia to a family with a long history of serving in political office. Harrison's father, Benjamin Harrison V, was a famous patriot. He served in the Virginia legislature for twenty-seven years before the Revolutionary War, where he was opposed to British policies including the Stamp Act. He signed the Declaration of Independence in 1776. After the Revolution, he served in various offices including five years as the governor of Virginia during his son's youth. While little is known of Harrison's mother, Elizabeth Bassett, their home was attacked during the American Revolution and many of their belongings were stolen or destroyed. Luckily, he and his family fled before the attack.

Harrison was privately tutored and decided that he would like to become a doctor. He first attended Hampden-Sydney College and went on to the University of Pennsylvania Medical School in 1791 but had to drop out when he could no longer afford it. He then joined the military.

First Lady: Anna Tuthill Symmes Harrison

On November 25, 1795, Harrison married Anna Tuthill Symmes behind her father's back. In fact, her father had never approved of Harrison as a husband for his daughter because of his career in the military. He would not approve of Harrison until the future president became a war hero.

Anna had been raised in a wealthy family that owned a large part of present-day Cincinnati, Ohio. Her father, John Cleves Symmes, had at one time been the chief justice of the New Jersey Supreme Court. Anna was extremely well educated for her time. She met Harrison while visiting Lexington, Kentucky. She never occupied the White House because her husband died one month after taking office, and she became the first recipient of a federal pension for a president's widow. The Harrisons had nine children, five of whom died before he became president. Their son John Scott would be the father of the twenty-third president, Benjamin Harrison.

War Hero and Public Servant

William Henry Harrison joined the military in 1791 and served until 1798, fighting in the Indian Wars in the Northwest Territory. In 1794, he led his men at the Battle of Fallen Timbers. During this battle, U.S. forces faced a confederacy of about 1,000 Native Americans including members of the Shawnee, Miami, Ottawa, and Chippewa tribes, among others. The tribes were forced to retreat.

This victory led to the signing of the Treaty of Greenville in 1795, for which Harrison was present. This treaty required the tribes to give up claims to lands in the Northwest Territory in exchange for money and the right to hunt in the territory. Harrison was commended for his actions at the battle and promoted to captain.

IN THEIR OWN WORDS...

William Henry Harrison, in addition to being hailed as a war hero, was well respected by his men. Major Richard M. Johnson, who would later become Martin Van Buren's vice president, said in 1812: "He has the confidence of the forces without a parallel in our History except in the case of General Washington in the revolution."

Harrison left military service in 1798 to become first the secretary of the Northwest Territory and then the governor of the Indiana Territory.

Tippecanoe

Even though Harrison was not in the military in 1811, he led a force against the Indian Confederacy in Indiana. Tecumseh and his brother, the Prophet, were Shawnee leaders of this confederacy. The Native Americans launched a surprise attack on Harrison and his men while they slept at Tippecanoe Creek, but Harrison was able to rouse his men and stop the attack. They then moved against the confederacy, burning their village, which was called Prophetstown. This is how Harrison came by his nickname: "Old Tippecanoe."

War of 1812

Harrison did not officially rejoin the military until he decided to fight in the War of 1812. He began the war as a major general of Kentucky militia and by the war's end was named a major general of the Northwest Territories. His forces were able to retake Detroit from British colonel Henry Procter. He then became a national hero at the Battle of the Thames where his forces defeated the British and their Indian allies, including the Shawnee leader Tecumseh. He resigned from the army in May 1814.

Road to the Presidency

Harrison ran an unsuccessful campaign to become president in 1836 and was defeated by Martin Van Buren. He was nominated again by the Whig party in 1840 with John Tyler as his vice president. This time President Van Buren was the incumbent. However, the huge economic depression that occurred during his first term in office hurt his popularity. During the campaign, Harrison was viewed as coming from a humble background while Van Buren was seen as an elite who was out of touch with the people.

Van Buren could not even carry his home state of New York and Harrison easily won the election with 80 percent of the electoral votes.

PRESIDENTIAL TRIVIA

The election of 1840 featured the first modern campaign. The parties used advertising and campaign slogans such as "Tippecanoe and Tyler Too." Further, his supporters contrived an image of Harrison as having been born in a log cabin even though he was actually raised on a wealthy estate. The image stuck and enabled him to gain the majority of votes on the Western frontier.

Tecumseh's Curse

When Harrison took office in March 1841, he delivered the longest inaugural address ever on an extremely cold day. He then got caught in a rainstorm and came down with a cold. This grew worse and eventually led to his death on April 4, 1841, one month after taking office. Many have claimed over the years that his death was a result of "Tecumseh's Curse." This was the legend that developed over time that claimed that any president who won an election in years that ended in zeroes—for example 1840, 1860, etc.—would die while serving as president. Many saw this as retribution for Harrison's participation in defeating Tecumseh and burning Prophetstown.

SCANDALS & GOSSIP

Whether or not there is any truth to the myth, Tecumseh's Curse seemed to be in effect until Ronald Reagan, who was elected in 1980, survived an assassination attempt. Prior to that, Abraham Lincoln (1860), James Garfield (1880), William McKinley (1900), Warren G. Harding (1920), Franklin Roosevelt (1940), and John F. Kennedy (1960) all died naturally or by assassination while serving as president.

Because Harrison's time in office was so brief, he did not have a significant impact on the nation. His time was mainly spent dealing with individuals wishing to seek offices under his administration.

Harrison was the first president to die in office. Following the dictates of the U.S. Constitution, John Tyler then took over the presidency. Harrison's body lay in state at the U.S. Capitol and thousands of mourners paid their respects before he was buried.

John Tyler: First Presidential Successor

Born:	March 29, 1790
Died:	January 18, 1862
Two First Ladies:	Letitia Christian Tyler and Julia Gardiner Tyler
Political Party:	Whig
Presidential Term:	April 4, 1841 to March 3, 1845
Famous Quote:	"Let it, then, be henceforth proclaimed to the world, that man's conscience was created free; that he is no longer accountable to his fellow man for his religious opinions, being responsible therefore only to his God."

Timeline

1807 . . . . .Graduated from the College of William and Mary
1809 . . . . .Admitted to the bar
1811–1816 . . . . . . .Member of Virginia House of Delegates
1813 . . . . .Married Letitia Christian
1816–1821 . . . . . . .U.S. representative
1823–1825 . . . . . . .Member of Virginia House of Delegates
1825–1827 . . . . . . .Governor of Virginia
1827–1836 . . . . . . .U.S. senator
1838–1840 . . . . . .Member of Virginia House of Delegates
1841 . . . . .Vice president of the United States under William Henry Harrison
1841–1845 . . . . . .Tenth president of the United States
1844 . . . . .Married Julia Gardiner
1861 . . . . .Elected to Confederate House of Representatives

Childhood and Education

Not a great deal is known about the childhood of John Tyler. He grew up on a plantation in Virginia where his mother, Mary Armistead, died when he was only seven years old. His father, John Sr., was a huge supporter of not only the American Revolution but also of Thomas Jefferson. He also believed strongly in states' rights and did not support the ratification of the Constitution because he felt that it gave the federal government too much power.

When John Tyler was twelve, he entered the College of William and Mary Preparatory School. He continued his studies there and graduated from the upper college in 1807. He was a good student, especially in economics. After graduation, he studied law under his father and later under Edmund Randolph, the first U.S. attorney general. In 1809, he was admitted to the Virginia bar.

Two First Ladies: Letitia Christian Tyler and Julia Gardner Tyler

John Tyler married Letitia Christian when he was twenty-three years old on March 29, 1813. They were married for twenty-nine years. She was a pious woman who was devoted to her family, and she did not get involved in political life when her husband served in Congress. In 1839, she experienced a stroke and when Tyler won the presidency, she was unable to perform her duties as first lady. Instead, their daughter-in-law Priscilla Cooper acted as the official hostess in her stead. Letitia suffered a second stroke and died on September 10, 1842.

Married While President

Tyler was married again, during his presidency, to Julia Gardiner, who was thirty years his junior. They married in New York City on June 26, 1844, in a very low-key ceremony in an attempt to avoid intense public scrutiny. The wedding was kept so secret that none of his children (except one) knew about it in advance. Julia was actually five years younger than Tyler's eldest daughter, Mary, who resented his quick marriage to the socialite.

SCANDALS & GOSSIP

Julia Gardner was no stranger to scandal. She was a beautiful young woman and at the age of nineteen she appeared in an advertisement for a department store which called her the "Rose of Long Island." This was just not something that women from the wealthy class did at that time, and Julia was sent to Europe to avoid further gossip.

Julia was a consummate hostess and enjoyed her time as first lady. She loved to hold dances at the White House. It was Julia who began the custom of playing "Hail to the Chief" when the president entered a room.

Children

John Tyler had fourteen children who lived to maturity, seven by each of his wives. Five of his children served the Confederacy during the Civil War. They were:

Robert Tyler—Register of the treasury
John Tyler Jr.—Assistant secretary of war
Tazewell Tyler—Surgeon in the Confederate Army
David Gardner Tyler—Joined the Confederate Army
John Alexander Tyler—Joined the Confederate Army

Tyler's daughter Elizabeth was married at a White House wedding in 1842. One of Tyler's youngest children, Lyon Gardiner, was a writer and educator who served as the president of the College of William and Mary from 1888 until 1919.

Career Before the Presidency

John Tyler had a long career serving in both the state and federal legislatures. Two years after being admitted to the bar, he was elected to the Virginia House of Delegates and served in that capacity from 1811 to 1816. He then moved into the U.S. House of Representatives where he served for six years, espousing states' rights and fighting against federal incursions on the Constitution.

Tyler disagreed wholeheartedly with the Missouri Compromise, which prohibited slavery north of 36 degrees 30 minutes latitude, excluding the Missouri Territory. Tyler believed that any restriction of slavery by the federal government was illegal. He resigned in 1821 when he did not see that he was making a difference and in 1823 went back to the Virginia House of Delegates.

Tyler served as the governor of Virginia from 1825 to 1827 before being elected as a U.S. senator for Virginia. He served two terms before resigning in 1836. He was elected president pro tempore of the Senate for a brief time. While the vice president is officially the head of the Senate, the president pro tempore takes over when he is not present.

PRESIDENTIAL TRIVIA

John Tyler was the only president to openly side with the secessionists in the Civil War. At first, he tried to bring about a peaceful solution but when he saw that was impossible he joined the Confederacy. He was elected as a Virginia representative to the Confederate Congress.

Presidential Succession

In 1840, William Henry Harrison was the Whig nominee for president with John Tyler as his vice president. While Harrison was known as a war hero, Tyler was chosen to balance the ticket because he was from the South. When Harrison died after only one month in office, Tyler became the first president to succeed to the presidency from the vice presidency. John Tyler was sworn in on April 6, 1841, and did not have a vice president because no provisions had been made for one in the Constitution.

Presidential Administration

Tyler made his mark on history because his presidency was extremely important for its role in legitimizing the succession of the vice president to the presidency upon the death or removal of the president. When he assumed the presidency, many—including Henry Clay and other Whigs in Congress—felt that they could control Tyler. Opponents claimed that he should only be considered the "acting president" until the next election since he was truly not elected to be president.

QUIRKS & ODDITIES

Tyler worked hard at ensuring that people accepted him as the true president. When he received mail addressed to "Acting President Tyler" or "Ex-Vice President Tyler," he would return it unopened. This did not stop the press and Congress, however, from dubbing him "His Accidency."

Tyler fought against this perception and assumed the full power of the presidency. By his actions, he was able to claim legitimacy for himself and future vice presidents who succeeded to the office.

Resignation of the Cabinet

When Tyler took over the office, he inherited Harrison's cabinet. This would cause problems because they were not loyal to him as president. In fact, soon after taking his oath, Henry Clay pushed through a measure to create a new national bank. This was an institution that Tyler openly opposed even though the Whig party was in favor of the bill. Therefore, when Tyler vetoed the bank, his entire cabinet resigned except for the secretary of state, Daniel Webster. He filled the empty cabinet posts with conservative Democrats. This party strife meant that not much was accomplished on the domestic front during his time in office.

Diplomatic Treaties and the Annexation of Texas

Tyler had more luck in the realm of foreign affairs. In 1842, Tyler agreed to, and Congress ratified, the Webster-Ashburton Treaty with Great Britain. This treaty was important as it set the Northern boundary between the United States and Canada all the way to Oregon. In 1844, the Treaty of Wanghia was created, which allowed Americans to trade in Chinese ports. Further, the treaty ensured that U.S. citizens were not under the jurisdiction of Chinese law while in China.

Three days before leaving office, Tyler signed into law a joint resolution annexing Texas.

IN THEIR OWN WORDS...

Tyler claimed that he was the reason Texas became a state. As he said: "It would be indeed strange if my enemies could deprive me of credit of having annexed Texas to the Union. I presented the question . . . fought the battle . . . , and . . . adopted and enforced the . . . resolution. . . . My successor did nothing but confirm what I had done."

The resolution annexing Texas was important because it extended latitude 36 degrees 30 minutes as the mark dividing free and slave states. Keeping the balance between free and slave states was an important part of holding off the beginning of the Civil War.

Life After the Presidency

In 1844, John Tyler had no party willing to back him for reelection. He went ahead and organized his own party called the Democratic-Republican party to fight for the annexation of Texas. Henry Clay of the Whig party opposed him and the measure. When the Democrats nominated James K. Polk, who also believed in the annexation of Texas, Tyler decided to step aside to help ensure that Clay would be defeated and that Polk would win. He and his family retired to his farm in Virginia, and Tyler eventually became chancellor of the College of William and Mary.

Tyler died on January 18, 1862. He was preparing to attend the first session of the Confederate Congress in Richmond, Virginia. Tyler was denounced as a traitor by the Union and his death went unrecognized by the federal government for sixty-three years. In 1915, a memorial stone was erected for his grave by Congress.

11

James K. Polk:
Dark Horse Candidate

Born:	November 2, 1795
Died:	June 15, 1849
First Lady:	Sarah Childress Polk
Political Party:	Democratic
Presidential Term:	March 4, 1845 to March 3, 1849
Famous Quote:	"The world has nothing to fear from military ambition in our Government."

Timeline

1816. . . . . .Graduated from the University of North Carolina
1823–1825. . . . . . .Member Tennessee House of Representatives
1825–1839. . . . . . .Member of U.S. House of Representatives
1835–1839. . . . . . .Speaker of the House
1839–1841. . . . . . .Governor of Tennessee
1845–1849 . . . . . .Eleventh president of the United States
1845 . . . . .Texas admitted to the Union
1846 . . . . .Iowa admitted to the Union
1846–1848. . . . . .Mexican War
1848 . . . . .Wisconsin admitted to the Union

Childhood and Education

James Knox Polk was born on November 2, 1795, in Mecklenburg County, North Carolina. His father, Samuel, was a planter and landowner and was friends with Andrew Jackson. His mother, Jane Knox, was a staunch Presbyterian. James was the eldest of ten children and was often sickly as a youth. He moved with his family at the age of ten to Tennessee.

QUIRKS & ODDITIES

Polk often experienced pain due to gallstones. When he was seventeen, they became so severe that he went ahead and had them surgically removed in a risky surgery. The surgeon used no sterilization or anesthesia. Amazingly, Polk survived and his health improved.

Polk did not begin his formal education until 1813 at the age of eighteen but he was a quick student and was accepted at the University of North Carolina by 1816. He graduated with honors in 1818 and decided to enter politics.

First Lady: Sarah Childress Polk

Sarah Childress was raised on a plantation in Murfreesboro, Tennessee. She was extremely well educated for her time, having been sent to the Salem Female Academy in North Carolina, one of the few institutions of higher learning available to women during that era. She used her education to aid her husband in his political career by helping him draft speeches and correspondence, among other things.

As first lady, she was noted for her sobriety. As a devout Presbyterian, she did not believe in dancing and would not attend the theater.

Sarah performed her duties with grace, including entertaining officials and politicians. She asked for Dolley Madison's advice on being an effective first lady. As first lady, she was well respected for her manner and tactful conversation, even by those who disagreed with her husband.

Polk died just three months after leaving the presidency. As his widow, Sarah turned their home, Polk Place, into a shrine in his honor. During the Civil War, she remained neutral and entertained leaders from both the Union and the Confederacy. She died at the age of eighty-eight.

Career Before the Presidency

James K. Polk focused on a political career throughout his life. After a brief time clerking for the Tennessee Senate, he won a seat in the Tennessee House of Representatives (1823–1825). In 1825, Polk became a member of the U.S. House of Representatives and served there for fourteen years.

As a congressman, Polk became known as a huge supporter and ally of Andrew Jackson. Because of his support, Polk was given the nickname "Young Hickory" in reference to Andrew Jackson's nickname "Old Hickory." When Jackson won the presidency, Polk became very powerful in the House. He fought for lower taxes and against the Bank of the United States, and was chosen to be speaker of the House from 1835 to 1839. He left Congress to become governor of Tennessee from 1839 until 1841.

Nomination and Election

In 1844, former president Martin Van Buren attempted to win the Democratic nomination for president but lost support due to his belief that Texas should not be annexed. At the beginning of the convention, Polk was only being considered as a vice presidential candidate. However, the delegates were having a difficult time getting the necessary two-thirds-majority vote to nominate a candidate. Polk was nominated as the candidate on the ninth ballot. Because of this, he is considered to be the first dark horse candidate for president. A dark horse is a person who no one expected to be a viable candidate to win an election.

Polk was opposed in the election by Whig candidate Henry Clay. The campaign itself centered on the annexation of Texas, which Polk supported and Clay opposed. Due to Polk's support and popularity, the annexation passed three days before the end of John Tyler's term in office. For the election itself, each candidate received 50 percent of the popular vote, but Polk managed to win 170 out of 275 electoral votes.

Presidential Administration

President Polk spent most of his time in office dealing with foreign affairs. In fact, the term "Manifest Destiny" is often mentioned when discussing Polk. Manifest Destiny is the idea that it was the destiny of the United States to span from the Atlantic to the Pacific. This view was held by Polk and those of his time as they worked to consolidate the territories that would eventually become the present-day United States.

IN THEIR OWN WORDS...

Polk during his inaugural address: "[E]ighty years ago our population was confined on the west by the ridge of the Alleghenies. Within that period . . . our people . . . have filled the eastern valley of the Mississippi, adventurously ascended the Missouri . . . , and are already engaged in establishing the blessings of self-government in valleys of which the rivers flow to the Pacific. The world beholds the peaceful triumphs of the industry of our emigrants."

In 1846, the Oregon Treaty, which was created between the United States and Great Britain, fixed the boundary of the Oregon territory at the forty-ninth parallel. Further, Washington and Oregon would become U.S. territories while Vancouver would remain a British territory.

Mr. Polk's War

The Mexican War lasted for much of Polk's time in office, from 1846 to 1848. The annexation of Texas hurt relations between Mexico and America, and further, the border between the two countries was disputed. The United States felt that the border should be set at the Rio Grande River. When Mexico would not agree, wanting a border further north, President Polk prepared for war and ordered General Zachary Taylor to the border area. Some believe that he also wanted to go to war with Mexico as a way to gain California. Contemporary critics called this conflict "Mr. Polk's War." America had attempted to purchase the territory twice from Mexico but was rebuffed both times. Polk's belief in Manifest Destiny would drive him to acquire as much of the North American continent as he could.

Mexican troops fired on U.S. troops in April 1846. Polk used this incident to gain a declaration of war against Mexico. The war progressed steadily, favoring the United States with American forces invading Mexico. By the end of 1847, Mexico was ready to make peace. The cost in human lives was high, many of the troops having died of disease.

Treaty of Guadalupe Hidalgo

In February 1848, the Treaty of Guadalupe Hidalgo was signed, officially ending the Mexican War. This treaty fixed the border between Texas and Mexico at the Rio Grande, as the United States wished. Further, the United States gained California and Nevada, among other present-day territories, amounting to more than 500,000 square miles of land. This was the largest increase in territory for the United States since Thomas Jefferson's Louisiana Purchase. In exchange for the concessions of the treaty, the United States agreed to pay Mexico $15 million. The agreement had the important effect of reducing Mexico to half of its former size.

Life After the Presidency

Before he ever took office, President Polk announced that he was not going to seek a second term as president. He did not attempt to run for reelection and instead retired at the end of his first term in office. Unfortunately, he only lived three months after his retirement.

Polk died on June 15, 1849, possibly due to cholera. Polk is remembered as one of the best one-term presidents that America has had due to his leadership during the Mexican War and the fact that he was able to keep all of his campaign promises.

Zachary Taylor: Old Rough and Ready

Born:	November 24, 1784
Died:	July 8, 1850
First Lady:	Margaret "Peggy" Mackall Smith Taylor
Political Party:	Whig
Presidential Term:	March 5, 1849 to July 9, 1850
Famous Quote:	"It would be judicious to act with magnanimity toward a prostrate foe."

Timeline

Childhood and Education

Zachary Taylor was born on November 24, 1784, in Orange County, Virginia. When he was young, his family moved to a plantation near Louisville, Kentucky. Taylor's father, Richard Taylor, was a Revolutionary War veteran and later served in various public offices. Taylor's mother, Sarah Dabney Strother, was well educated for her time.

PRESIDENTIAL TRIVIA

Zachary Taylor's family had a long history in America. In fact, he was a direct descendant of William Brewster, who arrived on the Mayflower and was seen as the religious head of the Plymouth Colony. Taylor also shared the same great-grandfather as James Madison, making them second cousins.

Taylor received a rudimentary education with a series of tutors. However, he never went to college. He spent the years before becoming president serving in the military.

First Lady: Margaret "Peggy" Mackall Smith Taylor

Margaret "Peggy" Mackall Smith was born on September 21, 1788, in Calvert County, Maryland. She grew up in a wealthy family. According to tradition, her father, Walter Smith, was a major in the Revolutionary War.

Peggy met her future husband at her sister's home in Kentucky and they were married in June 1810. She followed her husband to all the frontier military posts in which he served. Together, the Taylors had six children, four of whom lived to maturity: Ann Mackall, Sarah Knox, Mary Elizabeth, and Richard. Sarah married Jefferson Davis while he was serving under Taylor in the military, but she died only a few months after their marriage. Davis would later become the president of the Confederate States during the Civil War. Taylor's son, Richard, would vote for the secession of South Carolina at the beginning of the Civil War and would then fight in the Confederate Army. He was the last Confederate general to surrender at war's end.

Peggy Taylor found military life hard and did not wish her husband to become president because she did not relish following him to the White House. As first lady, she did not attend any formal social occasions and did not leave the second floor of the White House very often. Instead, her youngest daughter, Mary Elizabeth, served as hostess in her place. Peggy Taylor died two years after her husband on August 14, 1852.

Military Career

Zachary Taylor served forty years in the military. He joined the army in 1808 at the age of twenty-four. In the War of 1812, he successfully defended Fort Harrison in present-day Indiana from Native American forces. He was promoted to major during the war. Over the subsequent eighteen years, he was promoted first to lieutenant colonel and then to colonel. Taylor participated in the Black Hawk War that occurred in 1832. In this war, Chief Black Hawk led Sauk and Fox Indians against the U.S. Army for possession of lands in the Indiana Territory.

Second Seminole War

Taylor fought in the Second Seminole War, which occurred from 1835 to 1842. Led by Chief Osceola, Seminole Indians refused to migrate west of the Mississippi River, as required by the Treaty of Paynes Landing, and attacked American soldiers.

QUIRKS & ODDITIES

Despite being a career military man, Taylor was not necessarily a model soldier in the way he dressed. In fact, during the Second Seminole War he was nicknamed "Old Rough and Ready" by his troops not only because of his toughness but also because of his disregard for military dress and dislike of pomp and circumstance.

The Seminoles hid in the Everglades and fought the U.S. Army for seven years. Taylor led 800 troops in the Battle of Lake Okeechobee against 400 Seminole Indians on December 25, 1837. Because of this battle, Taylor was promoted to brigadier general. It was also during this battle that he earned his nickname. On May 15, 1838, Taylor was named commander of all U.S. forces in Florida. By 1842, almost all Seminoles in Florida were killed or captured and sent to Oklahoma.

Mexican War

Zachary Taylor was an important leader during the Mexican War. Mexico and the United States disagreed about the border of Texas. In 1846, President James K. Polk sent General Taylor to the Rio Grande to protect the border. When Mexican troops attacked his forces, Taylor defeated them despite being outnumbered. Because of the aggressive Mexican actions, President Polk was able to get a declaration of war against Mexico from Congress.

Taylor led a successful mission against the city of Monterrey but then allowed the Mexican forces a two-month armistice upon their retreat. This upset Polk and caused a rift between him and Taylor. In fact, the president moved some of Taylor's troops and placed them under General Winfield Scott, but Zachary Taylor did not accept this as defeat. It was at this point that the most important battle for Taylor occurred with the Battle of Buena Vista, which made him a national hero. Mexican general Santa Anna led 15,000 troops against Taylor's 4,600. However, Taylor was able to force Santa Anna's retreat. Taylor used his success at this battle as part of his campaign for the presidency in 1848.

Nomination and Election

In 1848, the Whig party nominated Zachary Taylor based on his status as a national hero, even though he had never espoused any party. Millard Fillmore was nominated as Taylor's vice president.

Taylor was not at the nominating convention so the Whig party sent a letter to inform him of his nomination. The letter was sent without postage, meaning that Taylor would have to pay to receive it. However, Taylor had been receiving so many letters from admirers that he refused any that was not already postage paid. As a result, he did not realize he had been chosen as the Whig party candidate for weeks after the fact.

Taylor was opposed by two opponents in the election. The Democrats nominated Lewis Cass, a senator from Michigan, and former president Martin Van Buren ran for the Free Soil party. The main campaign issue was whether to ban or allow slavery in territories captured during the Mexican War, but Taylor did not take sides. The fact that he owned numerous slaves made people assume that he would be in favor of allowing the extension of slavery. Cass came out for allowing the residents of individual territories to decide for themselves. Van Buren was against allowing the extension of slavery and took antislavery votes from Cass. While he didn't win any states in the electoral college, Van Buren took enough votes to allow Taylor to win.

Presidential Administration

Taylor only served as president from March 5, 1849, until July 9, 1850, before suffering an untimely death. During this time, the Clayton-Bulwer Treaty was created between the United States and Great Britain, providing that any canals across Central America were to be neutral. Further, according to the treaty neither country was to colonize Central America. This treaty remained in effect until 1901.

Compromise of 1850

As stated previously, during the campaign for president Taylor had not taken a stand concerning the extension of slavery into the territories. The South's assumption that he would be in favor of adding new slave states was unfounded. In fact, he opposed extending slavery into the territories.

The Compromise of 1850 came about during Taylor's time in office. The purpose of the legislative compromise was to create a balance between free and slave states in newly created states and territories. It was a package of five separate legislative acts.

IN THEIR OWN WORDS...

Taylor's feelings about using the veto: "The power given by the Constitution to the Executive to interpose his veto is a high conservative power; but in my opinion it should never be exercised except in cases of clear violation of the Constitution, or manifest haste and want of due consideration by Congress."

Taylor stated that he would most probably veto the compromise when it passed. He did not believe in giving concessions to the South, and he denied the right of states to secede. Unfortunately, Taylor never got the chance to veto the compromise.

Death

During the hot summer Taylor got sick after eating some fresh cherries and drinking some milk. It is believed that he contracted cholera from the food. In fact, this was a common condition because of the lack of sanitation in Washington, D.C. He died on July 8, 1850. His last words were, "I am about to die. I expect the summons very soon. I have tried to discharge my duties faithfully. I regret nothing, but I am sorry that I am about to leave my friends." In 1991, Taylor's body was exhumed to see if he had been poisoned. The tests proved that the amount of arsenic in his body was normal and therefore no foul play was involved.

Had he lived to veto the Compromise of 1850, the events of the mid-nineteenth century would have been significantly different. This compromise helped avert Civil War for eleven years while at the same time polarized abolitionist forces in the North due to the inclusion of the Fugitive Slave Act, which made the federal government responsible for returning escaped slaves.

Millard Fillmore: His Accidency

Born:	January 7, 1800
Died:	March 8, 1874
First Lady:	Abigail Powers Fillmore
Political Party:	Whig
Presidential Term:	July 10, 1850 to March 3, 1853
Famous Quote:	"An honorable defeat is better than a dishonorable victory."

Timeline

1823 . . . . Admitted to the bar
1826 . . . . Married Abigail Powers
1829–1831 . . . . . . New York state assemblyman
1833–1835 . . . . U.S. representative
1837–1843 . . . . U.S. representative
1848–1849 . . . . . . Comptroller of New York
1849–1850 . . . . . . Vice president of the United States under President Taylor
1850–1853 . . . . Thirteenth president of the United States
1850 . . . . California admitted to the Union
1858 . . . . Married Caroline Carmichael McIntosh

Childhood and Education

Millard Fillmore was born on January 7, 1800, on a small farm in Summerhill, New York. He grew up in relative poverty with five brothers and three sisters. His mother, Phoebe Millard Fillmore, and father, Nathaniel Fillmore, provided him with a basic education before apprenticing him to cloth makers. Fillmore continued to educate himself during his apprenticeship and in 1819 was able to enroll in the New Hope Academy in Buffalo, New York. Over the next five years, he alternatively studied law and taught school until he was admitted to the New York bar in 1823.

First Lady: Abigail Powers Fillmore

Fillmore fell in love with one of his teachers at the New Hope Academy, Abigail Powers. She was only two years older than Fillmore. Abigail was born in Moravia, New York, and was the daughter of a Baptist minister. They both shared a love of learning that would last the rest of their lives. The two did not marry until 1826. The Fillmores had two children: Millard Powers and Mary Abigail.

White House Library

Abigail shared duties for social functions with her daughter Mary Abigail, typically only attending the larger functions. She enjoyed her private time, which she spent reading and playing music among other activities. She is credited with helping to create the White House library and spent much of her time selecting books for inclusion.

PRESIDENTIAL TRIVIA

Believe it or not, Congress at first did not want to provide the executive branch with its own library. Appropriations to create an executive library had been defeated previously because there was a fear that the executive office would become too powerful with its own library. In September 1850, $2,000 was finally appropriated to create the library.

In 1853, Abigail developed pneumonia after the completion of Fillmore's term in office. She died within a month.

Fillmore's Second Wife

In 1858, Fillmore married for a second time to Caroline Carmichael McIntosh. She was the widow of a wealthy businessman named Ezekial McIntosh and had Fillmore sign a prenuptial agreement before marrying him. When they married, Fillmore became the administrator of her estate until his death.

Political Career and Presidential Succession

Fillmore became active in politics soon after being admitted to the bar. In 1829 he was elected to the New York State Assembly. He then began ten years in the U.S. Congress representing New York. He grew in prominence in the Whig party throughout this time. In 1848, he became the comptroller of New York State and served in that capacity until he was nominated as the Whig vice presidential candidate with Zachary Taylor in 1849. Interestingly, Fillmore and Taylor did not meet until after the election. His role as vice president was minimal, although he did preside over the Senate during the debate for the Compromise of 1850. Fillmore succeeded to the presidency upon Taylor's death on July 9, 1850.

Presidential Administration

Millard Fillmore was in office from July 10, 1850, until March 3, 1853. He disagreed with his predecessor, Zachary Taylor, concerning slavery in the territories. Fillmore felt that it was important to allow the Compromise of 1850 through to preserve sectional peace, and that new territories should be added as slave states to appease the South. Taylor's cabinet resigned and Fillmore began filling positions with moderate Whigs like Daniel Webster to signal his change in policy.

Compromise of 1850

When the Compromise of 1850 was delivered to him as president, he signed it into law. The compromise consisted of five separate laws:

1. California was admitted as a free state.
2. Texas received compensation for giving up claims to Western lands.
3. Utah and New Mexico were established as territories.
4. The slave trade was abolished in the District of Columbia.
5. The Fugitive Slave Act was passed, which required the federal government to help return runaway slaves.

The last of the above items was the most odious to antislavery forces.

IN THEIR OWN WORDS...

Fillmore's thoughts on slavery: "God knows that I detest slavery, but it is an existing evil, for which we are not responsible, and we must endure it, till we can get rid of it without destroying the last hope of free government in the world."

While the compromise temporarily held off the Civil War for a time, Fillmore's support of it—especially the Fugitive Slave Act—cost him not only support during his presidency but also the Whig party's nomination in 1852.

Opening of Japan

One other important event that occurred during Fillmore's time in office was the opening of Japan. Commodore Matthew Perry created the Treaty of Kanagawa in 1854 that provided for peace between the two nations, the ability to trade in two Japanese ports, help for any American ships wrecked off the Japanese coast, and permission for American ships to purchase provisions in Japan. This treaty was significant because it opened inroads for American merchants to trade with the Far East.

Life After the Presidency

During his presidency, Fillmore had tried to take the Whig party, with himself as its leader, to the middle ground between pro- and antislavery forces. However, the division was so strong that his efforts only resulted in abandonment by the majority of his party. He chose not to run in the election of 1852 and instead retired to Buffalo, New York. Soon after his retirement, both his wife, Abigail, and his daughter Mary Abigail died.

Know-Nothing Party

The Whig party was in its death throes and would soon disappear altogether. While Fillmore was traveling through Europe, the Know-Nothing party, an anti-Catholic, anti-immigrant party, had nominated him to run for president again in 1856. Fillmore accepted the nomination by mail and returned to the United States to run.

PRESIDENTIAL TRIVIA

The Know-Nothing party was officially called the American Republican party, but it was dubbed Know-Nothing because when people tried to find out who the leaders were or what the party's goals were, party members said they knew nothing.

In the election Fillmore only carried one state, Maryland, and 22 percent of the popular vote. He lost to Democrat James Buchanan.

Public Life in Buffalo

Fillmore spent the rest of his life involved in public affairs in Buffalo, New York. He helped establish the city's first high school, the University of Buffalo, Buffalo General Hospital, and other important civic organizations.

Fillmore supported the Union during the Civil War even though he personally opposed President Lincoln's actions. His past enforcement of the Fugitive Slave Act while president tarnished his reputation so much that when Lincoln was killed, Fillmore's home was vandalized. He died on March 8, 1874, of a stroke.

14

Franklin Pierce: Party Animal

Born:	November 23, 1804
Died:	October 8, 1869
First Lady:	Jane Means Appleton Pierce
Political Party:	Democratic
Presidential Term:	March 4, 1853 to March 3, 1857
Famous Quote:	"The storm of frenzy and faction must inevitably dash itself in vain against the unshaken rock of the Constitution."

Timeline

1824 . . . . Graduated from Bowdoin College

1827 . . . . Admitted to the bar

1834 . . . . Married Jane Means Appleton

1846–1848 . . . . . . Mexican War

1829–1833 . . . . . . Member of the New Hampshire legislature

1831–1832 . . . . Speaker of the New Hampshire legislature

1833–1837 . . . . Member of the U.S. House of Representatives

1837–1842 . . . . . . U.S. senator from New Hampshire

1845–1847 . . . . . . U.S. district attorney for state of New Hampshire

1846–1848 . . . . . . Served in the army during Mexican-American War

1853–1857 . . . . Fourteenth president of the United States

Childhood and Education

Franklin Pierce was born on November 23, 1804, in Hillsborough, New Hampshire. His father, Benjamin Pierce, had fought in the Revolutionary War and later became an important official in New Hampshire. Eventually, he was elected as governor of the state. His mother, Anna Kendrick Pierce, was prone to bouts of depression and alcoholism, which Pierce seemed to inherit.

Pierce went to a local school and two academies before attending Bowdoin College in Maine.

PRESIDENTIAL TRIVIA

Franklin Pierce studied at Bowdoin College with both Nathaniel Hawthorne and Henry Wadsworth Longfellow. He became good friends with Hawthorne. Hawthorne would write his campaign biography in 1852. In 1853, when Pierce was president, he appointed Hawthorne to be a consul in Liverpool, England.

At first Pierce was a poor student, spending much of his time on the social scene and being ranked last in his class. He then decided to increase his effort and by the time he graduated from college, he was fifth in his class. He then went on to study law with various individuals in Massachusetts and New Hampshire. He was admitted to the New Hampshire bar in 1827.

First Lady: Jane Means Appleton Pierce

Pierce married Jane Means Appleton on November 19, 1834. She was a deeply religious woman from New Hampshire and the daughter of the former president of Bowdoin College and Congregationalist Minister, Jesse Appleton, who died when she was thirteen. Jane had different beliefs than Pierce, especially when it came to politics and drinking. She was quiet and shy, the opposite of her husband. Further, she had been raised in a Whig household and Pierce was a staunch Democrat.

The Pierces had three sons, all of whom died by the age of twelve. Tragically, the youngest, Benjamin, was killed in a train accident soon after Pierce had been elected president but before he took office. Even before the terrible accident, Jane had not wished her husband to become president. This, combined with her child's death, caused her to spend most of her time as first lady immersed in grief. She had help with her duties from her aunt by marriage, Abigail Kent Means, and from her friend Varina Davis, who was the wife of Pierce's secretary of war, Jefferson Davis. Jane died of tuberculosis on December 2, 1863.

Preparing for the Presidency

Franklin Pierce practiced law for two years before being elected as a member of the New Hampshire legislature in 1829 where he rose to the role of Speaker of the House by 1832. In 1833, at the age of twenty-seven, he was elected as a U.S. representative. He served in the House until 1837 when he was elected to one term as a senator representing New Hampshire. During his time as a representative and senator, Pierce did not take a strong stance for any cause except for opposing the abolitionist movement. He was friendly with southerners, including the future president of the Confederacy, Jefferson Davis.

SCANDALS & GOSSIP

Pierce was known more for his society life than for his legislation while he was in Congress. In fact, stories of his partying and drinking to excess were common knowledge. His wife was unhappy with his life in Washington and his bouts of heavy drinking. She finally convinced him to resign from the Senate and return to private life in 1842.

Pierce left the Senate to practice law. During his time as an attorney, Pierce also remained active in the Democratic party, helping Polk to win the presidency in 1844. Pierce was then asked by President James Polk to be the attorney general of the United States, but he declined the position to be able to continue in his law practice. His decision was probably based at least partially on Mrs. Pierce's dislike of the social scene in the capital.

In 1846, Pierce joined the military to fight in the Mexican War. Despite having no military experience, he appealed to President Polk and was given the rank of brigadier general over a force of volunteers. He led his troops to help fight at the Battle of Contreras, where his leg was crushed when he fell from his horse. He had to be carried off the field of battle. He returned a month later to help with the capture of Mexico City. He left the military in 1848.

Nomination and Election

In 1852, Pierce was nominated as the candidate for the Democratic party. He was proslavery, which appealed to southerners, but at the same time he hailed from the North, so he was chosen as a compromise candidate. Senator William King was his vice president. He was opposed by Whig candidate and war hero General Winfield Scott, under whom he had served in the Mexican War.

While the issue of slavery in territories and appeasing the South were important parts of the campaign, in the end the election was determined by personality. In fact, both sides used mudslinging to hurt the other's chances—for example, each side called its opponent a drunk.

PRESIDENTIAL TRIVIA

By the 1850s, campaigns were becoming more sophisticated. For example, Pierce's campaign put its best foot forward by having Nathaniel Hawthorne write a campaign biography for the candidate. Campaign slogans were also becoming more commonplace, including this famous one: "We Polked you in 1844; we shall Pierce you in 1852!"

Winfield Scott was running for the divided Whig party and his antislavery beliefs hurt him in the South. Despite being proslavery, Pierce was supported by virtually all of the Democratic party. In the end, Pierce won with 51 percent of the popular vote and 86 percent of the electoral vote.

Presidential Administration

Franklin Pierce's time in office was marked by criticism and contention from both the North and the South. The entry of new territories into the United

States continued to be a cause of dissension between the North and South. While the North wanted to keep new territories free, the South wished to add more slave territories and states to the nation.

IN THEIR OWN WORDS...

Pierce made it clear in his inaugural address what he thought about the slavery question: "I believe that involuntary servitude, as it exists in different States of this Confederacy, is recognized by the Constitution. I believe that it stands like any other admitted right, and that the States where it exists are entitled to efficient remedies to enforce the constitutional provisions."

When in 1854 an internal memo called the Ostend Manifesto was printed in the *New York Herald* advocating aggressive action to take Cuba if Spain was unwilling to sell it, the North saw this as an attempt to extend slavery to another territory. This memo caused so much criticism that Pierce and his cabinet were discredited.

Bleeding Kansas

While the Ostend Manifesto caused northerners concern because they opposed the extension of slavery, the Kansas-Nebraska Act, passed in 1854, actually caused them to take direct action—the Republican party was created in protest to the act. The law, which had been created by Stephen Douglas, divided the Kansas-Nebraska territory into two separate regions, each of which would be able to decide for itself whether to allow slavery. This idea of allowing the people to decide for themselves is known as popular sovereignty. Pierce strongly supported this bill and actively fought for its passage.

The real issue at stake was that the Missouri Compromise of 1820 had provided that no slavery would be allowed above the 36 degree, 30 minute latitude line. Therefore, the Kansas-Nebraska Act effectively repealed the Missouri Compromise. While Nebraska was strongly antislavery and posed no real problems, Kansas was another story. After the passage of the act, proponents of both sides rushed into the territory to try and sway public opinion their way. Eventually, open hostility erupted and the territory gained the nickname "Bleeding Kansas."

Two legislatures were created: One proslavery legislature that was comprised mainly of nonresidents who came across the Missouri border and one antislavery legislature based in Topeka. Pierce proclaimed in 1856 that the proslavery legislature was legitimate. Later, in 1856, proslavery forces invaded the antislavery center of Lawrence, Kansas. Violence also erupted on the floor of the U.S. Senate when, after Massachusetts senator Charles Sumner gave an antislavery speech, South Carolina senator Andrew Butler beat him severely with a cane. Upset over these actions by proslavery proponents, John Brown and his sons attacked and killed five proslavery advocates in May 1856. Antislavery forces would eventually prevail in 1861, but the violence continued until then.

Gadsden Purchase

In 1853, the United States had bought a stretch of land consisting of areas in modern-day Arizona and New Mexico as part of the Gadsden Purchase. This purchase completed the current boundaries of the continental United States. As in other areas of the country, the debate over whether to organize the territories as free or slave states continued to cause problems. The territories would not be organized and admitted as states until after the beginning of the Civil War.

Life After the Presidency

All of the dissension and criticism of Pierce for the Ostend Manifesto and his inability to stop the fighting in the Kansas territory led to his not being nominated to run for a second term in 1856. In fact, his support of slavery made the sectional divisions even more pronounced. Franklin Pierce retired to New Hampshire at the end of his term in office, and he traveled to Europe and the Bahamas with his wife.

Pierce opposed secession as the Civil War loomed but at the same time spoke in favor of the South. Once the war began, he spoke in support of the Confederacy and his onetime secretary of war-turned-president, Jefferson Davis, which led many to call Pierce a traitor. He died on October 8, 1869, in Concord, New Hampshire, from cirrhosis of the liver.

James Buchanan: Old Buck

Born:	April 23, 1791
Died:	June 1, 1868
First Lady:	Never married
Political Party:	Democratic
Presidential Term:	March 4, 1857 to March 3, 1861
Famous Quote:	"The ballot box is the surest arbiter of disputes among freemen."

Timeline

1809 . . . . Graduated from Dickinson College
1812 . . . . Admitted to the bar
1814 . . . . Fought in the War of 1812
1815–1816 . . . . Member of the Pennsylvania House of Representatives
1821–1831 . . . . Member of the U.S. House of Representatives
1832–1833 . . . . U.S. minister to Russia
1834–1845 . . . . . . U.S. senator from Pennsylvania
1845–1849 . . . . . . Secretary of state
1853–1856 . . . . U.S. minister to Great Britain
1857–1861 . . . . Fifteenth president of the United States
1858 . . . . Minnesota admitted to the Union
1859 . . . . Oregon admitted to the Union
1861 . . . . Kansas admitted to the Union

Childhood and Education

James Buchanan was born in a log cabin on April 23, 1791, in Cove Gap, Pennsylvania, to James Buchanan Sr. and Elizabeth Speer Buchanan. His father was a wealthy merchant and farmer, and his mother was extremely well read. At the age of five, Buchanan and his family moved to Mercersburg, Pennsylvania. He was privately tutored before studying at the Old Stone Academy and then entering Dickinson College in 1807. He then studied law in Lancaster, Pennsylvania and was admitted to the Pennsylvania bar in 1812.

Bachelor President

Buchanan never married and never had any children. He was engaged to Anne Coleman, but she died before they were married.

SCANDALS & GOSSIP

Buchanan had a fight with his betrothed, Anne Coleman, in 1819. She called off the engagement. Later that year, she died suddenly. Although it can't be confirmed, some people believe that it was suicide. Author John Updike wrote a play in 1974 called *Buchanan Dying* where he takes a fictional look at what might have happened between the pair that resulted in her death.

Buchanan did have a ward who he sponsored and raised from childhood named Harriet Lane. She served the function of first lady while Buchanan was in office. She was an accomplished hostess and was well loved, which was especially difficult given the events that were occurring in the nation. She used tact and common sense to try to keep the peace at official functions. Lane did not marry until she was thirty-six and Buchanan was retired from the presidency.

Leading to the Presidency

Buchanan briefly began his career as a lawyer before joining the military to fight in the War of 1812. He did not join until near the end of the war after Washington, D.C., had been burned by the British. It was this event that spurred him to volunteer for a company of dragoons that marched to Baltimore. When the British were expelled from Baltimore, Buchanan was honorably discharged.

QUIRKS & ODDITIES

James Buchanan always kept his head cocked to the left. This was because he had one eye that was nearsighted and one that was farsighted. To see things correctly, he got in the habit of cocking his head and closing one eye. If he was looking at something close, he'd close the farsighted eye; if he needed to see something far away he'd close the nearsighted one.

Jackson Supporter

After his service, Buchanan was elected to the Pennsylvania House of Representatives. He served there for two years before losing his seat and going back to his law practice. In 1821, he was elected to the U.S. House of Representatives where he served until 1831. He had been elected as a Federalist but when the party dissolved he became a Democrat. He was a staunch supporter of Andrew Jackson and led the opposition against John Quincy Adams after the so-called corrupt bargain that had given him the presidency over Jackson in 1824.

Diplomatic Moves

In 1831, Andrew Jackson appointed Buchanan to be the minister to Russia, where he successfully completed a trade agreement. He returned home in 1834 to become a U.S. senator representing Pennsylvania and served in that capacity until 1845. He still continued in his staunch support of Jackson and, later, Van Buren.

In 1845, Buchanan was named secretary of state under President James K. Polk. As the secretary of state, he negotiated the Oregon Treaty with Great Britain that set the northern boundary of the territory at the forty-ninth parallel.

From 1853 to 1856, he served as President Pierce's minister to Great Britain, and during that time he created the Ostend Manifesto along with the U.S. ministers to Spain and France. This secret document stated that the United States should acquire Cuba by any means necessary. However, when it was leaked in the press, it caused Pierce's administration a lot of problems with Northern interests. Buchanan's involvement in the document's creation helped increase his popularity in the South.

Nomination and Election

Buchanan had been in the running for the Democratic presidential nomination since 1844. In 1856, he was one of the possible candidates against the Democratic president, Franklin Pierce, and Senator Stephen Douglas. The Democrats were having a hard time agreeing on a candidate because all three of those who were being considered believed that owning slaves was constitutionally protected. However, Buchanan was the compromise candidate since he had been in Great Britain during much of the previous administration and therefore appeared to be distanced from the issues such as the fighting in Kansas. He ran against Republican candidate John C. Fremont and Know-Nothing candidate and former president Millard Fillmore.

During the campaign, Buchanan upheld as constitutional the right of individuals to hold slaves. On the other hand, the Republicans claimed that being conciliatory toward the South would just perpetuate sectional strife. However, there was fear that if the Republicans won, civil war would result. In the end Fillmore took votes from Fremont, and Buchanan won with 45 percent of the popular vote and 174 out of 296 electoral votes.

Presidential Administration

During Buchanan's inaugural address, he asserted that the slavery issue was about to be decided by the Supreme Court, ending the sectional differences in the United States. He was referring to the *Dred Scott* court case.

Was James Buchanan a homosexual? This is the claim made by James Loewen in his book *Lies Across America: What Our Historic Sites Got Wrong.* Buchanan lived with William Rufus King for many years. As Loewen says, "The two men were inseparable. . . . Andrew Jackson dubbed King "Miss Nancy," and Aaron Brown . . . referred to him as Buchanan's "better half," and "his wife."

The court decided that slaves should be considered property and further that Congress had no right to exclude slavery in the territories. This would have wide-reaching effects in terms of how to deal with fugitive slaves. Buchanan felt that this case proved the constitutionality of slavery, but he was incorrect in his belief that this ruling would end sectional strife—it only fanned the flames that would erupt by the end of his term in office.

John Brown's Raid

One event that polarized the nation was John Brown's Raid on a federal armory in Harper's Ferry, Virginia, in October 1859. Brown led eighteen men—five of whom were African American—to seize the armory. He believed that his actions would lead to an uprising of African Americans that in turn would result in a war against slavery. President Buchanan sent Robert E. Lee and the U.S. Marines to stop the raiders. Brown was captured and stood trial for murder, treason, and conspiring with slaves to rebel. He was sentenced to death and hanged in December 1859. Southerners saw this rebellion as one more example of the North plotting to end slavery. Northerners, while disagreeing with the way Brown acted, agreed with his ultimate goal of ending slavery.

Kansas and the Lecompton Constitution

According to the Kansas-Nebraska Act passed under Franklin Pierce, popular sovereignty was to determine whether Kansas was a slave or free state. A number of constitutions were proposed for the new state, the most famous of which was the Lecompton Constitution, which would have made it a slave state. Believing that slavery was constitutional, Buchanan fought for the acceptance of the Lecompton Constitution using many means, including offering cash and office appointments in exchange for votes. The Lecompton Constitution reached a deadlock in Congress and was sent back to the territory to be voted on in a general election by Kansas residents, who overwhelmingly defeated it. The effect of this incident was the split of the Democratic party over the Constitution into northerners and southerners. Kansas did finally enter the Union in 1861 as a free state.

Secession

Buchanan had no plans to run for reelection. With the Democratic party divided, the Republican candidate Abraham Lincoln was able to win the election in November 1860. Upon Lincoln's election, seven states seceded from the Union to form the Confederate States of America. Buchanan did not believe that the federal government could force a state to remain in the Union and therefore did nothing. In fact, two incidents occurred that demonstrated his willingness to compromise to avoid Civil War.

After the secession of Florida, federal troops stationed in Pensacola moved into Fort Pickens to consolidate their forces. Buchanan sent supplies and troops by ship to reinforce the fort. However, when they arrived they only sent the provisions ashore. Buchanan had made a truce with Florida that no further troops would be stationed at the fort unless it was fired on.

In Charleston, South Carolina, troops moved off the mainland to occupy Fort Sumter. Similarly, provisions and troops were sent to reinforce the federal forces. However, confederate forces fired on the ship carrying the troops and it was forced to retreat, but Buchanan ignored this action. President Buchanan left office with the Union divided.

IN THEIR OWN WORDS...

In a message to the Senate and House of Representatives at the end of his term, Buchanan said: "I feel that my duty has been faithfully, though it may be imperfectly, performed; and, whatever the result may be, I shall carry to my grave the consciousness that I at least meant well for my country."

According to a survey of presidential historians conducted by the University of Louisville, Buchanan's failure to oppose the secession of the states was the number one presidential blunder in America's history.

Life After the Presidency

After leaving the presidency, Buchanan retired to Pennsylvania and was not involved in public affairs. He supported Abraham Lincoln throughout the Civil War. In 1866, he wrote a book entitled *Mr. Buchanan's Administration on the Eve of the Rebellion* in which he defended his actions at the end of his term. On June 1, 1868, Buchanan died of pneumonia.

Abraham Lincoln:
The Great Emancipator

Born:	February 12, 1809
Died:	April 15, 1865
First Lady:	Mary Todd Lincoln
Political Party:	Republican
Presidential Term:	March 4, 1861 to April 15, 1865
Famous Quote:	"As a nation, we began by declaring that 'all men are created equal.' We now practically read it, 'All men are created equal, except Negroes.' When the Know-Nothings get control, it will read, 'All men are created equal except Negroes, and foreigners, and Catholics.' When it comes to this I should prefer emigrating to some other country where they make no pretense of loving liberty—to Russia, for instance, where despotism can be taken pure, without the base alloy of hypocrisy."

Timeline

1832 . . . . Fought in the Black Hawk War
1833–1836 . . . . . . Postmaster of New Salem, Illinois
1834–1842 . . . . . . Member of the Illinois legislature
1842 . . . . Married Mary Todd
1847–1849 . . . . Member of the U.S. House of Representatives
1858 . . . . Lincoln-Douglas Debates
1861–1865 . . . . Sixteenth president of the United States

Childhood and Education

Abraham Lincoln was born in Hardin County, Kentucky, on February 12, 1809. He moved to Indiana by the age of seven and lived there for the rest of his youth. His father, Thomas Lincoln, was a farmer and carpenter. When his mother, Nancy Hanks, died in 1818, his father soon remarried to Sarah Bush Johnston. Lincoln grew very close to his stepmother, and she had an important role in urging him to read and learn. He had one sister, Sarah Grigsby, live to maturity.

Abraham Lincoln had only about one year of formal education. He was tutored by various individuals throughout the years, and he also played an important role in his own education. He had a lifelong love of learning and reading.

First Lady: Mary Todd Lincoln

Mary Todd Lincoln was born in Lexington, Kentucky. Her family was relatively wealthy and she was well educated. Unfortunately, she was also mentally unstable and her condition caused a great deal of stress for Abraham Lincoln.

SCANDALS & GOSSIP

Many detractors claimed that Mary was a Southern sympathizer—four of her siblings did fight for the South during the Civil War. There was even some talk of her being a spy. Of course, this did not help her emotional stability.

Mary Todd Lincoln also suffered from migraines that impacted her ability to function effectively as first lady. Her time as first lady was further hampered by her jealousy of those around her husband. These actions did not endear her to others and made her an unpopular figure in the White House.

The Lincolns had three sons, but only one lived past the age of eighteen. During Lincoln's time as president, his second son, William "Willie" Wallace Lincoln, died of a fever. He was the only president's child to die in the White

House. His death caused Mary to sink further into her mental illness. In 1871, their youngest son, Thomas "Tad" Lincoln, died at the age of eighteen.

QUIRKS & ODDITIES

Lincoln was very permissive with Tad, allowing him to interrupt important meetings as necessary. In 1863, a turkey had been sent to the White House for Christmas dinner. Tad adopted the bird and nicknamed it Jack. One day as Christmas neared, Tad burst into one of his father's cabinet meetings in tears. After hearing the boy's case for the bird, Lincoln ordered a reprieve to save the turkey's life.

From that point on, Mary Todd began having hallucinations. She was committed to a mental institution in 1875 where she stayed for three months before moving in with her sister. After her death in 1882, an autopsy revealed that she had "cerebral disease."

Early Career

Lincoln briefly worked as a clerk before joining the military in 1832, when he enlisted to fight in the Black Hawk War. He was quickly elected to be the captain of a company of volunteers that joined regulars under Colonel Zachary Taylor. However, he only served thirty days in this capacity before signing on as a private in the mounted Rangers and later joining the Independent Spy Corps. He saw no real action during his short stint in the military.

Political Aspirations

Lincoln decided on a political rather than a military career. He was defeated in his first attempt at office when he ran for the Illinois state legislature in 1832. He was appointed as postmaster of New Salem, Illinois, by Andrew Jackson and served from 1833 until 1836. During this time, he taught himself law and was admitted to the Illinois bar in 1837. At the same time, he was elected as a Whig to the Illinois legislature in 1834, where he served until 1842.

From 1847 to 1849, Lincoln was a member of the U.S. House of Representatives and was elected yet again to the state legislature in 1854. He helped form the Republican party in 1856 and resigned from the Illinois state legislature in 1858 when he was nominated to run for the U.S. Senate. In his acceptance speech for the nomination he gave his famous "house divided" speech in which he said, "A house divided against itself cannot stand. I believe this government cannot endure permanently half slave and half free."

Lincoln-Douglas Debates

Lincoln's main opponent in the 1858 Senate race was Stephen Douglas. During the campaign, they debated each other seven times. While they agreed on many issues, they disagreed over the morality of slavery. While Douglas argued for popular sovereignty—allowing the citizens of each state or territory to decide if slavery would be legal within its borders—Lincoln did not believe that slavery should spread any further. Lincoln explained that while he was not asking for equality, he believed that African Americans should get the rights granted in the Declaration of Independence: life, liberty, and the pursuit of happiness. Even though Lincoln lost the Senate seat to Douglas, he became a national figure based on his oratory and debates.

Bid for the Presidency

Lincoln was nominated for the presidency in 1860 by the Republican party with Hannibal Hamlin as his running mate. He ran on a platform denouncing disunion and calling for an end to slavery in the territories. He had three main opponents, two of whom were Democrats. The Democratic party was divided along sectional lines. Stephen Douglas represented the Northern Democrats and John Breckinridge the National (Southern) Democrats. Lincoln's third opponent, John Bell, ran for the Constitutional Union party. Bell basically took votes from Douglas, which helped pave the way for Lincoln to win the election with 40 percent of the popular vote and 180 of the 303 electors.

Presidential Administration

Obviously the most momentous event of Lincoln's time in office was the Civil War, which lasted from 1861 until 1865. In fact, seven Southern states seceded from the Union upon word that Lincoln had won the election of 1860. By the beginning of the war, eleven states had seceded, forming the Confederate States of America. Lincoln firmly believed in preserving the Union and reuniting North and South.

Emancipation Proclamation

In September 1862, Lincoln issued the Emancipation Proclamation. With this proclamation, Lincoln freed the slaves in all Southern states. While not a congressional act, Lincoln used his war powers to free the slaves of seceded states.

IN THEIR OWN WORDS...

In a letter, Lincoln wrote: "My paramount object in this struggle is to save the Union, and is not either to save or to destroy slavery. If I could save the Union without freeing any slave I would do it, and if I could save it by freeing all the slaves I would do it; and if I could save it by freeing some and leaving others alone I would also do that."

Lincoln did not believe that he had the constitutional power to free slaves in states that were still part of the Union.

Suspending Civil Liberties

A point of contention for Lincoln's opponents was his curbing of civil liberties during the Civil War. Lincoln suspended habeas corpus, which provided prisoners the right to be brought before a court to determine whether they were being justly held. He also allowed for military arrest of civilian antiwar activists. Conversely, when the war ended, Confederate officers were allowed to return home with their side arms and horses—not in disgrace.

End of the Civil War

In 1864, Lincoln promoted Ulysses S. Grant to be commander of all Union forces. General William T. Sherman marched on and captured Atlanta and then continued to Savannah to confront Robert E. Lee. This Union victory was a decisive blow to the Confederacy and helped clench Lincoln's reelection in 1864. In April 1865, Richmond fell and Lee surrendered to General Grant at Appomattox courthouse in Virginia. In the end, Lincoln hoped to be lenient toward the South as they rejoined the Union. However, his assassination and Andrew Johnson's weak presidency resulted in the Radical Republicans enacting strict punitive measures against the South during Reconstruction.

Other Actions During His Presidency

In 1862, the Homestead Act was passed allowing squatters to take title to 160 acres of land after having lived on it for five years. This act was important for helping populate the Great Plains.

In opposition to Virginia's secession from the Union, West Virginia broke off from the state in 1863. It was admitted to the Union as a separate state.

Reelection in 1864

In 1864, the Republican party temporarily changed its name to the National Union party. There was concern that Lincoln could not win the election due to problems that were occurring in the war along with Lincoln's curbing of civil liberties. However, they went ahead and nominated him again with Andrew Johnson as his vice president. Their platform demanded unconditional surrender and the official end to slavery.

Lincoln's opponent, George McClellan, had been relieved as the head of the Union armies by Lincoln in 1862. His platform was that the war was a failure and that Lincoln had taken away too many civil liberties. Luckily for Lincoln, the war turned in the North's favor during the campaign and he won with 55 percent of the popular vote and 91 percent of the electoral vote.

Assassination Conspiracies

On April 14, 1865, Abraham Lincoln was assassinated while attending a play at Ford's Theater in Washington, D.C. Actor John Wilkes Booth and a group of conspirators had come up with a plan to kill not only Lincoln but also Andrew Johnson and William Seward. One of the conspirators, Lewis Powell, managed to injure Seward but George Atzerodt did not go through with the assassination of Johnson.

Booth jumped from the theater box after shooting Lincoln in the head, broke his leg, and ran as well as he could out of the theater shouting "Sic semper tyrannus," or "As always to tyrants." Booth and another conspirator named David Herold traveled to Mary Surratt's tavern in Maryland. There they picked up supplies before visiting Dr. Samuel Mudd who set Booth's leg.

Herold and Booth both fled and were found hiding in a barn on April 26. While Herold surrendered, Booth would not. The barn was set on fire, and Booth was shot and killed. Eight conspirators were eventually captured and punished for their roles in the assassination. Four of them—Lewis Powell (Paine), David Herold, George Atzerodt, and Mary Surratt—were hanged. Mary Surratt was the first woman to be executed in the United States.

Numerous assassination conspiracy theories have been advanced over the years. Two of the more fantastic theories involve Andrew Johnson and the Catholic Church. A congressional committee looked into the allegation that Johnson was behind it all but found no evidence to support it. The other unproven theory was that the Catholic Church was unhappy with Lincoln's defense of a former priest.

After being shot, President Lincoln was taken across the street to the Petersen House. He died the next day, April 15, at 7:22 A.M. Vice President Andrew Johnson then succeeded to the presidency.

17

Andrew Johnson:
First Impeached President

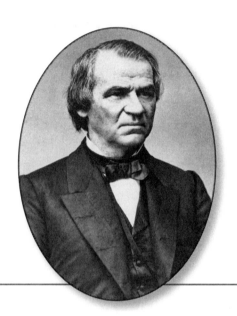

Born:	December 29, 1808
Died:	July 31, 1875
First Lady:	Eliza McCardle Johnson
Political Party:	No party affiliation
Presidential Term:	April 15, 1865 to March 3, 1869
Famous Quote:	"Honest conviction is my courage; the Constitution is my guide."

Timeline

1827. . . . . .Married Eliza McCardle
1830–1833. . . . . . .Mayor of Greeneville, Tennessee
1841–1843. . . . . . .Tennessee state senator
1843–1853. . . . . . .Member of the U.S. House of Representatives
1853–1857. . . . . . .Governor of Tennessee
1857–1862. . . . . . .U.S. senator
1862–1864. . . . . . Military governor of Tennessee
1865 . . . . .Vice president of the United States under President Lincoln
1865–1869 . . . . . .Seventeenth president of the United States
1867. . . . . .America purchased Alaska
1867. . . . . .Nebraska admitted to the Union

Childhood and Education

Born on December 29, 1808, in Raleigh, North Carolina, Andrew Johnson was raised in relative poverty. His father, Jacob Johnson, died when he was only three. His mother, Mary McDonough Johnson, was eventually remarried to Turner Dougherty, a man that Johnson and his brother, William, never liked.

Johnson's mother bound him and his brother out as indentured servants to a tailor. In exchange for working and learning the trade, the pair received their food and lodging.

PRESIDENTIAL TRIVIA

In 1824, after two years of working for James Selby, the brothers ran away and thereby broke their contract. On June 24, 1824, their "master," James Selby, announced their escape in an ad in the local newspaper. He offered a $10 reward for anyone who would return the brothers to him.

Having successfully escaped indenture, Johnson opened his own tailoring shop at the age of seventeen to make money. At the same time, he taught himself to read—in fact, he never attended school at all.

First Lady: Eliza McCardle Johnson

Eliza McCardle was the daughter of shoemaker John McCardle and Sarah Phillips. Born on October 4, 1810, in Leesburg, Tennessee, she was an only child. Her father died when she was very young. Nonetheless, she had a good education and in fact, when she married Andrew Johnson at the age of sixteen, she helped him with his reading and writing skills. The pair were married on May 17, 1827 in Greeneville, Tennesse. Together, Eliza and Andrew Johnson had three sons and two daughters: Martha, Charles, Mary, Robert, and Andrew Johnson Jr.

Eliza was an invalid after 1865 and while first lady she stayed in her room on the second floor of the White House. Their daughter Martha Patterson took over the social duties of being first lady with Eliza appearing publicly only twice. She died in 1876, six months after her husband's death.

Early Career

Johnson worked as a tailor in his own shop in Greeneville, Tennessee. By the age of twenty-two, he was elected the mayor of Greeneville. He served in that capacity for four years until 1833. In 1835, Johnson was elected to the Tennessee House of Representatives and by 1841 he became a Tennessee state senator.

Move to National Politics

Having done well for himself in the state legislature, Johnson moved into national politics. In 1843, he was elected to be a U.S. representative for his district. He remained a representative until he was elected as governor of Tennessee in 1853. By 1857, he was elected to be a U.S. senator from Tennessee. While in his legislative roles, he worked hard to defend the rights of the common man, even advocating the Homestead Act, which would give free farms to the poor. He also defended slavery and supported the Fugitive Slave Act, which was part of the Compromise of 1850. Despite this, he was the only Southern senator who did not agree with secession and retain his seat upon the secession of his state. In the South, he was viewed as a traitor. Johnson saw not only the secessionists but also the abolitionists as enemies of the Union.

Military Governor of Tennessee

Due to Johnson's loyalty to the Union, Abraham Lincoln made him the military governor of Tennessee in 1862. When Lincoln ran for reelection in 1864, he chose Johnson as his vice president to balance the ticket, as Johnson was a southerner who was also pro-Union. They won a huge victory against the Democrats.

The conspirators who killed Lincoln had also planned to kill Johnson. However, the conspirator who was to kill him did not follow through, and Johnson became president following Abraham Lincoln's assassination on April 15, 1865.

SCANDALS & GOSSIP

On Inauguration Day, Vice President Johnson's drunken behavior caused an uproar. One observer wrote that he was "too drunk to perform his duties and disgraced himself." In truth, Johnson was not known to be a drinker and had drank more than normal as part of his recovery from a recent illness. However, his behavior was reported in the newspapers and used against him by his enemies.

Presidential Administration

President Johnson felt that it was important to continue with Lincoln's vision of how to deal with the postwar South. This era in American history is known as Reconstruction. Both Lincoln and Johnson thought it was necessary to be lenient toward those who had seceded from the Union to heal the rift of the Civil War. Johnson's reconstruction plan would have allowed southerners who swore an oath of allegiance to the federal government to regain citizenship. He also wanted to allow the states to quickly return to self-governance. However, his plan was never given a chance because more radical elements in the government prevailed. In fact, reconstruction was controlled by the Radical Republicans, who wanted to punish the South.

When the Radical Republicans passed the Civil Rights Act in 1866, Johnson tried to veto the bill. He did not believe that the North should force its views concerning civil rights on the South. His vetoes on this and fifteen other bills were overridden. During his administration, the thirteenth and fourteenth amendments to the Constitution were passed. The thirteenth amendment freed all slaves, and the fourteenth provided civil rights and liberties to freed slaves.

Seward's Folly

In 1867, Secretary of State William Seward arranged for the United States to purchase Alaska from Russia for $7.2 million. Some in Congress argued that this was not a good deal for the United States and termed this agreement "Seward's Folly." Critics felt that it had no value. However, it did pass through Congress and it proved in the long run to be a wonderful investment. It provided the United States with gold and oil while drastically increasing the size of the country. It also removed Russian imperialism from the North American continent.

Impeachment

In 1867, the Tenure of Office Act was passed. This bill denied the president the right to remove his own appointed officials from office. When President Johnson dismissed his secretary of war, Edwin Stanton, from his position in 1868 and replaced him with Ulysses S. Grant, the House of Representatives brought articles of impeachment against him. In the end, the House voted to impeach Johnson, making him the first president to be impeached while in office.

Upon his impeachment, the Senate met to decide if the president should be removed from office. Johnson narrowly escaped removal by one vote.

IN THEIR OWN WORDS...

The book *Profiles in Courage* describes eight senators who made decisions that went against either party lines or public opinion. One of these was Edmund G. Ross, the one man who voted against removing Johnson from office. As he wrote to his wife: "Millions of men cursing me today will bless me tomorrow for having saved the country from the greatest peril through which it has ever passed, though none but God can ever know the struggle it has cost me."

Life After the Presidency

In 1868, Andrew Johnson was not nominated to run for presidency. Instead, he retired to his home in Greeneville, Tennessee. During the years after his retirement, he tried to reenter politics by running for both the U.S. House and Senate. He lost on both accounts until 1875, when he was elected to the Senate. He died of cholera on July 31, 1875, shortly after taking office.

Ulysses S. Grant: Civil War Hero

Born:	April 27, 1822
Died:	July 23, 1885
First Lady:	Julia Boggs Dent Grant
Political Party:	Republican
Presidential Term:	March 4, 1869 to March 3, 1877
Famous Quote:	"I have never advocated war except as a means to peace."

Timeline

1843 . . . . Graduated from West Point

1846–1848 . . . . . . Fought in the Mexican War

1848 . . . . Married Julia Boggs Dent

1861–1865 . . . . . . Civil War

1864 . . . . Made commander of all Union armies

1869–1877 . . . . . . Eighteenth president of the United States

1876 . . . . Colorado admitted to the Union

Childhood and Education

Ulysses S. Grant was born Hiram Ulysses Grant on April 27, 1822, in Point Pleasant, Ohio. He was always called Ulysses and when he enrolled in West Point he put down his name as Ulysses H. Grant, which was then mistakenly recorded as Ulysses S. Grant.

Grant was raised in Georgetown, Ohio, on a farm with his father, Jesse Root Grant, and his mother, Hannah Simpson Grant. His father was a tanner and merchant. Grant helped out on the farm though he hated assisting with the tanning as he could not stand the sight of blood.

Grant attended local schools, then went to the Presbyterian Academy and was later appointed to West Point Military Academy. Though not necessarily the best student, he was good at math and working with horses. Due to his equestrian skills, Grant wanted to be assigned to the cavalry. However, his low grades and class rank resulted in him being placed in the infantry.

First Lady: Julia Boggs Dent Grant

Grant married Julia Boggs Dent, the daughter of a St. Louis merchant and slaveholder. He had been roommates at West Point with Julia's brother Fred. They were married on August 22, 1848.

PRESIDENTIAL

TRIVIA

Grant's father and mother were both strict abolitionists. Therefore, the fact that Julia Dent's family owned slaves was very upsetting to them—in fact, they would not attend the wedding for this reason. They did not meet their new daughter-in-law until the couple's honeymoon in Kentucky.

Together, the Grants had three sons and one daughter: Frederick Dent, Ulysses S. Jr., Ellen Wrenshall, and Jesse Root. His son Frederick was appointed the U.S. minister to Austria-Hungary by Benjamin Harrison. He was also assistant secretary of war under William McKinley.

Julia was devoted to her husband and was often at his side even while he was serving in the military during the Civil War. While first lady, she refurbished the White House with new rugs and furnishings. She was a gracious hostess and held Tuesday afternoon receptions where anyone could come meet and talk to her. Their daughter, Nellie, got married while Grant was president and had an elaborate White House wedding. Julia truly relished her role as first lady and was very saddened when their time in the White House ended. She died on December 14, 1902, in Washington, D.C.

Career Before the Presidency

Upon his graduation from West Point, Grant was stationed at Jefferson Barracks, Missouri. He then was on frontier duty in Louisiana and participated in the military occupation of Texas.

Mexican War

In 1846, the United States went to war with Mexico. Grant was sent to fight and served with Generals Zachary Taylor and Winfield Scott. He proved himself a valuable officer and by the end of the war was promoted to first lieutenant.

He had been involved in the major battles of the war including the assault and capture of Mexico City.

IN THEIR OWN WORDS...

Grant disagreed with the war in Mexico. He saw ultimate retribution for it in the tragedy of the Civil War: "The Southern rebellion was largely the outgrowth of the Mexican War. Nations, like individuals, are punished for their transgressions. We got our punishment in the most sanguinary and expensive war of modern times."

Life Away from the Military

After the war ended, Grant was stationed in New York and Michigan before being sent out west for frontier duty again. In 1854, he decided to resign from the military. According to Grant, he did not think that he would be able to support his family out of his pay as an army officer. He moved to St. Louis to work a farm that his wife owned. By 1858, he decided to give up on farming and sold it. He then went into different forms of business, including real estate, to try to support his family.

U.S. Civil War

With the outbreak of the Civil War, Grant rejoined the military. As the colonel of the Twenty-first Illinois Infantry, he captured Fort Donelson, Tennessee, in February 1862. This was the first major Union victory, and as a result he was promoted to major general of the U.S. volunteers. It was also at Fort Donelson that he earned the nickname "Unconditional Surrender Grant" because he would only accept "unconditional and immediate surrender."

Grant went on to other important victories at Lookout Mountain and Missionary Ridge, and the Siege of Vicksburg from May 22 until July 4, 1863. At that point, he was a made a major general in the regular army. He continued to have victories over Southern forces until March 1864, when President Lincoln named him commander of all Union forces.

Grant accepted General Robert E. Lee's surrender at Appomattox, Virginia, on April 9, 1865, allowing for generous terms. He continued to serve as a general in command of the armies of the United States until 1869. He was also secretary of war under Andrew Johnson from 1867 until 1868.

Bids for the Presidency: 1868 and 1872

The public hailed Grant as a war hero, and he was unanimously nominated by the Republicans in 1868 to run for president. The Republican platform allowed for black suffrage in the South and a less lenient form of reconstruction than that espoused by Andrew Johnson. Grant was opposed by Democrat Horatio Seymour. Grant won the presidency with 53 percent of the popular vote and 72 percent of the electoral vote.

In 1872, Grant was nominated to run for the presidency even though a split had occurred in the Republican party. Horace Greeley was nominated to represent both the liberal Republican party and the Democratic party. Grant won 55 percent of the popular vote. However, before the Electoral College could vote, his opponent Horace Greeley died. Grant received 256 out of 352 electoral votes to win his second term in office.

Presidential Administration

The most significant political issue of Grant's presidency was Reconstruction in the South. Grant continued the military occupation of the South that was begun during Andrew Johnson's time in office. Further, he fought for the right of African Americans to vote because many states had begun denying them this right. In 1870, the fifteenth amendment was passed providing that no one could be denied the right to vote based on race.

PRESIDENTIAL TRIVIA

Even though Theodore Roosevelt's name is most often mentioned when discussing conservation, it was actually Ulysses S. Grant who created the first national park. On March 1, 1872, he dedicated Yellowstone National Park. It was not only the first of its kind in America but also, according to the National Park System, the first in the world.

In 1875, the Civil Rights Act was passed. This ensured that African Americans would have the same rights for public accommodation, transportation, and entertainment, among other things. It remained in effect until it was ruled unconstitutional in 1883.

Black Friday

Unfortunately, Grant's time as president is most remembered for the major scandals that occurred. The first of these involved speculation by Jay Gould and James Fisk in the gold market. They attempted to corner the market by buying up gold—keeping Grant and his treasury from realizing what was occurring. The two speculators quickly drove up the price of gold. When Grant saw what was happening, he had the treasury add gold into the market to bring the price down on September 24, 1869. This date was known as Black Friday because many investors and businesses that held gold were ruined by the sudden drop in its price.

Credit Mobilier and the Whiskey Ring

In 1872, the Credit Mobilier scandal occurred. Officers in the Credit Mobilier Company were stealing money from the Union Pacific Railroad. To cover up their wrongdoings, they sold stocks at a huge discount to members of Congress. This was revealed during the election of 1872. An investigation by Congress hurt the political reputations of Vice President Schuyler Colfax and other senators and representatives.

The Whiskey Ring scandal occurred in 1875. The government had placed a tax on liquor, and many distillers and federal agents were illegally keeping money that should have been turned over to the government from these taxes. Grant called for punishment of those involved, but upon learning that his personal secretary had been involved, the president acted to protect him from prosecution.

Other Scandals

Two other scandals that occurred during Grant's administration involved his secretaries of the treasury and war. Grant's secretary of the treasury, William A. Richardson, gave John Sanborn a job collecting delinquent taxes. At that time, they were experimenting with outsourcing the collection of taxes to private individuals. Sanborn was allowed by Richardson to keep 50 percent of what he collected. Eventually, he got greedy and started collecting taxes even from those not known to be delinquent. Congress investigated and in the end the private collection of taxes was officially ended.

Finally, in 1876, it was revealed that Grant's secretary of war, W. W. Belknap, had taken bribes from traders selling at Indian posts. The House voted unanimously to impeach him. Belknap resigned.

In the end, the corruption and scandals of Grant's administration had a huge impact on national politics. For one thing, the Republican party was weakened. Further, prior to his administration, Reconstruction had been the big national issue but these scandals, along with an economic depression that began in 1873, replaced the Reconstruction of the South as the top news stories of the day.

Little Big Horn

While Grant was president, conflicts were occurring between Native Americans and the military in the West. In 1875, Sioux and Cheyenne Indians decided to fight against the settlers who were intruding on their sacred lands. They gathered with chief Sitting Bull to fight. Lieutenant Colonel George Custer was sent to attack the Lakota and Northern-Cheyenne at Little Big Horn but instead was massacred and scalped. Retribution against the Indians was swift and the Sioux nation was defeated within a year.

Life After the Presidency

Grant retired from the presidency after his second term. He and his wife traveled extensively through Europe, Asia, and Africa before returning home to Illinois in 1880.

When his son, Ulysses Jr., joined with a friend named Ferdinand Ward to set up a brokerage firm, Grant borrowed money to help him get started. However, the firm went bankrupt—in fact, Ward had been scamming Grant and the other investors. Grant and many investors lost everything; Ward was convicted and sent to prison.

When Grant found out that he was dying of throat cancer, he began to look for ways to provide for his wife before his death. Mark Twain contracted with him to write his memoirs, and he spent every waking moment writing. He finished only five days before his death, which occurred on July 23, 1885. He is buried in Grant's Tomb in New York City.

19

Rutherford B. Hayes: His Fraudulency

Born:	October 4, 1822
Died:	January 17, 1893
First Lady:	Lucy Ware Webb Hayes
Political Party:	Republican
Presidential Term:	March 3, 1877 to March 3, 1881
Famous Quote:	"The President of the United States of necessity owes his election to office to the suffrage and zealous labors of a a political party, . . . but he should strive to be always mindful of the fact that he serves his party best who serves the country best."

Timeline

1852 . . . . Married Lucy Ware Webb

1861–1865 . . . . . . Fought in the Civil War, rising to rank of major general

1865–1867 . . . . . . U.S. representative

1868–1872 . . . . . . Governor of Ohio

1876–1877 . . . . . . Governor of Ohio

1877–1881 . . . . Nineteenth president of the United States

Childhood and Education

Rutherford B. Hayes was born on October 4, 1822, in Delaware, Ohio. He was named after his father who had died eleven weeks before his birth. Hayes was raised by his mother, Sophia Birchard Hayes. Sophia was able to make ends meet by renting out a small farm near their family home. According to Hayes's diary, he remembered spending time visiting the farms as a child and being treated kindly by the tenants. Hayes also had an uncle who helped out by providing Hayes and his elder sister, Fanny, with books and other luxuries.

Hayes was very close to Fanny. He fondly remembered growing up with her and taking care of her as she was recovering from dysentery. When Fanny died in 1856 after giving birth to stillborn twins, Hayes was devastated. He wrote in his diary, "The dearest friend of childhood, the affectionate adviser, the confidante of all my life, the one I loved best, is gone."

Early Interest in Politics

Hayes attended a local district school, the Norwalk Seminary, a residential Methodist school, and a college preparatory academy before attending Kenyon College. He was an excellent student and graduated first in his class. During his time at the college, the election of 1840 occurred. It was one of the first that incorporated some of the elements of the modern campaign including local meetings, slogans, and more. Hayes, a Whig, was very interested in the campaign and wrote about it in his diary. When William Henry Harrison won the election, Hayes said, "The long agony is over. The 'whirlwind' has swept over the land and General Harrison is undoubtedly elected President. I never was more elated by anything in my life."

Harvard and the Law

Hayes studied law in Columbus, Ohio, before being admitted to Harvard Law School. He graduated from Harvard in 1845 and was admitted to the Ohio bar. Throughout his time at Harvard, he continued to display an intense interest in politics. When the Whigs lost in the election of 1844, Hayes wrote, "I would start in the world without a penny if by my sacrifice

[Henry] Clay could be chosen President." Hayes enjoyed learning about the law and began practicing it in Ohio soon after graduation.

First Lady: Lucy Ware Webb Hayes

Hayes married Lucy Ware Webb on December 30, 1852. Her father was a physician who had died when she was an infant. She met Hayes in 1847 in Delaware, Ohio. She attended Wesleyan Women's College in Cincinnati becoming the first first lady to have graduated from college. Hayes felt that she had "a quick, sprightly intelligence." Together they had four sons and one daughter: Sardis Birchard, James Webb, Rutherford Platt, Frances, and Scott Russell. His son James served first as his secretary and then became a military hero in the Spanish-American War.

PRESIDENTIAL TRIVIA

President and Mrs. Hayes began the custom of the Easter egg roll on the south lawn of the White House in 1878. Prior to that, families had gathered at the capitol for the Easter egg roll. However, a law passed that outlawed using the capitol as a playground, so the event officially moved to the White House.

Lucy was a staunch opponent of slavery and very strict in her Methodist religion. She believed wholeheartedly in temperance, or the banning of alcohol. Because of this, she earned the nickname "Lemonade Lucy" for banning alcohol at White House state functions. Despite this, she was an excellent hostess and held many informal and formal gatherings as first lady.

Early Career

Hayes began his law practice in lower Sandusky, Ohio. However, he did not have much luck there and moved to Cincinnati in 1849. From that point on, his law career began to flourish—in fact, in 1858 Hayes was chosen to be the Cincinnati city solicitor. He served in that position until he joined the fight in the Civil War.

Civil War

Hayes's family was known for their long history of military service. In fact, both of his grandfathers fought in the American Revolution. When the Civil War began, he could not simply stand by and watch; in 1861, he joined the military to fight in the war. He began as a major in the Twenty-third Ohio Volunteer Infantry. He was wounded four times, including a serious injury in 1862 at the Battle of South Mountain, but continued to serve until the end of the war. Hayes eventually rose to the rank of major general of volunteers.

In 1864, Hayes was elected to be a U.S. representative even though he was still in the military. He did not take his seat until the end of the war. Once the war ended, he took his seat and quickly won again for a second term. He served as a U.S. representative from 1865 until 1867.

IN THEIR OWN WORDS...

Excerpt from Hayes's diary concerning the Civil War: "[T]his was a just and necessary war and that it demanded the whole power of the country; that I would prefer to go into it if I knew I was to die or be killed in the course of it, than to live through and after it without taking any part in it."

Governor of Ohio

In 1867, Hayes was elected to be the governor of Ohio. He served as governor until 1872 and then was reelected as governor in 1876. As governor, he proved to be especially honest and created civil service and other reforms in the state. He left the office in 1877 to become president of the United States.

Bid for the Presidency

Hayes was chosen in 1876 as a compromise candidate by the Republican party. The fact that he was not well-known led to his nickname, "The Great Unknown." His platform centered on reform—especially civil service reform—a sound currency, and the "permanent pacification" of the South.

Opponent Samuel Tilden

Hayes was opposed by Democrat Samuel J. Tilden, who was the governor of New York. He was well-known for causing the demise of the Tweed Ring. William Marcy "Boss" Tweed, an active member of the Democratic party in New York, had gathered a group of associates who exchanged jobs and contracts for bribes and political support. The group had New York City in a stranglehold. Tilden's conviction of Boss Tweed made him a national figure. Tilden's platform spoke against the many years of scandal under the Republican President Grant. He also argued for civil service reform.

Tilden Comes Close

Each candidate had reformers on their side. However, it appeared that Tilden was the favorite for the election. The corruption of the Grant administration was fresh in the voters' minds. In the end, Tilden ended up winning the popular vote. However, foreshadowing the election of 2000, the vote in three Republican-controlled states was in confusion. Tilden only needed one electoral vote to win while Hayes needed every vote from all three states. During the recount, many Democratic ballots were ruled invalid in Florida and Louisiana.

A fifteen-person investigative commission was convened. In the end, they voted eight to seven along party lines, giving all of the electoral votes to Hayes and allowing him to win. Many Democrats clamored in outrage against this, but Tilden did not allow open rebellion to occur due to the Compromise of 1877.

PRESIDENTIAL TRIVIA

Rutherford B. Hayes was the first president to have the oath of office administered twice. Because the normal date for inauguration, March 4, fell on a Sunday in 1877, Hayes was privately given the oath of office by Chief Justice Morrison R. Waite at the White House on Saturday, March 3. Chief Justice Waite then delivered the oath again on Monday, March 5.

Compromise of 1877

To satisfy the South, Hayes agreed to the Compromise of 1877, which included many measures, the largest of which was ending the military occupation of the South. Further, the Democratic party was promised certain administrative positions once Hayes became president. The deal held and Hayes became the president. Unfortunately the removal of the military from the South meant that freed African Americans would have a hard time getting the equal treatment that should have been theirs.

Presidential Administration

Unfortunately for President Hayes, he began his term with the electoral controversy still fresh. He was nicknamed "His Fraudulency" by his enemies and many felt that he had stolen the election. However, he was a man of strong convictions and believed that he truly had won the election. During his time in office, he attempted to get civil service reform passed, which was especially important after all the scandals during Grant's administration. The patronage system was so well established, however, that he, not only failed to pass the civil service reform, but also managed to anger members of his own party, which would lead to his party abandoning him before the end of his term.

Currency Issues

A major issue during Hayes's time in office centered on the nature of currency in the United States. At this time, currency was backed by gold or silver, but as silver became more readily available, it began to lose its value. Because of its availability, some politicians argued that silver should be bought and turned into coins to help make money more readily available. Others, however—including Hayes—felt that "greenbacks" should be redeemable in gold as a more stable form of currency. The Bland-Allison Act, passed in 1878 over Hayes's veto, required the government to buy silver to create more coins. This was short lived, and in 1879 the Resumption of Specie Act passed providing that greenbacks created after January 1, 1879, would be backed with gold.

Chinese Immigration

Another major issue in the 1880s was Chinese immigration. There was a strong anti-Chinese sentiment, especially in the West, as many claimed they were taking too many jobs. Congress tried to pass a law, which Hayes vetoed, restricting Chinese immigration. In 1880, Hayes had his secretary of state, William Evarts, make an agreement with China that restricted immigration. This helped to ameliorate those who wanted to completely deny any further Chinese immigration.

Life After the Presidency

Hayes never planned to run for a second term in office. He retired in 1881 and spent the rest of his life devoted to causes of importance to him. He provided many scholarships to African Americans, fought for temperance, and became one of the trustees of Ohio State University. He died on January 17, 1893, of a heart attack.

James A. Garfield: Compromise Candidate

Born:	November 19, 1831
Died:	September 19, 1881
First Lady:	Lucretia Rudolph Garfield
Political Party:	Republican
Presidential Term:	March 4, 1881 to September 19, 1881
Famous Quote:	"I love agitation and investigation and glory in defending unpopular truth against popular error."

Timeline

1858 . . . . .Married Lucretia Rudolph
1859–1861. . . . . . .Ohio state senator
1861–1863. . . . . . .Fought in the Civil War, rising to rank of major general
1863–1880. . . . . . U.S. representative
1881. . . . . .Twentieth president of the United States

Childhood and Education

James Garfield was born on November 19, 1831, in Ohio, the last American president to have been born in a log cabin. Garfield's father, Abram, died when Garfield was only eighteen months old. His mother, Eliza Ballou Garfield, tried to make ends meet on their farm, but Garfield and his three siblings grew up in poverty. Garfield went to a local school before moving in 1849 to the Geauga Academy located in Chester, Ohio. He worked his way through school, taking on odd jobs. Garfield was baptized into the Disciples of Christ during his time at the Academy.

QUIRKS & ODDITIES

Garfield was the first of only seven left-handed presidents. The others were Herbert Hoover, Harry Truman, Gerald Ford, Ronald Reagan, George H. W. Bush, and Bill Clinton. Garfield was actually able to write with both hands. In fact, he could write Latin with one while he was writing Greek with the other.

Garfield entered the Eclectic Institute in Hiram, Ohio, which was the primary college of his chosen faith. He spent some time teaching to help pay for his education. In 1854, he attended Williams College in Massachusetts and graduated with high honors in 1856.

First Lady: Lucretia Rudolph Garfield

Garfield had met his future wife, Lucretia Rudolph, while they were both students at the Geauga Academy; they both then attended the Eclectic Institute. In fact, Lucretia—or "Crete"—was Garfield's student in 1853, the year they began dating. They carried on a long-distance courtship, marked by many years of correspondence. The pair was finally married on November 11, 1858. Together, the Garfields had four sons and one daughter live to maturity: Harry Augustus, James Rudolph, Mary, Irvin McDowell, and Abram. Harry and James both entered public service. Harry was the president of Williams College before being appointed by President Woodrow Wilson to work with the U.S. Food Administration during World War I. He received a distinguished service medal in 1921 for his work. James served as President Theodore Roosevelt's secretary of the interior.

Reluctant First Lady

Lucretia was very intelligent and enjoyed literary pursuits. At the same time, she did not feel at home in social situations. When he was elected to be president, she saw her role as a "terrible responsibility." Lucretia understood her role as first lady, holding receptions and performing her duties at state functions as required.

As first lady, Lucretia spoke with her husband often about political issues and even spoke with the press. She did not bow to political pressures. For example, when the temperance groups tried to get her to continue with Lucy Hayes's banning of alcohol at the White House, she would not agree.

Lucretia contracted malaria and fell seriously ill during her time as first lady. She was still convalescing away from Garfield and the White House when her husband was shot. After her husband's untimely death, Lucretia lived on until March 14, 1918, all the while making sure to preserve correspondence and other papers from her husband's career.

Early Career

Garfield decided to become an instructor at the Eclectic Institute, which he had previously attended, and he taught classical languages there before becoming its president from 1857 to 1861. He was only twenty-six when he became president of the college. While serving in this capacity, Garfield studied law and served as an Ohio state senator. In his role as senator he showed himself to be a staunch abolitionist who welcomed the Civil War to defeat the South. He was admitted to the Ohio bar in 1860.

In 1861, Garfield joined the Union Army to fight in the Civil War, rising through the ranks to become a major general. He fought in the Battles of Shiloh and Chickamauga. In 1863, Garfield was made chief of staff to the army of the Cumberland's commander, William Rosecrans. However, Garfield was elected to Congress while still in the military and resigned to take his seat as a U.S. representative.

PRESIDENTIAL TRIVIA

Garfield was a Radical Republican while in Congress. After the Civil War, he attempted to find a middle ground between the leniency for the South that was espoused by Lincoln and Johnson and the harsher treatment championed by the Radical Republicans. When he saw that no compromise could be reached, he decided to side with the Radicals. In 1868, he voted for Johnson's impeachment.

Garfield served as a congressman from 1863 until 1880. During the final years of the Civil War, he complained that Lincoln did not exhibit enough military aggression. During Grant's time in office, Garfield had to appear before a congressional committee having been accused of accepting bribes. He denied any wrongdoing, saying that any money he had been given was repaid in full. In 1876, he was a member of the fifteen-man investigative committee that awarded the election to Hayes after votes had been contested in three states.

Bid for the Presidency

In 1880, Garfield was elected to become a senator. However, he would never take office because in the meantime he would win the presidency. He was chosen as the Republican nominee for president after much discussion. The Republican convention could not decide, even in thirty-three previous ballots, who would be their presidential candidate. Garfield's mild manner and continued support for one of the candidates under consideration allowed him to gain momentum for his own candidacy. On the thirty-sixth ballot he won the nomination as a compromise candidate between conservatives and moderates. Conservative candidate Chester A. Arthur was nominated as vice president. Garfield was opposed by Winfield Hancock in the presidential election.

In his inaugural address, Garfield proclaimed: "The elevation of the negro race from slavery to the full rights of citizenship is the most important political change we have known since the adoption of the Constitution.... No thoughtful man can fail to appreciate its beneficent effect upon our institutions and people."

The campaign was more about personality than issues, with both sides claiming that the other would bring corruption into the White House. The popular vote was extremely close, with Garfield receiving only 1,898 more votes than his opponent. However, he ended up with 58 percent (214 out of 369) of the electoral vote.

Presidential Administration

Garfield was only in office for a little more than six months, but in that time he showed that he was one to fight against political corruption. He spent much of that time dealing with patronage issues and fighting against those who tried to jockey their way into governmental jobs. Garfield found that the number of people wanting to be appointed to jobs based on patronage was overwhelming and disheartening.

Star Route Scandal

The one major issue that Garfield dealt with before his death was corruption in the postal service. Many postal routes out West and in the South were contracted out to private organizations. In numerous instances, those private companies would come in with low bids and then the postal officials would go to Congress asking for higher payments. The officials would then keep the difference for themselves or pay off members of Congress. In 1881, Garfield ordered an investigation—even though it could show that members of his own party were profiting. In the end, the so-called Star Route Scandal resulted in important civil service reforms.

Assassination

On July 2, 1881, Charles J. Guiteau, a mentally disturbed office seeker, shot President Garfield in the back. Guiteau had been denied a position as the ambassador to France and had been following the President for weeks before actually shooting him. According to Guiteau, he wanted to kill Garfield "to unite the Republican Party and save the Republic." Garfield ended up dying on September 19, 1881, of blood poisoning.

PRESIDENTIAL TRIVIA

The earliest attending doctors who probed into Garfield's bullet wound caused so much damage that it was unclear what path the bullet took. To help find the bullet, Alexander Graham Bell rigged up a rudimentary metal detector. Because the president was lying on a metal spring mattress, however, the detector did not work properly.

Garfield's death was more related to the unsanitary manner in which the physicians attended to him than to the actual wounds. Guiteau, who had readily given himself up, was convicted of murder and hanged on June 30, 1882.

Chester A. Arthur: Gentleman Boss

Born:	October 5, 1829
Died:	November 18, 1886
First Lady:	None. His wife, Ellen Lewis Herndon Arthur, died before he took office.
Political Party:	Republican
Presidential Term:	September 19, 1881 to March 3, 1885
Famous Quote:	"I may be President of the United States, but my private life is nobody's damned business."

Timeline

1848 . . . . Graduated from Union College

1854 . . . . Admitted to the bar

1858–1862 . . . . . . Served in the New York state militia

1859 . . . . Married Ellen Lewis Herndon

1871–1878 . . . . . . .Collector of the port of New York

1881 . . . . .Vice president of the United States under President Garfield

1881–1885 . . . . . . .Twenty-first president of the United States

Childhood and Education

Chester Arthur was born on October 5, 1829, in North Fairfield, Vermont. His father, William Arthur, was a Baptist minister. William Arthur often moved the family—including Chester's mother, Malvina Stone, Chester himself, his six sisters, and his only brother—as he took up new ministerial posts.

PRESIDENTIAL TRIVIA

In the 1830s, William Arthur was a founding member of the New York Anti-Slavery Society, which quickly became a national organization. By 1840, the society had more than 240,000 members, including such national figures as William Lloyd Garrison and Frederick Douglass. William Arthur's abolitionist views had a huge impact on his son.

Arthur attended an academy in New York before entering the Lyceum in Schenectady at age fifteen. In 1845, he enrolled at Union College and graduated in 1848. Arthur went on to study law and was admitted to the New York bar in 1854.

Marriage: Ellen "Nell" Lewis Herndon Arthur

Ellen Herndon was born on August 30, 1837, in Culpepper Court House, Virginia. Her father, William Lewis Herndon, was in the navy and died in a hurricane when she was twenty. Nell, as she was called, met Arthur when she was on the way to visit her mother, Frances Hansbrough Herndon, after her father's death. On October 25, 1859, the two were married. Nell was a talented singer who performed around New York City where they lived. Together, they had two children live to maturity: Chester Alan Jr. and Ellen Herndon.

In 1880, Nell caught pneumonia after waiting outside in the cold. She drifted into a coma and died two days later on January 10, 1880. Arthur was away when she got sick and wasn't able to speak to her before her death, which greatly troubled him for the rest of his life. Arthur's sister Mary McElroy acted as his unofficial first lady during his term in office.

Early Career

After graduating from Union College, Arthur taught school and then became the principal of an academy in New York. While teaching, he also studied law. In 1854, Arthur was admitted to the bar and began practicing law in New York City. One important case that he defended resulted in the desegregation of public transportation in New York City.

Arthur was very active in the Republican party from 1856 on. He held several different party leadership positions in New York and was a staunch supporter of President Abraham Lincoln.

QUIRKS & ODDITIES

Arthur was nicknamed "Elegant Arthur" because of his manner of dress. In fact, he had a huge wardrobe and would change often—sometimes several times a day. It was reported that he owned eighty pairs of trousers.

In 1858, Arthur joined the New York state militia and served until 1862. He was eventually promoted to quartermaster general in charge of inspecting troops and providing equipment for the military. Arthur was appointed by President Grant in 1871 to the lucrative job of collector of the port of New York. He served in this capacity until 1878, when he was removed from office by President Hayes due to bribery and corruption charges that were never proven. In 1881, Arthur was elected to run as vice president with presidential nominee James Garfield.

Presidential Administration

President James Garfield was shot on July 2, 1881, but did not die until September 19, 1881, from blood poisoning. On September 20, Chester Arthur was sworn in as president. Upon Garfield's death, Arthur said, "Men may die, but the fabrics of free institutions remains unshaken."

PRESIDENTIAL

TRIVIA

When Arthur was sworn in as president, Congress was not in session and no Senate president pro tempore or speaker of the House had been selected. Upon Arthur's leaving the office, there was also no vice president. At that point, if Arthur had died, there would have been no president and no provision to select a president.

Chinese Exclusion Act

Despite the restrictions placed on Chinese immigration through a treaty agreement between former President Hayes and China, anti-Chinese sentiment was still widespread. Opponents of Chinese immigration convinced Congress to pass an act that would have excluded the Chinese from immigrating for twenty years. However, Arthur vetoed this bill but signed a compromise—the Chinese Exclusion Act of 1882. This halted immigration for ten years and made other provisions restricting the naturalization of Chinese immigrants. The act was renewed twice and was not completely repealed until 1943, when China was an ally of the United States during World War II.

Modern Civil Service System Begins

Before his death, President Garfield had paved the way for civil service reform. He investigated wrongdoings in the awarding of mail contracts, which revealed major corruption involving individuals pocketing tax money. The fact that Garfield was assassinated by an unhappy office seeker just made the issue that much more timely. After his death the Pendleton Act was passed, creating the modern civil service system.

President Arthur signed the bill into law and immediately began enforcing the new reform. The act created a three-man body to oversee the civil service system and Arthur immediately showed his willingness to support the bill by appointing three well-known reformers. Another important part of the act was the provision that jobs classified as civil service could only be attained after passing an open exam.

Arthur's staunch support of the law meant the loss of many followers who had previously supported him. This was a large factor in his losing the Republican nomination for president in 1884.

Mongrel Tariff

In 1883, the Mongrel Tariff was passed. This was a group of measures designed to reduce tariff rates and intended to be a compromise between protectionists and the proponents of free trade. However, the act actually only reduced duties by 1.5 percent—a small amount for the many people that it made unhappy. It was significant because it heightened a debate that would last for decades about tariffs and their use. It was at this point that the Republicans began to be seen as the party of protectionism while the Democrats were portrayed as the party of free trade.

IN THEIR OWN WORDS...

Following are two sections of the Pendleton Act: "[N]o person habitually using intoxicating beverages to excess shall be appointed to, or retained in, any office, appointment, or employment to which the provisions of this act are applicable." And: "[W]henever there are already two or more members of a family in the public service . . . , no other member of such family shall be eligible to appointment to grades."

Life After the Presidency

Chester Arthur did not receive the nomination to run for president in his own right. He had angered members of his party by his hard line when it came to civil service reforms. Arthur retired to New York City and returned to practicing law; he no longer held public office and, in fact, only lived a little more than a year after his retirement. He had kept the fact that he suffered from Bright's disease, a fatal kidney disease, secret throughout his presidency. He died on November 18, 1886, of a stroke at his home in New York City. While Arthur had become president by default and his integrity had been questioned by many, he ended his term in office respected for doing what was right as opposed to what was politically expedient.

22

Grover Cleveland: Lone Democrat

Born:	March 18, 1837
Died:	June 24, 1908
First Lady:	Frances Folsom Cleveland
Political Party:	Democratic
First Presidential Term:	March 4, 1885 to March 4, 1889
Famous Quote:	"He mocks the people who proposes that the government shall protect the rich and that they in turn will care for the laboring poor."

Timeline

1859 . . . . Admitted to the bar
1871–1873 . . . . Sheriff of Erie County, New York
1882 . . . . Mayor of Buffalo, New York
1883–1885 . . . . . . Governor of New York
1885–1889 . . . . . . Twenty-second president of the United States
1886 . . . . Married Frances Folsom
1893–1897 . . . . . . Twenty-fourth president of the United States
1896 . . . . Utah admitted to the Union
1904 . . . . President of Princeton University's board of trustees

Childhood and Education

Grover Cleveland was born on March 18, 1837, in Caldwell, New Jersey. He grew up in New York and started attending school at the age of eleven. His father, Richard Falley Cleveland, was a Presbyterian minister who died when Cleveland was sixteen. Prior to his death, Reverend Cleveland had moved the family around many times as he was transferred from post to post. His untimely death caused Cleveland to leave school to help support his mother, Ann Neal Cleveland, and his five sisters and three brothers. In 1855, Cleveland moved to Buffalo, New York, to live and work with his Uncle. While there, he studied law and was admitted to the bar in 1859.

First Lady: Frances Folsom Cleveland

Cleveland became the only president to marry in the White House when he wed Frances Folsom. At the time, he was forty-nine and she was twenty-one.

QUIRKS & ODDITIES

Cleveland was a law partner with Frances Folsom's father. Cleveland had actually bought her first baby carriage. When her father died, Frances was eleven years old and Cleveland became her unofficial guardian, helping her to gain an education. It was while she was in college that he asked Frances's mother if he could court her.

Together, the Clevelands had three daughters and two sons: Ruth, Esther, Marion, Richard Folsom, and Francis Grover. Their daughter Esther was the only president's child born in the White House.

Before his marriage, Cleveland's sister Rose had acted as the official White House hostess. Once married, however, Frances took over these duties as the nation's youngest first lady and became an instant celebrity. In fact, at that time there were no laws protecting people from having their image used in advertising without their permission. As such, Frances Cleveland's image was used everywhere to advertise products ranging from perfume to ashtrays and more. She was also a trendsetter, with women emulating her hairstyle and clothing. Frances remarried after Cleveland's death in 1908, becoming the first wife of a president to do so.

Early Career

After being admitted to the bar, Cleveland entered private law practice. At the same time, he became an active member of the Democratic party in New York. He was elected Sheriff of Erie County, New York, in 1871 and became known for fighting against corruption. In 1882, he was elected mayor of Buffalo, New York, and one year later he became the governor of New York in which capacity he served from 1883 to 1885. While he earned the enmity of those who were corrupt and dishonest, his own honesty helped propel him to the presidency.

Bid for the Presidency

In 1884, Cleveland was nominated by the Democrats to run for president with Thomas Hendricks as his running mate. His opponent was Republican James Blaine. Blaine was a career politician who had often been in the running for the Republican nomination in years past.

Ma, Ma, Where's My Pa?

During the campaign, the Republicans began to use an episode from Cleveland's past against him. Apparently, Cleveland had been involved with a widow named Maria C. Halpin in the 1870s. In 1874, Mrs. Halpin gave birth to a son who she named Oscar Folsom Cleveland, naming Grover Cleveland as the father. Even though he was unsure of his responsibility, he agreed to pay child support. When Mrs. Halpin began drinking incessantly, he paid to have the child put into an orphanage. When the Republicans brought this up during the campaign, Cleveland met it head on. A common chant during this time was, "Ma, Ma, where's my Pa? Gone to the White House, ha, ha, ha!" Cleveland's honesty and forthright manner when dealing with this issue helped remove the stigma from him and did not cost him the election.

SCANDALS & GOSSIP

Mrs. Halpin wished to get her child back from the orphanage. The courts would not agree, so in 1876 she kidnapped her son from the orphanage, but the authorities were able to recover him. Eventually he was adopted by a New York family and became a doctor.

Election Results

In the end, Cleveland was able to win the election. Blaine had hurt his own chances for success when he was seen dining with industrialists like John Jacob Astor during a time when labor was hurting with a huge amount of unemployment. Cleveland won with only 49 percent of the popular vote and 55 percent of the electoral vote.

Presidential Administration

Grover Cleveland's time in office was marked by his strict sense of honesty and his desire to do what was morally right in his opinion. His strict views about being fair to everyone actually led him to make some decisions that would be questioned today. For example, he would not allow an appropriation for seed to be given to struggling farmers in Texas because he felt that such acts by the federal government made people rely more on the government's help than on their own wits and strength.

Cleveland angered veterans with his vetoes. At that time, many requests for pensions from Civil War veterans were being presented to Congress, and Cleveland vetoed any request that he felt did not have merit or was fraudulent. He also vetoed a bill, which would later become law under Harrison, that allowed veterans who were disabled for reasons other than military service to receive benefits.

As the first Democratic president since the Civil War, Cleveland was petitioned by many Democrats for patronage jobs. The Democratic leaders wanted to place as many Democrats in the government as possible. However, Cleveland would not appoint anyone who he believed was unsuited for a particular job, angering many of the party's leaders.

Cleveland said this upon vetoing the bill that would have helped individual farmers in Texas: "I can find no warrant for such an appropriation in the Constitution; and I do not believe that the power and duty of the General Government ought to be extended to the relief of individual suffering which is in no manner properly related to the public service or benefit."

Presidential Succession Act

Garfield's death in office had revealed a problem with presidential succession in that if the vice president succeeded to the presidency while there was no speaker of the House or president pro tempore of the Senate, then there would be no one to take over the presidency if the new president should die. Therefore, the Presidential Succession Act was passed during Cleveland's administration providing that upon the death or resignation of both the president and vice president, the line of succession would go through the cabinet in chronological order of creation.

Interstate Commerce

An important act that passed in 1887 was the Interstate Commerce Act. This act created the Interstate Commerce Commission, which was the first federal regulatory agency. The ICC was tasked with regulating interstate railroad rates. The act required the railroads to publish their rates so that they would not fluctuate depending on the individuals involved. However, the commission was not given the necessary resources to truly enforce all aspects of the act. In spite of this shortcoming, the creation of the ICC was an important first step in controlling corruption and protecting small businesses.

Native American Rights

In 1887, the Dawes Severalty Act passed, granting citizenship and title to reservation land for Native Americans who were willing to renounce their tribal allegiance, thus replacing tribal holdings with individual land allotments. Land could be sold after twenty-five years. The purpose of the act was to move the Native Americans from a tribal culture to one resembling white America, with individuals living on their own private property. In the end, it was a failure as it resulted in a weakening of tribal ties but did not help Native Americans to become more accepted by the dominant culture.

Defeat for Reelection

Cleveland ran for president again in 1888. He was opposed by Republican Benjamin Harrison. One of the main issues of the campaign was the use of a protective tariff. In fact, protective tariffs had resulted in a decrease in the goods available for sale and higher prices for those goods. Cleveland had argued ineffectively for a new, lower tariff during his time in office, while Republicans argued that protective tariffs were necessary to help American producers and businesses. After a close election, Harrison won with less of the popular vote but the majority of the electoral vote. Cleveland was kept from winning the presidency because he was unable to carry his home state of New York, where the powerful political machine Tammany Hall opposed his election. Cleveland returned to his law practice in New York City after his defeat. He would run again in 1892 and win, becoming the only president to serve two nonconsecutive terms.

Benjamin Harrison: Human Iceberg

Born:	August 20, 1833
Died:	March 13, 1901
First Lady:	Caroline Lavinia Scott Harrison
Political Party:	Republican
Presidential Term:	March 4, 1889 to March 3, 1893
Famous Quote:	"We Americans have no commission from God to police the world."

Timeline

1852 . . . . Graduated from Miami University

1853 . . . . Married Caroline Lavinia Scott

1862–1865 . . . . . . Served in the Civil War, rising to the rank of brigadier general

1881–1887 . . . . . . U.S. senator

1889–1893 . . . . . . Twenty-third president of the United States

1889 . . . . Montana, Washington, and North and South Dakota admitted to the Union

1890 . . . . Wyoming and Idaho admitted to the Union

1896 . . . . Married Mary Scott Lord Dimmick

Childhood and Education

Benjamin Harrison was born on August 20, 1833, in North Bend, Ohio. He grew up on a 600-acre farm that had been given to his father by his grandfather, William Henry Harrison, the ninth president of the United States. Harrison would become the only president whose grandfather had also been president. His father, John Scott Harrison, was a member of the U.S. House of Representatives. His mother, Elizabeth Irwin Harrison, died when Harrison was almost seventeen. Harrison was a deeply religious man and was raised a Presbyterian. He was a deacon and church elder and also taught Sunday school. He was so devout that he would not conduct state business on Sundays.

PRESIDENTIAL TRIVIA

Benjamin Harrison has been called the "human iceberg." He was not a people person and did not like to engage in small talk. He was very intelligent but was not known for his charisma. As Theodore Roosevelt said when he was a civil service commissioner, "He is a cold-blooded, narrow-minded, prejudiced, obstinate, timid . . . politician."

Harrison was a very bright student. He was tutored at home and then attended a small, local school. In 1847 he attended Farmer's College, a college preparatory school located in Cincinnati. Harrison entered Miami University in Oxford, Ohio, as a junior in 1850. He graduated in 1852, studied law, and then was admitted to the Ohio bar in 1854.

First Lady: Caroline Lavinia Scott Harrison

Caroline Lavinia Scott was born on October 1, 1832. Caroline was an accomplished musician and graduated from the Oxford Female Institute with a music degree. Her father, John W. Scott, was a Presbyterian minister and also a professor of chemistry and physics at Farmer's College. Harrison was a student at the college at that time and was introduced to Caroline by her father. Harrison courted and then married Caroline on October

20, 1853, in Oxford, Ohio. Together they had two children: Russell Benjamin and Mary Scott.

Active First Lady

Caroline was very involved as the president's wife. Using money granted from Congress, she performed major renovations in the White House including adding new floors, plumbing, and bathrooms.

**QUIRKS &
ODDITIES**

The Harrisons were the first family to have electricity installed in the White House. Legend has it that after Harrison got an electrical shock while switching off a light, he and his wife were afraid to touch the light switches. In fact, they would sometimes even go to bed with the lights on.

Artistically talented, Caroline painted the White House china. She had the first Christmas tree put up inside the White House. Politically, she was also a huge proponent of increasing women's rights. She also served as the first president-general of the Daughters of the American Revolution while her husband was president. Tragically, she came down with tuberculosis in 1892 and died in the White House only four months before the end of her husband's term in office.

Second Marriage

Four years after Caroline's death, Harrison married Mary Scott Lord Dimmick. She was the niece of Harrison's first wife and had in fact spent some time at the White House with the president and the first lady before her death. At the time of their marriage, Harrison was sixty-two and Mary was thirty-seven. His children by his first marriage would not attend the wedding. Together they had one daughter, Elizabeth, who was born in 1897. Harrison died five years after their marriage but Mary lived until 1948.

Early Career

Harrison entered private law practice in 1854 and became active in the Republican party in Ohio. He supported Abraham Lincoln's bid for the presidency in 1860. During this time he was appointed as a reporter for the Indiana Supreme Court.

In 1862, Harrison joined the military to fight in the Civil War. He served with valor under Major General Joseph Hooker. During the fight for Atlanta, Harrison led his men to an important victory. He then participated in the march on Atlanta with General Sherman and was promoted to brigadier general.

At the end of the war, he resumed his law practice in Ohio and his activities with the Republican party. He was chosen by President Hayes to be on the Mississippi River Commission. In 1881, he won a seat in the U.S. Senate representing Indiana. While in office, Harrison was a staunch protectionist but proved to be one of the first conservationists in America. He served in the Senate until 1887.

Bid for the Presidency

In 1888, Harrison received the Republican nomination for president with Levi Morton as his running mate. His opponent was incumbent President Grover Cleveland. After a very close campaign, Cleveland actually won the popular vote by more than 100,000 votes. However, he failed to carry his home state of New York, which cost him that state's electoral vote and the election. Harrison won with 58 percent of the electoral vote.

Presidential Administration

One of the main issues that Harrison faced during his presidency was civil service reform. Congress was deeply divided on this issue, creating a no-win situation for the president. Therefore, not much was accomplished on this front during Harrison's term in office. In fact, because he appointed people to positions based on merit rather than on political patronage, he created an enemy in the powerful speaker of the house, Thomas Reed. Because of the enmity between the two of them, legislation that was important to Harrison was often voted down or ignored.

Harrison experienced a lot of firsts while he was president. As already stated, he was the first to have electricity in the White House. He was also the first to attend a baseball game, and the first to have his voice recorded. A strong believer in civil rights, Harrison held afternoon receptions open to the public that for the first time African Americans were allowed to attend.

New States and Relations

Six states entered into the Union during Harrison's time in office—more than during any other president's administration. It was also during his term that relations were established with Central America. The Pan American Congress met in 1889 in Washington, D.C. Its purpose was an increase in cooperation between North, Central, and South America.

Fighting Monopolies

At the end of the nineteenth century, reformers were beginning to set their sights on the unfair business practices of many trusts and monopolies. To combat this, the Sherman Anti-Trust Act was passed in 1890. This bill was the first to attempt to stop businesses from forming unfair monopolies and using other means to reduce competition. The law itself was vague and did not have much effect on the trusts that it was targeting. However, it did have the unwanted effect of being used against labor unions. In fact, labor unions that tried to use collective bargaining practices like strikes were targeted through this law as having created unfair monopolies.

Nonetheless, the Sherman Anti-Trust Act was an important first step toward making sure that trade was not limited by the existence of monopolies.

Economics Issues

In 1890, Representative William McKinley sponsored a tariff that required those wishing to import products to pay a whopping 48 percent tax. This was seen as a response to a recession that was occurring in America. The goal was to encourage people to buy American goods. However, consumer prices rose for imported items and in many cases a reduction of supply occurred. Consumers blamed Republicans—including Harrison—for their economic woes and this led to his defeat in the election of 1892.

IN THEIR OWN WORDS...

Harrison realized the importance of keeping workers happy, presaging the future changes to help protect laborers. As he said: "We cannot afford in America to have any discontented classes, and if fair wages are paid for fair work we will have none."

Life After the Presidency

Harrison retired to Indianapolis after his term as president, remarried, and went back to practicing law. In 1900, he actually served as counsel to the Republic of Venezuela during a boundary dispute between Venezuela and Great Britain. In Febuary 1901, Harrison developed the flu. Despite various treatments, Harrison's conditioned worsened and on March 13, 1901, he died of pneumonia.

Grover Cleveland: Second Term

24

Second Presidential Term: March 4, 1893 to April 15, 1897

Election of 1892

Grover Cleveland decided to run for president again in 1892. At the time, New York City was dominated by a group called Tammany Hall, which was notorious for trading bribes for positions of power.

In the election of 1888, Tammany Hall had kept Cleveland from winning the presidency because they opposed his reforms. They attempted to keep him from winning the nomination in 1892, but he was able to scrape by, winning with a margin of only ten votes. Cleveland's vice presidential running mate was Adlai Stevenson. He was opposed by incumbent Benjamin Harrison, and James Weaver ran as a third party candidate for the People's party. The tariff issue dominated this campaign just as it had in 1888. Harrison defended protectionist tariffs like the McKinley Tariff, which was passed in his term, while Cleveland spoke strongly against this tariff, promising to lower it if elected. In the end Cleveland won with 277 out of a possible 444 electoral votes.

PRESIDENTIAL

TRIVIA

In between his two terms in office, Grover and Frances Cleveland had a baby girl they named Ruth. Born in 1891, she was very sickly and died in 1904. According to the National Confectioner's Association and the Curtiss Candy Company, the "Baby Ruth" candy bar was named after Ruth Cleveland, even though she had died sixteen years before it was first offered.

Second Presidential Administration

As strong in his convictions as he was during his first term in office, Cleveland began by forcing the withdrawal of a treaty that would have annexed Hawaii in 1893. He was by nature an anti-imperialist and believed that America was wrong in helping with the overthrow of Queen Liliuokalani. The queen had attempted to create a new Constitution for the island that would have restored power to the monarchy. This power had been previously removed when the former king had agreed to a reduction in authority. Cleveland learned that most Hawaiians did not support her ousting or annexation and believed that American troops should not have been involved.

Panic of 1893

In 1893, America experienced an economic depression resulting in the collapse of thousands of businesses and leaving millions of Americans out of work. During this depression, called the Panic of 1893, riots broke out and many asked the government for help. Cleveland, however, along with many others in the government, saw the business cycle with its highs and lows as a natural state of affairs and did not believe that the government had a place in helping people who were harmed by its extreme lows. It was not until much later that the government would take an active role in helping flatten the business cycle through overt actions.

Cleveland on the Hawaii issue: "It has been the boast of our government that it seeks to do justice in all things.... I mistake the American people if they favor the odious doctrine that there is no such thing as international morality, that there is one law for a strong nation and another for a weak one, and that even by indirection a strong power may with impunity despoil a weak one of its territory."

Silver Purchase Act

Another major issue that had been debated since the end of the Civil War—and would continue to be part of the public discussion until Franklin Roosevelt's time—was how to back the U.S. currency. Cleveland was a strong believer in the gold standard, while others felt that currency should be backed by silver. Gold was more rare, but was also a more stable way to back currency. Silver was much more readily available, and so people were less inclined to hoard currency and it became more available to the public.

During Benjamin Harrison's term as president, the Sherman Silver Purchase Act had passed, requiring the federal government to purchase silver in exchange for silver certificates. These could then be turned back in for silver or gold. By the time Cleveland was president, he felt that the gold reserves had dangerously dwindled as people were turning their certificates in for gold, which was rarer and ultimately worth more. To combat this, he called Congress into session to repeal the Sherman Silver Purchase Act, although many in his own party did not agree with his assessment. In the end, the act was repealed.

Tariff Reduction

Cleveland had campaigned to lower the protective tariff created with the McKinley Tariff and he helped push forward the Wilson-Gorman Act in 1894. It had started as a serious reduction in the tariff but ended up only moving the 48 percent tax to 41 percent. To help make up for lost revenue, it imposed a 2 percent income tax. Cleveland was angered by this bill because, after going through the Senate, new items to be taxed were actually added to the bill even though its original purpose had been to lower tariffs. The bill became a law without his signature. In 1895, the Supreme Court ruled that the income tax imposed by the bill was unconstitutional.

Pullman Strike

The end of the nineteenth century saw an increase in laborers fighting for better working conditions. The Pullman Palace Car Company had reduced wages and on May 11, 1894, the workers in Illinois walked out under the leadership of Eugene V. Debs. The Pullman Strike resulted in violence in Chicago. Cleveland ordered federal troops in and arrested Debs and other leaders, ending the strike.

PRESIDENTIAL TRIVIA

Cleveland was able to send in federal troops and U.S. marshals to break up the Pullman strike on the basis that it was impeding the delivery of U.S. mail. In fact, the strike's main leader, Eugene V. Debs, was sent to jail for six months for interfering with the delivery of the mail.

The strike itself was important as it brought many issues before the national audience, including whether a strike should be legal and what the government's response should be.

Life After the Presidency

At the end of his second term, Cleveland decided to retire from active political life. He moved to Princeton, New Jersey, and became a lecturer and member of the board of trustees of Princeton University. He continued to campaign for various Democrats throughout the rest of his life. He also wrote articles for the *Saturday Evening Post*. Cleveland died in Princeton, New Jersey, on June 24, 1908, of heart failure.

25

William McKinley:
The Front Porch Campaigner

Born: January 29, 1843
Died: September 14, 1901
First Lady: Ida Saxton McKinley
Political Party: Republican
Presidential Term: March 4, 1897 to September 14, 1901
Famous Quote: "We need Hawaii just as much and a good deal more than we did California. It is Manifest Destiny."

Timeline

1861–1865 . . . . Served in the Civil War, rising to rank of brevet major
1865 . . . . Admitted to the Ohio bar
1871 . . . . Married Ida Saxton
1877–1883 . . . . . . U.S. representative
1885–1891 . . . . . . U.S. representative
1892–1896 . . . . . . Governor of Ohio
1897–1901 . . . . Twenty-fifth president of the United States
1898 . . . . Spanish-American War
1901 . . . . Assassination

Childhood and Education

William McKinley was born on January 29, 1843, in Niles, Ohio, to William McKinley Sr., a pig iron administrator, and Nancy Allison McKinley. McKinley attended public school and in 1852 went to the Poland Seminary. When he was seventeen, he enrolled in Allegheny College in Pennsylvania but soon dropped out due to illness. Unfortunately, he never returned to college because of financial difficulties. He taught school for a time before fighting in the Civil War. After the war ended, he studied law and was admitted to the Ohio bar in 1867.

First Lady: Ida Saxton McKinley

William McKinley met Ida Saxton in Canton, Ohio, in 1868. In 1870, they started dating. Ida was the daughter of a prominent banker and newspaper owner and had attended the best of schools and taken a tour in Europe. Ida agreed to marry McKinley on January 25, 1871. They had two daughters, neither of whom lived beyond infancy.

Ida suffered from illnesses including epileptic seizures, making her an invalid throughout most of their married life. She did, however, move with McKinley as he took various political positions. Despite her illness, she participated in state functions as first lady.

Ida survived her husband's assassination. She retired to Canton, Ohio, and died on May 26, 1907.

PRESIDENTIAL TRIVIA

The McKinleys had a very loving relationship, and William was solicitous of his wife's health. During functions, he insisted that his wife sit next to him and if he noticed that she was about to have a seizure he would place a handkerchief or other cloth over her so that others could not see her face.

Early Career

After dropping out of Allegheny College, McKinley found that he had to work in order to help his family survive an economic depression. He taught and then worked in a post office until 1861. At that time, he decided to fight to preserve the Union and stopped working to fight in the Civil War.

Civil War

McKinley joined the Twenty-third Ohio Volunteer Infantry at the age of eighteen and served from 1861 to 1865. He began his stint in the Union Army as a private, but he quickly moved up in the ranks. He participated in numerous smaller skirmishes before fighting at the Battle of Antietam in September 1862. He was promoted after the battle for showing valor as he moved rations to the front. By February 1863, he was made first lieutenant. By the end of the war he had received a battlefield promotion to brevet major.

Political Aspirations

At the end of the war, McKinley was admitted to the bar in 1867 and started practicing law. He also became involved with the Republican party in Ohio. By 1877, he was elected to the U.S. House of Representatives where he served until 1883 and then again from 1885 until 1891. During his time in the House, he was well-known as a proponent of protectionism. One of the highest tariffs in America's history was passed under his name, and he was voted out of office because of his support of this tariff, which caused a marked increase in consumer prices. In 1892, McKinley was elected to be the governor of Ohio.

Bid for the Presidency

In 1896, McKinley was nominated by the Republican party to run for president with Garret Hobart as his running mate. He was opposed by William Jennings Bryan. During Bryan's acceptance of the nomination, he gave his famous "Cross of Gold" speech where he spoke against the gold standard. He argued that America should endorse the free coinage of silver that would have increased the amount of money in circulation, helping farmers in debt.

Here is the most famous excerpt from Bryan's speech: "Having behind us the commercial interests and the laboring interests and all the toiling masses, we shall answer their demands for a gold standard by saying to them, you shall not press down upon the brow of labor this crown of thorns. You shall not crucify mankind upon a cross of gold."

As expected, the main issue of the campaign centered on the use of gold, silver, or a combination of the two to back U.S. currency. McKinley felt that the only safe method for backing currency was the more stable gold. In the end, McKinley won with 51 percent of the popular vote and 271 out of 447 electoral votes.

Election of 1900

After having served one term as president, McKinley easily won the nomination again in 1900. He was opposed yet again by William Jennings Bryan. This time, young Theodore Roosevelt was chosen as McKinley's vice president. Bryan and the Democrats still spoke out against the gold standard but because the economy had improved they had limited success with this tactic. He also campaigned against McKinley's and America's growing imperialism as evidenced by the Spanish-American War. In the end, McKinley won with 292 out of 447 electoral votes

Presidential Administration

McKinley had strong opinions concerning protectionism and the gold standard when he ascended to the presidency. Throughout his term in office, he attempted to shore up America's economy through what he saw as the best means possible.

McKinley was unafraid to move forward in gaining further land and other interests for America. He disagreed with President Cleveland's opinion concerning how America dealt with Queen Liliuokalani and Hawaii and approved its annexation. This would be the first step toward statehood for the island territory.

Remember the **Maine**

One of the main events of McKinley's administration was the Spanish-American War. At the time, many newspapers were in the business not only of reporting the news but also sensationalizing it—and in some cases making the news itself. This "yellow journalism" can be directly related to America's going to war with Spain in 1898.

On February 15, 1898, the U.S. battleship *Maine*, stationed in the Havana harbor, exploded and sank killing 266 members of the crew. The cause of the explosion has never been determined, but that did not stop newspapers from claming that Spanish mines were to blame. "Remember the *Maine!*" became the rallying cry of the Spanish-American War.

**QUIRKS &
ODDITIES**

Frederick Remington was sent to Cuba by William Randolph Hearst to report about what was happening before the start of the Spanish-American War. Writing back to Hearst, Remington said, "There is no war. . . . Request to be recalled." Hearst responded, "Please remain. You furnish the pictures, I'll furnish the war."

This event directly led to war being declared against Spain on April 25, 1898. America fought against the Spanish in both the Pacific and Atlantic Oceans. Commodore George Dewey destroyed Spain's Pacific fleet while Admiral William Sampson destroyed the Atlantic fleet. American troops captured Manila and took possession of the Philippines. In Cuba, Santiago was captured. The United States also took Puerto Rico before Spain asked for peace. The United States and Spain made peace with the Paris Peace Treaty on December 10, 1898. According to the treaty, Spain gave up its claim to Cuba and ceded Puerto Rico and Guam to America. It also gave the Philippine Islands to the United States in exchange for $20 million.

China

America wanted to ensure that it had equal rights to trade with China along with other nations around the world. In 1899, Secretary of State John

Hay created the Open Door policy to this effect. However, the Boxer Rebellion occurred in June 1900 as a backlash against Western influences in trade and culture in China. Western missionaries and foreign communities were targeted. America joined forces with eight nations—including Great Britain, France, Germany, Russia, and Japan—to stop the rebellion in 1900. China ended up having to pay war reparations. The war's outcome reduced the authority of the Chinese government in the eyes of its people, setting the scene for future rebellions.

Gold Standard

Economically, a significant action taken during McKinley's administration was the Gold Standard Act. According to this bill, America was officially placed on the gold standard, meaning that greenbacks were backed by gold held in reserve by the United States. This remained in effect until 1933 when President Franklin Roosevelt took America off the gold standard.

PRESIDENTIAL TRIVIA

Henry M. Littlefield published an article called "*The Wizard of Oz*: Parable on Populism," in which he describes hidden meanings throughout the book. According to Littlefield, L. Frank Baum, author and supporter of Bryan and free silver, wrote the story as an allegory of the problems with the gold standard. In the book, Dorothy's shoes—the means of her return to safety—are made of silver.

Assassination

On September 6, 1901, President McKinley was visiting the Pan-American exhibit in New York City, a fair with participants from the Western Hemisphere similar to a world's fair. While there, McKinley was shot twice by anarchist Leon Czolgosz. McKinley died eight days later on September 14, 1901. Czolgosz claimed that he assassinated McKinley because the president was an enemy of working people. The assassin was convicted of McKinley's murder and electrocuted on October 29, 1901.

26

Theodore Roosevelt: Trust Buster

Born:	October 27, 1858
Died:	January 6, 1919
First Lady:	Edith Kermit Carow Roosevelt
Political Party:	Republican
Presidential Term:	September 14, 1901 to March 3, 1909
Famous Quote:	"The American people are slow to wrath, but when their wrath is once kindled it burns like a consuming flame."

Timeline

1880 . . . . Graduated from Harvard

1880 . . . . Married Alice Hathaway Lee

1882–1884 . . . . . . New York state assemblyman

1886 . . . . Married Edith Kermit Carow

1889–1895 . . . . . . Member of U.S. civil service commission

1895–1897 . . . . . . President of New York City police board

1897–1898 . . . . . . Assistant secretary of the navy

1898 . . . . Spanish-American War

1898–1900 . . . . . . Governor of New York

1901. . . . . Vice president of the United States under President McKinley

1901–1909 . . . . . . Twenty-sixth president of the United States

1904–1905 . . . . . . Russo-Japanese War

1906 . . . . Won the Nobel Peace Prize

1907. . . . . Oklahoma admitted to the Union

Childhood and Education

Theodore Roosevelt was born on October 27, 1858, in New York City and grew up in a wealthy family. His father, Theodore Roosevelt Sr., was a merchant. He had a huge impact on Theodore Jr., who looked to him for guidance. His mother, Martha "Mittie" Bulloch Roosevelt, was a southerner from Georgia who was sympathetic to the Confederate cause.

Roosevelt was sickly as a youth, suffering from asthma and other illnesses. As he grew up, he exercised and boxed to try and build up his constitution. In fact, he turned what could have been a limitation into one of his strongest attributes. Roosevelt had wonderful experiences traveling to Europe and Egypt in his youth.

QUIRKS & ODDITIES

Roosevelt had a photographic memory. He read an average of three books a day. He also was an avid writer. He penned more than thirty books, including books on natural history, American History, and his own autobiography.

Roosevelt was tutored by his aunt, along with other private teachers, before entering Harvard in 1876. In 1880 he graduated magna cum laude and went to Columbia Law School. During law school, he researched and began writing his first book, entitled *The Naval War of 1812*, which would be published in 1882. Roosevelt only attended Columbia for one year before dropping out to begin his political life.

Marriages: Alice Hathaway Lee Roosevelt and Edith Kermit Carow Roosevelt

Theodore Roosevelt was married to Alice Hathaway Lee, who was the daughter of an important New York City banker named George Cabot Lee and his wife, Caroline Haskell Lee. Alice died at the age of twenty-two, two days after the birth of their daughter, Alice. Tragically, Roosevelt's mother also died the same day.

Roosevelt's daughter Alice was a true character. She was banned from the White House numerous times after her father's term ended. She became such a fixture in Washington that she gained the nickname "Washington's Other Monument." Her father found her hard to handle remarking once, "I can run the country or I can control Alice, but I can't possibly do both."

Alice was married in the White House East room to Representative Nicholas Longworth in 1906.

Roosevelt married long time acquaintance Edith Kermit Carow on December 2, 1886, in London. She had grown up next door to Theodore in New York City. Together, they had four sons and one daughter. Edith was an active first lady, remodeling the White House and arranging the wedding of her stepdaughter.

Early Career

At twenty-four, Theodore Roosevelt became the youngest member of the New York State Assembly, where he served until 1884. In that year after his mother and his first wife both died, he moved to the Dakota territory to work as a cattle rancher. By 1886, he had returned to New York City. From 1889 to 1895, Roosevelt was a U.S. civil service commissioner, a job in which he worked hard to ensure that civil service laws were enforced. He continued his efforts to stop corruption as president of the New York City police board from 1895 until 1897. In 1897, he became the assistant secretary of the navy, believing that America should go to war with Spain. In typical Roosevelt style, he resigned his position in the upper echelons of the government and joined the military to fight in the Spanish-American War.

Rough Rider

In 1898, Roosevelt joined the U.S. Volunteer Cavalry Regiment to fight in the Spanish-American War. His regiment became known by the nickname "Rough Riders." He only served for five months—from May through

September 1898—but in that time distinguished himself by his courage and initiative, quickly rising to the rank of colonel. On July 1, 1898, Roosevelt and the Rough Riders scored a major victory at San Juan, charging up Kettle Hill and causing a rout of troops from San Juan Hill. This then allowed the American troops to occupy Santiago. Roosevelt resigned from the military after hostilities ended.

Governor and Vice President

Roosevelt served as the governor of New York from 1898 to 1900, where he earned a reputation fighting corruption in government. In 1901, Roosevelt was nominated as vice president under William McKinley. However, he was only in this office until September when he succeeded to the presidency.

Unexpected Presidency

Roosevelt became president on September 14, 1901 upon President McKinley's assassination. At the age of forty-two, he was the youngest man to ever become president. At the end of this term in 1904, Roosevelt's popularity made him the obvious choice for the Republican nomination, with Charles W. Fairbanks as his vice presidential nominee. Roosevelt was opposed by Democrat Alton B. Parker. Since both candidates agreed on most of the major issues, the campaign became more of a popularity contest. In fact, neither candidate spent a lot of time campaigning. In the end, Roosevelt easily won with 336 out of 476 electoral votes.

Presidential Administration

As the first full term president of the twentieth century, Roosevelt helped usher in many changes and reforms that are still important today. He felt it was important for America to control a canal linking the Atlantic and Pacific oceans. Panama seemed the obvious choice due to its location and size. At the time, the country was controlled by Colombia. After attempts to make an agreement with Colombia concerning a canal failed, America aided Panama in gaining independence from Colombia. Once independent, the United States created a treaty with Panama to gain the canal zone in exchange for $10 million plus annual payments that continue to this day.

Diplomacy and Immigration

One of the cornerstones of American foreign policy was the Monroe Doctrine, which said that the Western Hemisphere would be off limits to foreign imperialism and encroachment. Roosevelt believed in what was called "Big Stick Diplomacy" based on his famous quote, "Speak softly and carry a big stick; you will go far." Therefore, he added the Roosevelt Corollary to the Monroe Doctrine that stated that America had a responsibility to intervene, with force if necessary, in Latin America to enforce the Monroe Doctrine.

Roosevelt was also interested in world affairs beyond the scope of American foreign interests. From 1904 to 1905, Russia and Japan went to war because they both had imperialistic designs on Manchuria and Korea. In 1905, Roosevelt offered his services to be the mediator of the peace between the two countries. The designees of each nation met at Portsmouth, New Hampshire. Roosevelt's successful mediation led to his being awarded the 1906 Nobel Peace Prize.

Just as anti-Chinese sentiment was prevalent in America during the late nineteenth and early twentieth centuries, anti-Japanese feelings were also on the rise. In 1907, Roosevelt made an agreement with Japan known as the Gentleman's Agreement. According to this agreement, Japan agreed to slow the immigration of laborers to America. In exchange, the United States would refrain from passing a law that would affect Japanese immigration as the Chinese Exclusion Act had done for Chinese immigration.

Square Deal

While in office, Roosevelt was known for his progressive policies and attempts to reform business. One of his nicknames was "Trust Buster" because his administration used antitrust laws to fight against corruption in the railroad, oil, and other industries. His policies concerning trusts and labor reform were part of what he called the "Square Deal."

Another area of reform passed during Roosevelt's term dealt with the meat packing and drug industries. Upton Sinclair had written a novel called

The Jungle describing the disgusting and unsanitary practices of the meat packing industry in graphic detail.

An excerpt from *The Jungle*: "[T]he meat would be shoveled into carts, and the man who did the shoveling would not trouble to lift out a rat even when he saw one—there were things that went into the sausage in comparison with which a poison rat was a tidbit."

The Jungle resulted in the Meat Inspection Act and the Pure Food and Drug Act in 1906. As the names suggest, the first law required the government to inspect meat packing plants and the second protected consumers from mislabeling and other dangerous practices for food and drug production.

Great Conservationist

Roosevelt was well-known for his conservation efforts and was nicknamed the "Great Conservationist." While known as a big-game hunter, he was also one who believed in preserving wildlife and natural habitats for future generations.

While president, Roosevelt was on a hunting trip. After days of searching, he finally cornered a bear, but the condition of the animal caused Roosevelt to show compassion and he did not take the animal as a hunting trophy. This was reported in the press and a shopkeeper got the idea to name bear toys "Teddy Bears." The name has stuck.

Roosevelt was influenced by John Muir, founder of the Sierra Club. During his time in office, more than 125 million acres in national forests were created. He also established the first national wildlife refuge in Florida.

Life After the Presidency

Roosevelt had pledged when he ran in 1904 that he would not seek another term as president. Therefore, he did not run in 1908 but instead retired to Oyster Bay, New York. He left for a safari to Africa from 1909 to 1910 where he collected important plant and animal specimens for the Smithsonian Institute. After returning home, he found himself disagreeing with successor William Howard Taft's policies and decided to run again for president in 1912.

Bull Moose

Roosevelt sought the Republican nomination again in 1912 but was denied the opportunity. He then left to form his own third party, called the Bull Moose party. His entry into the 1912 presidential race split the Republican vote to such an extent that Democrat Woodrow Wilson was able to win the election.

Assassination Attempt and Death

A would-be assassin named John Schrank attempted to kill Roosevelt in 1912 while he was campaigning in Milwaukee. Roosevelt's fifty-page speech and steel spectacle case kept a bullet from killing him by slowing it down. Roosevelt went ahead and gave his planned speech before being seen by a doctor. Surgeons left the bullet in him, and he did not seem to be affected by it for the rest of his life. However, it effectively ended his campaign for reelection in the election of 1912.

Roosevelt died on January 6, 1919, of a coronary embolism. Theodore Roosevelt would always be remembered as a fiery individualist who embodied the American culture of the early 1900s. To this effect, he is enshrined on Mount Rushmore along with George Washington, Thomas Jefferson, and Abraham Lincoln.

William Howard Taft: Chief Justice

Born:	September 15, 1857
Died:	March 8, 1930
First Lady:	Helen "Nellie" Herron Taft
Political Party:	Republican
Presidential Term:	March 4, 1909 to March 3, 1913
Famous Quote:	"Presidents come and go, but the Supreme Court goes on forever."

Timeline

1878 . . . . .Graduated from Yale University

1880 . . . . .Graduated from University of Cincinnati Law School

1886 . . . . .Married Helen "Nellie" Herron

1890 . . . . .U.S. solicitor general

1892 . . . . .Judge of the Sixth U.S. Circuit Court

1900–1904 . . . . . .Commissioner and later governor-general of the Philippines

1904–1908 . . . . . .Secretary of war

1909–1913 . . . . . .Twenty-seventh president of the United States

1912 . . . . .New Mexico and Arizona admitted to the Union

1921–1930 . . . . . . .Chief justice of the Supreme Court

Childhood and Education

William Howard Taft was born on September 15, 1857, in Cincinnati, Ohio. His father, Alphonso Taft, was a lawyer and helped found the Republican party in Cincinnati when Taft was an infant. He served as a public official and was President Ulysses S. Grant's secretary of war.

Taft was an excellent student. He attended a public school in Cincinnati, went to Woodward High School where he graduated second in his class, and then enrolled in Yale University in 1874, again graduating second in his class in 1878. He later went to the University of Cincinnati Law School and was then admitted to the Ohio bar in 1880.

First Lady: Helen "Nellie" Herron Taft

Taft married Helen "Nellie" Herron, the daughter of Judge John W. Herron and Harriet Collins, on June 19, 1886. Helen's parents were prominent members of society and friends of President and Mrs. Rutherford B. Hayes. Together, the Tafts had two sons and one daughter.

Shortly after becoming first lady, Helen had a stroke from which she never fully recovered. However, she continued with her duties as first lady, relishing the social events.

PRESIDENTIAL TRIVIA

Mrs. Taft was responsible for the planting of the Japanese cherry trees around the Tidal Basin in Washington, D.C. She had seen the trees on a visit to Japan and desired to have them in the capital. She and the Japanese ambassador's wife planted the first two saplings in an official ceremony on March 27, 1912.

On June 19, 1911, President and Mrs. Taft celebrated their twenty-fifth wedding anniversary in the White House. Helen Taft remembered this as the "greatest event" of her time as first lady. She continued to be involved in the Washington social scene after the end of her husband's presidency.

Early Career

Taft became assistant prosecutor in Hamilton County, Ohio, upon his graduation from the University of Cincinnati Law School. In 1883, he went into private law practice. Taft had a strong desire to become a judge, and by 1887 he was appointed as a judge of the Ohio Superior Court.

Judicial Appointments

In 1890, Taft was appointed by President Benjamin Harrison to be the U.S. solicitor general. Two years later, he was given the judgeship of the Sixth U.S. Circuit Court in 1892 and eventually became the chief justice. He excelled as a jurist, and the position was his real passion in life. While serving on the court, he also taught law from 1896 to 1900.

Governor of the Philippines

In 1900, Taft was selected by President McKinley to be commissioner and then governor-general of the Philippines. In this capacity, he helped to create a civil regime on the islands and at the same time brought a peaceful end to recurring rebellions. Even though his goal was to become a Supreme Court justice, he turned down the opportunity when President Roosevelt offered it to him so that he could finish his work in the Philippines.

Secretary of War

From 1904 to 1908, Taft served as President Roosevelt's secretary of war. As such, he helped establish the American protectorate in Cuba. He was very close to the president and in fact was handpicked by Roosevelt to succeed him in 1908.

Bid for the Presidency

Since Roosevelt had promised not to run again and had chosen Taft as his successor for the presidency, the nomination was pretty straightforward. Roosevelt was very popular and Taft became the nominee with James

Sherman as his vice president. He was opposed by William Jennings Bryan, who had unsuccessfully run against William McKinley in 1896 and 1900. The campaign was more about personality than issues. In fact, Roosevelt was so popular that both candidates tried to assert that they would be better at carrying out the former president's policies. In the end, Taft won with 52 percent of the popular vote and 66 percent of the electoral vote.

Presidential Administration

President Taft was not nearly as popular as President Roosevelt had been. For example, in 1909 the Payne-Aldrich Tariff Act passed with Taft's signature. The tariff deeply divided Taft's own party. Many progressive Republicans were unhappy with the previous tariff of 46 percent on imported goods. The new tariff lowered tariff rates to 41 percent. When Taft hailed this as an excellent bill, it upset the progressives who felt that it was just a patronizing token change.

QUIRKS & ODDITIES

As America's fattest president, Taft was the butt of many jokes. His weight when he left the White House was around 330 pounds. During his presidency, Taft once became stuck in the White House bathtub. A new tub brought in for his use was so large it could hold four average-size men.

Continuing to Fight Trusts

Taft followed Roosevelt's lead to continue the fight against unfair business practices by enforcing antitrust laws. One of his biggest suits was a Justice Department investigation of antitrust activity with Standard Oil. Eventually, a suit was brought before the Supreme Court that resulted in the corporation breaking up into thirty-four smaller companies in 1911. Many of the major oil companies today, such as Exxon-Mobil and Chevron, can trace their roots to the Standard Oil Company.

Even while fighting trusts, Taft did not publicly speak against trusts and unfair business practices, and his silence alienated him from progressive reformers. Further, his antitrust suits caused him to become very unpopular with big business, including powerful companies like U.S. Steel. President Taft found himself in a difficult position with both progressives and conservatives. His actions never seemed to go far enough for the progressive elements in his party and often went too far for the conservatives. Moreover, his policies caused a rift between him and former president Roosevelt that would come back against Taft in the election of 1912.

Dollar Diplomacy

President Taft made numerous foreign policy decisions based on something called Dollar Diplomacy. He felt as did his secretary of state, Philander Knox, that the purpose of diplomacy was to improve financial opportunities at home and abroad while also using capital to help U.S. interests overseas. In other words, America would use military and diplomatic actions to promote U.S. business interests abroad.

Taft used this policy in 1912 when he sent marines into Nicaragua to help stop a rebellion that the government deemed would be unfriendly to American business interests. In China, Taft had Secretary Knox secure an agreement that an American banking conglomerate would be able to join with Europeans who were financing a railway. Unlike his predecessor, Roosevelt, Taft did not want to stretch the powers of the president. He felt strongly that the actions of the president should be accomplished within the confines of the previously outlined presidential powers.

Life After the Presidency

In 1912, when Taft came up to be nominated by the Republicans, he was opposed by President Roosevelt who was disappointed with his actions in office. Roosevelt felt that Taft, whom he had handpicked, did not fulfill his vision for the presidency.

Taft realized that he was not as popular as Teddy Roosevelt and that he had lost support within his own party. As he said: "I am afraid I am a constant disappointment to my party. The fact of the matter is, the longer I am President the less of a party man I seem to become."

In the end, Roosevelt was defeated by Taft for the nomination and left the Republican party to form the Bull Moose party. Taft was then running against his former friend in addition to the Democratic candidate, Woodrow Wilson. Since both Taft and Roosevelt were pulling votes from Republicans, they ended up splitting the vote and allowing Wilson to win the election.

After retiring, Taft decided to teach law at Yale University from 1913 until 1921, but it was no secret that his ultimate goal was to become a Supreme Court justice. He got his wish in 1921 when President Warren G. Harding named him chief justice of the U.S. Supreme Court. One of his most famous decisions was for *Olmstead v. United States*, which found that the rule against unreasonable search and seizure did not apply to wiretapping. He served in this capacity until one month before his death on March 8, 1930. He was the only president to go on and become a Supreme Court justice. In fact, Taft viewed his time as a Supreme Court justice as his highest accomplishment.

Woodrow Wilson: Educator

28

Born: December 28, 1856

Died: February 3, 1924

Two First Ladies: Ellen Louise Axson Wilson and Edith Bolling Galt Wilson

Political Party: Democratic

Presidential Term: March 4, 1913 to March 3, 1921

Famous Quote: "The Constitution was not made to fit us like a straitjacket. In its elasticity lies its chief greatness."

Timeline

1879 . . . . Graduated from College of New Jersey (Princeton)

1885 . . . . Married Ellen Louise Axson

1886 . . . . Received Ph.D. in political science from Johns Hopkins University

1902–1910 . . . . . . President of Princeton

1911–1913 . . . . Governor of New Jersey

1913–1921 . . . . Twenty-eighth president of the United States

1914–1918 . . . . World War I

1915 . . . . Married Edith Bolling Galt

Childhood and Education

Woodrow Wilson was born on December 28, 1856, in Staunton, Virginia. His father, Joseph Ruggles Wilson, was a Presbyterian Minister. Along with Wilson's mother, Janet "Jessie" Woodrow, Joseph soon moved their family to Augusta, Georgia. Wilson was a sickly youth and was taught at home by his parents. He started attending school at the age of twelve. In 1873, he went to Davidson College but soon dropped out due to health issues.

Wilson entered the College of New Jersey (now called Princeton) in 1875 and graduated in 1879. He studied law and was admitted to the Georgia bar in 1882. However, he was not interested in law but instead decided to go back to school to become an educator. He earned a Ph.D. in political science from Johns Hopkins University making him the only president to earn a doctorate.

Two First Ladies: Ellen Louise Axton Wilson and Edith Bolling Galt Wilson

In 1885, Woodrow Wilson married Ellen Louise Axton, the daughter of a Presbyterian minister. Ellen was a painter and actually had a studio set up for her in the White House. Together, the Wilsons had three daughters, two of whom were married in the White House. Ellen also worked to help alleviate the living conditions for African Americans and for the poor in Washington, D.C. She died on August 6, 1914 of Bright's disease. She was the only first lady to die in the White House.

After Ellen's death, Wilson's cousin took on the traditional first lady's duties. It was she who introduced Wilson to his next wife, Edith Bolling Galt. A little more than a year after the death of his first wife, Wilson married Edith on December 18, 1915.

In 1919, Edith Wilson basically took control of the presidency after her husband suffered a stroke. She only took items she considered important to the president. She was criticized for this, but she always claimed that she made no decisions herself except for deciding what the president should or should not see. But in the end, it is not known how much power she truly wielded. Edith died on December 28, 1961.

SCANDALS & GOSSIP

The sudden engagement of Wilson so soon after his wife's death led many to gossip. In fact, there were even rumors that the president and Edith Galt had murdered his first wife, but in the end it did not make enough of a difference to cost him the election of 1916.

Early Career

Wilson began his professional career as a professor, first at Bryn Mawr College from 1885 to 1888, then at Wesleyan University as a professor of history from 1888 to 1890, and finally at Princeton as a professor of political economy. In 1902, Wilson was appointed president of Princeton University, a position in which he served until 1910. As president of the University, he made reforms to curriculum and tried to change the elitist system of dividing classes at the school.

In 1911, Wilson decided to try his hand at politics and was elected as the governor of New Jersey. He served the state as a progressive Democrat, which alienated many of the traditional Democrats of the time. As a progressive, he was able to get many important reforms instituted, including one that helped labor. He served in this role until 1913 when he ran for the presidency.

Bid for the Presidency

Wilson decided that he wanted to run for president and campaigned for the nomination. It took forty-six ballots at the national convention, but in the end he received the Democratic nomination with Thomas Marshall as his vice president. Wilson was opposed by two Republican candidates: incumbent President William Taft, and former Republican-turned-Bull Moose party candidate Theodore Roosevelt. Since both had come from the Republican party, they split the vote allowing Wilson to easily win. Roosevelt received 27 percent of the popular vote and Taft had 23 percent, while Wilson won with 42 percent of the popular vote and 435 out of 531 electoral votes.

Wilson was nominated to run for the presidency in 1916 on the first ballot with Marshall returning as his vice president. He was opposed by

Republican Charles Evans Hughes. At the time of the election, Europe was at war and Wilson ran on with the slogan, "He kept us out of war." The race was a really close one, especially since Theodore Roosevelt brought many progressives to Wilson's opponent. In the end, California was the deciding state allowing Wilson to win with only 277 out of 534 electoral votes.

Presidential Administration

Wilson was the most educated president, and he could also be stern. Having grown up in the South, he had Southern sensibilities that influenced his attitude toward civil rights, on which he did not have a good record. In 1913, he ordered the segregation of the civil service. W. E. B. DuBois wrote him a letter that same year asking him about the abhorrent treatment of blacks in America. He said in his letter, "Sir, you have now been President of the United States for six months and what is the result? It is no exaggeration to say that every enemy of the Negro race is greatly encouraged; that every man who dreams of making the Negro race a group of menials and pariahs is alert and hopeful." In response, Wilson claimed that "The purpose of these measures was to reduce the friction. It is as far as possible from being a movement against the Negroes. I sincerely believe it to be in their interest."

Throughout the late nineteenth and early twentieth centuries, proponents of temperance had attempted to get state and federal laws passed limiting or outlawing the sale and consumption of alcohol. In 1919, they finally got their wish with the passage of the eighteenth amendment. The amendment took effect on January 16, 1920, and thus began the period of Prohibition. The era gets its name from the amendment itself, which said that "the manufacture, sale, or transportation of intoxicating liquors within, the importation thereof into, or the exportation thereof from the United States and all territory subject to the jurisdiction thereof for beverage purposes is hereby prohibited." The amendment would not be repealed until 1933 when Franklin Roosevelt was president.

Helping the Economy and Labor

Wilson inherited the tariff issues from his predecessors with groups arguing either for more protection through high tariffs or more free trade through tariff reductions. He and the Democratic party believed in the latter and the allowance of more free trade. This resulted in the passage of the Underwood Tariff during his presidency, which reduced tariff rates from 41 to 27 percent.

America had experienced many economic ups and downs since its inception. The nature of the business cycle is such that good times are eventually followed by bad times that can lead into depressions. Up until the early twentieth century, it was not seen as the government's responsibility to try to smooth out these ups and downs in the cycle. However, in 1913 the Federal Reserve Act created the federal reserve system to help deal with this. It provided banks with loans and the treasury with a system for adding or removing money from the economy as necessary.

Rampant unregulated capitalism had resulted in the rise of monopolies and unfair business practices. The passage of the Sherman Anti-Trust Act in 1890 was meant to help fight against this corruption. However, due to its loose wording, the law was actually used to fight against workers who were trying to protect themselves by creating unions and using collective bargaining tools, such as strikes, to get better working conditions. To alleviate this and help protect labor from being prosecuted under a law that was meant to help them, the Clayton Anti-Trust Act was passed in 1914. The act allowed for important labor tools like strikes, pickets, and boycotts.

Mexico and Pancho Villa

From 1910 until 1917, a revolution was occurring in Mexico. When Victoriano Huerta took over the government in 1913, the United States did not recognize his rule as legitimate. Instead they decided to wait and see what happened over time. Huerta was unable to truly consolidate his power and resigned in 1914. He was replaced by Venustiano Carranza.

Carranza could not control all of the uprisings in the nation. Revolutionary Pancho Villa controlled a large amount of territory in the North. Villa crossed into America in 1916, attacking the town of Columbus, New Mexico, and killing seventeen Americans. Wilson sent 6,000 troops under General John Pershing to the area. Pershing pursued Villa into Mexico trying to capture him, but his efforts were in vain. The only thing Pershing did do was upset the Mexican government and Carranza for invading their territory. Wilson recalled American troops without capturing Villa.

World War I

In 1914, Archduke Francis Ferdinand of Austria-Hungary was assassinated by a Serbian nationalist. At the time, many European nations had made agreements to protect each other if attacked. Therefore, most of the European nations were pulled into a war that became World War I. The two groups fighting each other were the Central Powers, consisting of Germany, Austria-Hungary, Turkey, and Bulgaria, and the Allies, consisting of Britain, France, Russia, Italy, Japan, Portugal, China, and Greece.

At first America remained neutral, following an isolationist policy. However, events combined to cause America to enter the war.

IN THEIR OWN WORDS...

Woodrow Wilson in his 1917 address to Congress asking for a declaration of war: "The world must be made safe for democracy. Its peace must be planted upon the tested foundations of political liberty. We have no selfish ends to serve. We desire no conquest, no dominion. We seek no indemnities for ourselves, no material compensation for the sacrifices we shall freely make."

German submarines were harassing American ships traversing the Atlantic, and in 1917 the British ship *Lusitania* was sunk, killing 120 Americans and resulting in a major uproar in America against Germany. Later attacks sunk American merchant ships. Further, the Zimmerman telegram was released revealing that Germany had approached Mexico with an agreement to form an alliance if the United States entered the war. Due to this, America officially declared war on April 6, 1917.

General Pershing led American troops into battle to help the Allies defeat the Central Powers. On January 8, 1918, while the Allies were still fighting, Wilson delivered a speech to Congress where he outlined his fourteen points for how to bring a lasting peace to Europe. His plan included the abolition of secret treaties between nations, freedom of the seas and free trade, the redrawing of numerous territorial lines, the removal of forces from various occupied countries, and the creation of a League of Nations.

QUIRKS & ODDITIES

During the war, the government asked people to conserve gas and meat. For example, Wilson asked people to have meatless Mondays. To do his part, Wilson had a flock of sheep brought onto the White House lawn. This had the double benefit of keeping the cost of lawn maintenance down while selling the wool to give money to the Red Cross.

The war ended a year and a half later when an armistice was signed on November 11, 1918.

The End of War and the League of Nations

The Treaty of Versailles, which officially ended the war, was signed in 1919. In it, Germany was given most of the blame for the war and had to pay huge war reparations. The treaty was based on Wilson's fourteen points. However, it was his last point—the creation of a League of Nations—that caused America to take issue with the treaty. Many people did not believe that the United States should join the League of Nations. Wilson worked tirelessly trying to get support for the League, but in the end the Senate would not agree and did not ratify the treaty. Their refusal to join the League meant that it was never able to be an effective body and it eventually dissolved. Wilson, however, was awarded the Nobel Peace Prize in 1919 for his work in creating the League of Nations.

After the war ended, countries met to try and control military buildup. In December 1920, the Washington Arms Conference occurred where the former allies and Japan met. As a result of these talks, tonnage ratios were created to regulate each participating nation's supply of battleships. The ratio ended up being 5-United States, 5-Great Britain, 3-Japan, 1.75-France, and 1.75-Italy.

Life After the Presidency

Wilson decided not to run again in 1920. Instead, he retired in Washington, D.C., ill from overwork in his efforts to gather support for the League of Nations. On February 3, 1924, he died of complications from a stroke.

29

Warren G. Harding: Poor Judge of Character

Born:	November 2, 1865
Died:	August 2, 1923
First Lady:	Florence Mabel Kling DeWolfe Harding
Political Party:	Republican
Presidential Term:	March 4, 1921 to August 2, 1923
Famous Quote:	"Let the black man vote when he is fit to vote, prohibit the white man voting when he is unfit to vote."

Timeline

1882 . . . . .Graduated from Ohio Central College

1891. . . . . .Married Florence Mabel Kling DeWolfe

1900–1904 . . . . . .Member of Ohio State Senate

1904–1906 . . . . . .Lieutenant governor of Ohio

1915–1921. . . . . . .U.S. senator from Ohio

1921–1923. . . . . . .Twenty-ninth president of the United States

Childhood and Education

Warren G. Harding was born on November 2, 1865, in Corsica, Ohio, to George Tryon Harding and Phoebe Elizabeth Dickerson, both of whom were doctors. Harding grew up on a small farm and attended a local school. At fifteen, he attended Ohio Central College and graduated in 1882.

First Lady: Florence Mabel Kling DeWolfe Harding

Florence Mabel Kling was born in Marion, Ohio, in 1860, the daughter of one of the wealthiest men in town. She married Henry DeWolfe at the age of nineteen, and together they had one son, but Florence left her husband soon after the birth of their child. Florence was an accomplished pianist and made money by giving piano lessons. One of her pupils was Harding's sister Charity. She pursued him and they were eventually married on July 8, 1891. Together, the Hardings had no children.

Savvy First Lady

Florence had good business sense and helped Harding make a newspaper he owned a success and pushed him along the path to become president. She relished the job of first lady and held numerous societal events. She also opened the White House to the public. She was with her husband when he died and she retired to Washington, D.C., after his death. Florence died on November 21, 1924.

Extramarital Affairs

It was rumored that Harding had two extramarital relationships—one with Carrie Fulton Phillips and another with Nan Britton. Both of these were long-lasting affairs. Phillips happened to be the wife of one of his good friends.

SCANDALS & GOSSIP

When the Republican party discovered that Harding was having an extramarital relationship with Carrie Fulton Phillips, it was too late to get another nominee. To keep the affair quiet, they sent her and her family away to Japan and paid them a lot of money. Letters proving their affair were sealed by court order until 2023, the one-hundredth anniversary of Harding's death.

Nan Britton claimed that her daughter, Elizabeth Ann, was Harding's. In fact, Harding paid child support for her care.

Early Career

Harding attempted a few other professions before becoming a politician. He was a teacher, an insurance salesman, and a reporter. In the early 1880s, Harding purchased a newspaper called the *Marion Daily Star*. He took the failing paper and turned it into one of the biggest newspapers in the country. However, his editorials had a decidedly Republican bent, which upset the owner of one of his rival newspapers, Amos Kling. Kling was the father of Harding's future wife—in fact, when he found out that they were going to be married, Kling refused to attend the wedding and did not have any contact with the Hardings for years. Florence helped make the *Marion Daily Star* an even greater commercial success.

In 1899, Harding decided to run for and was elected to the Ohio State Senate. In 1903 he was elected to be lieutenant governor of Ohio. He attempted to run for the governorship but lost in 1910. From 1915 to 1921, Harding served as a U.S. senator from Ohio, during which time he was a strong opponent of Wilson's proposal that the United States join the League of Nations.

Bid for the Presidency

Harding was nominated to run for president for the Republican party as a dark horse candidate. The convention could not decide on a candidate, so a group of party leaders got together to choose him even though he was relatively unknown outside of Ohio. His running mate was Calvin Coolidge. He was opposed by Democrat James Cox and Cox's vice presidential running mate, Franklin D. Roosevelt. Harding ran under the theme, "Return to Normalcy."

IN THEIR OWN WORDS...

Harding never seemed fully suited to be president, as evidenced by this comment: "I don't know what to do or where to turn on this taxation matter. Somewhere there must be a book that tells all about it, where I could go to straighten it out in my mind. But I don't know where the book is, and maybe I couldn't read it if I found it!"

The campaign was noteworthy for many reasons. For one thing, it was the first to be widely covered by the press and to use Hollywood to its advantage. Notably, Florence Harding courted the press and had an active role in getting her husband elected to the presidency. More importantly, however, it was the first election in which women had the right to vote. Harding ended up winning easily with 61 percent of the popular vote and 404 out of 531 electoral votes.

Presidential Administration

When Harding became president, he brought many friends into his administration and his time in office was marked by many scandals. Officials under Harding were implicated or convicted of bribery, fraud, conspiracy, and other forms of wrongdoing. As Harding said, "I have no trouble with my enemies. I can take care of my enemies in a fight. But my friends . . . they're the ones who keep me walking the floor at nights."

There is no evidence that Harding was ever personally involved in these scandals.

PRESIDENTIAL TRIVIA

Harding fought against unfair treatment of African Americans. He spoke out against lynchings and ordered the White House and the District of Columbia to desegregate. His actions in support of better treatment for blacks were part of what caused a rumor to circulate claiming that Harding was part black. Historians do not believe that he was.

Teapot Dome Scandal

The most significant scandal of Harding's presidency was the Teapot Dome scandal. Harding's secretary of the interior, Albert Fall, secretly sold the right to tap into oil reserves in Teapot Dome, Wyoming, to a private company in exchange for some cattle and $308,000. He also sold the rights to other national oil reserves. In the end he was caught and sentenced to one year in jail.

Ending World War I

During his time in the Senate, Harding had not supported the League of Nations. His opposition meant that America would never join the League, especially once he became president. Without ratifying the Treaty of Paris, World War I was not officially at an end. To rectify this situation, a joint resolution was passed, which Harding signed, officially ending the state of war between Germany and the United States.

During the Harding administration, America entered into numerous treaties with foreign nations. Three of the major treaties were the Five Power Treaty, the Four Power Treaty, and the Nine Power Treaty.

Five Power Treaty: The United States, Great Britain, France, the USSR, and Italy agreed to halt battleship production for ten years and developed tonnage ratios between the nations.

Four Power Treaty: The United States, Great Britain, France, and Japan discussed the need for the four nations to respect each other's Pacific possessions and not seek further expansion.

Nine Power Treaty: The United States, Great Britain, France, Japan, Italy, Belgium, China, the Netherlands, and Portugal made the Open Door Policy official while respecting the sovereignty of China.

Social Issues

Harding pardoned Socialist Eugene V. Debs. Debs was an important figure in American politics through the early twentieth century. He actually ran for the presidency five times, including once while he was in jail. During World War I, Debs spoke out against American involvement in the war. In 1918, he was sent to jail for ten years because of his antiwar demonstrations. Harding pardoned Debs in 1921 and actually met with him in the White House.

Death in Office

In June, 1923, Harding and his wife set out on a "voyage of understanding" across America. He visited Alaska and made his way to San Francisco. On the way he got very sick and developed pneumonia. On August 2, 1923, Harding died of what naval physicians determined was a heart attack. However, an autopsy was never performed. His early death probably saved him from impeachment over the many scandals of his administration.

30

Calvin Coolidge: Silent Cal

Born:	July 4, 1872
Died:	January 5, 1933
First Lady:	Grace Anna Goodhue Coolidge
Political Party:	Republican
Presidential Term:	August 2, 1923 to March 3, 1929
Famous Quote:	"The business of America is business."

Timeline

1895. . . . . .Graduated from Amherst College

1897. . . . . .Admitted to the bar

1905. . . . . .Married Grace Anna Goodhue

1910–1911. . . . . . .Mayor of Northampton, Massachusetts

1912–1915. . . . . . .Member of the Massachusetts State Senate

1916–1918. . . . . . .Lieutenant governor of Massachusetts

1919–1920 . . . . . .Governor of Massachusetts

1921–1923. . . . . . .Vice president of the United States under President Harding

1923–1929 . . . . . .Thirtieth president of the United States

Childhood and Education

Calvin Coolidge was born John Calvin Coolidge Jr. on July 4, 1872, in Plymouth, Vermont. He stopped using the name John after he graduated from college. His father, John Calvin Coolidge Sr., was a storekeeper and local public official. Coolidge's mother, Victoria Josephine Moor, died when he was twelve. He had one sister, Abigail Gratia Coolidge, who died at the age of fifteen.

QUIRKS & ODDITIES

Coolidge loved animals and owned many. According to him, "Any man who does not like dogs and want them about, does not deserve to be in the White House." Other than dogs and cats, he had a donkey, a goose, canaries, mockingbirds, and wombats. He was known to walk around with his pet raccoon, Rebecca, curled around his neck.

Coolidge attended a local school before enrolling in 1886 at the Black River Academy in Ludlow, Vermont. He studied at Amherst College from 1891 to 1895 and graduated cum laude. He then studied law and was admitted to the Massachusetts bar in 1897.

First Lady: Grace Anna Goodhue Coolidge

Grace Anna Goodhue was born on January 3, 1879, and grew up in Burlington, Vermont. She went to the University of Vermont and upon graduation worked at the Clarke School for the Deaf. When Grace married Coolidge in October, 1905, they were not terribly wealthy and lived in a duplex, continuing to do so even when he was governor. Together they had two sons: John and Calvin Jr.

As first lady, Grace was a very popular hostess. She dressed fashionably and upheld her duties admirably, even when their son died at the age of sixteen. Calvin Jr. died at the White House while home from school. He had spent an entire day playing tennis and had developed a blister on his foot. However, he continued to play for hours more without any socks on his feet.

The blister became infected and without the benefit of the antibiotics available today, he died of blood poisoning in 1924.

In 1931, Grace was voted one of America's twelve greatest living women.

Early Career

Coolidge practiced law beginning in 1897. He quickly became active in the Republican party in Massachusetts. His journey to the presidency occurred by steps: first locally, and then in the state of Massachusetts. In 1899, he was elected to his first political office as a Northampton City councilman. From 1907 to 1908, he served as a member of the Massachusetts General Court. He was then elected to be mayor of Northampton in 1910.

In 1912, Coolidge moved to the Massachusetts State Senate before becoming lieutenant governor in 1916 and governor in 1919. He gained national prominence in 1919 as governor when he ordered the Massachusetts National Guard to end a Boston police department strike. It was his opinion that "There is no right to strike against the public safety by anybody, anywhere, anytime." In 1921, he ran with Warren Harding to become vice president of the United States.

Bid for the Presidency

Coolidge became president on August 3, 1923, taking over after Harding died in office.

PRESIDENTIAL TRIVIA

Coolidge was informed that he was succeeding to the presidency when a messenger came to his home. His father, who was a notary public, became the first and only parent to swear in their child to the presidency. Coolidge was then officially sworn in by Chief Justice William Howard Taft when he returned to Washington, D.C.

At the end of that term, Coolidge was nominated by the Republicans to run for president in his own right. Charles Dawes was his running mate. He ran against Democrat John Davis and Progressive Robert M. LaFollette. The economy was booming during the "Roaring Twenties," and Coolidge was able to win in a landslide. In the end, Coolidge won with 54 percent of the popular vote and 382 out of 531 electoral votes.

Presidential Administration

Immigration was a huge issue in the period between the world wars. There was much prejudice, especially against immigrants from Southern European and Asian countries. The Immigration Act of 1924 was created to cut the number of immigrants who would be allowed into the United States so that only 150,000 total individuals were allowed each year. The law favored immigrants from Northern Europe over Southern Europeans and Jews. Japanese immigrants were not allowed in at all under this law, negating the Gentleman's Agreement that Theodore Roosevelt had made with Japan.

Economic Issues

While the economic situation during Coolidge's time seemed on the surface to be one of prosperity, the foundation was being laid for the Great Depression. Taxes that had been imposed during World War I were cut in 1924 and 1926.

These tax cuts were focused more on helping the rich than the poor. With the increase in the money that individuals had access to, speculation and investment in the stock market increased. This would become very important during President Hoover's administration with the stock market crash and the beginning of the Great Depression.

In 1924, Coolidge tried to veto the Veteran's Bonus that had passed through Congress. This bill provided veterans with insurance that would be redeemable in twenty years. During Hoover's term in office, veterans who had no money and no jobs would march on Washington to demand early payment of these policies.

Calvin Coolidge was noted for his quiet nature. He was given the nickname, "Silent Cal." One humorous story tells that a lady once approached him and said, "Mr. Coolidge, I've made a bet against a fellow who said it was impossible to get more than two words out of you." To this, Coolidge replied: "You lose."

Farm Relief Bills

In 1927 and 1928, Congress tried to help out farmers who were having economic problems with a series of farm relief bills. These bills would have the government buy crops at a set price and then be responsible for selling the produce. Coolidge did not believe that the government should be involved in setting prices for goods, instead preferring to allow the forces of supply and demand to set prices, and so he vetoed the bill twice. Within the coming years and the period of the Great Depression, farmers would be some of the hardest hit.

Kellogg-Briand Pact

The Kellogg-Briand Pact, or the Pact of Paris, was created on August 27, 1928, by U.S. Secretary of State Frank Kellogg and French Foreign Minister Aristide Briand. Its point was to assert that war was not a viable method for settling international disputes. Before it was to go into effect on July 24, 1929, fifteen nations had agreed to the pact. Over time more nations agreed to the pact and ultimately sixty-two would sign it.

Calvin Coolidge realized that he would be judged on his everyday words and actions, and he took this responsibility seriously. As he said: "The President has tended to become the champion of the people because he is solely responsible for his acts, while in the Congress where responsibility is divided it has developed that there is much greater danger of arbitrary action."

The Senate agreed to the pact with the proviso that America reserved the right to defend itself. This treaty is still binding today. Even though the pact did not stop aggression and war completely, it has set the standard that military action against other nations should only be used for self- or collective defense.

Life After the Presidency

Coolidge chose not to run for another term in office and did not give a reason for his decision. Instead, he retired to Northampton, Massachusetts, and became involved in various enterprises. For example, he was the chairman of the Railroad Commission, the honorary president of the Foundation of the Blind, and a trustee of Amherst College. He published *The Autobiography of Calvin Coolidge* before his death and even had a column in the newspaper that was called "Calvin Coolidge Says." He died at home on January 5, 1933, of a coronary thrombosis or blood clot.

31

Herbert Hoover:
Great Depression President

Born:	August 11, 1874
Died:	October 20, 1964
First Lady:	Lou Henry Hoover
Political Party:	Republican
Presidential Term:	March 4, 1929 to March 4, 1933
Famous Quote:	"It is a paradox that every dictator has climbed to power on the ladder of free speech. Immediately on attaining power each dictator has suppressed all free speech except his own."

Timeline

1895...........Graduated from Stanford University
1897–1899 ......Worked as a mining engineer in Australia and China
1914–1919.......Head of the Commission for the Relief of Belgium
1917–1918.......Head of the American Food Administration
1918–1921.......Head of the American Relief Administration
1921–1928.......Secretary of commerce
1929–1933 ......Thirty-first president of the United States
1947...........Headed Hoover Commission

Childhood and Education

Herbert Hoover was born on August 11, 1874, in West Branch, Iowa. His father, Jesse Clark Hoover, was a blacksmith and salesman and died when his son was six. His mother, Huldah Minthorn Hoover, was a Quaker minister. Unfortunately, she died when Hoover was nine. Hoover, his brother, and his sister were separated and sent to live with relatives. Hoover would become the first Quaker president.

Hoover attended a local school as a youth, but never graduated from high school. He enrolled as part of the first class at Stanford University in California. He worked his way through college studying geology and participating in many extracurricular activities.

First Lady: Lou Henry Hoover

Herbert Hoover met Lou Henry during his senior year at Stanford. She also received a degree in geology. The daughter of a banker, her family moved from Iowa to California when she was ten years old. Hoover and Lou Henry got married on February 10, 1899, and left the next day for China where Hoover had been hired as a mining engineer. Together, they had two sons: Herbert Hoover Jr. and Allan Hoover.

QUIRKS & ODDITIES

Lou and Herbert Hoover learned to speak Mandarin Chinese while they were in China. Lou even created her own English-Chinese dictionary. It was said that the two of them would sometimes speak in Chinese when they did not want to be overheard.

Lou Hoover was very involved in the Girl Scouts, even serving as the organization's president at one point. She was a well respected first lady. As first lady she spent time restoring rooms in the White House. When the country was in its deepest depression, the Hoovers used their own money to pay for entertaining.

Early Career

Hoover worked for a consulting firm in San Francisco right out of college before being sent as a mining engineer to Australia. He worked there until 1899 when he was given a job in China. On the way to his new position, he stopped by California to marry Lou Hoover. He and his wife were in China during the Boxer Rebellion, which targeted Westerners. They were trapped in China with very little protection. Hoover showed his leadership skills during this time by directing the building of barricades and the provisioning of food to anti-Boxer Chinese. They managed to escape capture on a German boat.

War Relief Efforts

During World War I, Hoover played an important role in war relief efforts. First, he headed the American Relief Committee, which helped approximately 120,000 Americans who had been stranded in Europe. He was then made the head of the Commission for the Relief of Belgium, which had been suffering since its invasion by Germany. He spent his time and energy ensuring that food and other necessities reached the Belgian people.

IN THEIR OWN WORDS...

Herbert Hoover was pivotal in helping those hurt the worst by World War I. Here is what he had to say about war: "Older men declare war. But it is youth that must fight and die. And it is youth who must inherit the tribulation, the sorrow, and the triumphs that are the aftermath of war."

He also led the American Food Administration, which helped America avoid rationing through cutting overseas food consumption, and the American Relief Administration, which provided food and supplies to Central Europe.

Secretary of Commerce

From 1921 to 1928 he served as the secretary of commerce for Presidents Harding and Coolidge. He was a very visible secretary and made many important changes and innovations. He saw the Commerce Department as a partner to business, not an adversary. To that end, he instituted policies that would help businesses overseas and at home. Hoover was again brought upon the national stage when he helped organize relief efforts after a devastating flood affected six states in 1927.

Bid for the Presidency

In 1928, Herbert Hoover was nominated as the Republican candidate for president on the first ballot, with Charles Curtis as his running mate. He ran against Alfred Smith, the first Roman Catholic to be nominated for president. Smith's religion was an important part of the campaign against him even though Hoover himself did not bring it up. Instead, Hoover ran on the idea of continuing prosperity. Hoover ended up winning with 58 percent of the vote and 444 out of 531 electoral votes.

Presidential Administration

Hoover was president during one of the worst economic disasters in America's history. He had only been president for seven months when Black Thursday hit. On Thursday, October 24, 1929, stock prices began falling sharply. Some tried to halt the freefall by buying up large amounts of stock, but this only stopped the drop for a couple of days. On Tuesday, October 29, 1929, the stock market crashed, beginning the Great Depression. The crash meant that thousands of people lost all of their money. During the market's prosperous times, many individuals had taken advantage of the widespread amount of borrowing that was being allowed to purchase stocks. Because there was little regulation at the time, brokerages were lending money to speculators with very little collateral. The goal of the speculator was that they would borrow money to purchase stock, wait until the stock went up, sell it, and then pay back their loan keeping all the profit. When the crash came, however, those investors were unable to pay back their debts. Most of these speculators were ruined and bankrupt, and the suicide rate among them at the time was tremendous.

The Great Depression was much more than just a stock market crash and its aftermath. It was a nationwide event.

PRESIDENTIAL

TRIVIA

Hoover's name was used to describe many of the deplorable situations during the Great Depression. For example, "Hoovervilles" were groups of shanties where many were forced to reside, "Hoover Blankets" was a nickname given to newspapers that many used for covers in the cold, and "Hoover Leather" was the cardboard that individuals used to replace worn-out soles in their shoes.

During the Depression, unemployment rose to 25 percent and approximately 25 percent of all banks failed. President Hoover did not see the enormity of the problem soon enough, and instead of providing direct relief to the unemployed, he felt that helping businesses would trickle down to help the people. However, the Depression was too widespread for this to have much of an effect. Hoover did, however, refuse to accept any pay for his time in office because of the plight of the poor. Instead, he donated his pay to charity.

Hawley-Smoot Tariff

In 1930, an attempt was made to help protect farmers and others from foreign competition. The idea was that by taxing foreign imports, American farmers and manufacturers would be able to make and keep more money. Unfortunately, this had the opposite effect as other nations enacted their own tariffs, which hurt American exporters. In the end, trade around the world slowed down.

Bonus March

Due to their economic situation, veterans who had been awarded bonus insurance over President Coolidge's veto demanded immediate payment instead of waiting the full twenty years. In May 1932, approximately 15,000 veterans marched on Washington, D.C., to issue their demands in what became known as the Bonus March. When Congress did not answer their demands, marchers who had no homes to return to stayed and lived in makeshift homes and shantytowns. President Hoover sent in General Douglas MacArthur to move the veterans out. He and his troops used tear gas and tanks to make them leave, setting fire to their tents and shacks upon their retreat.

Twentieth Amendment

The twentieth amendment was passed during Hoover's time in office, decreasing the time that an outgoing president would be in office after the November election by moving the date of inauguration up from March 4th to January 20th. It was called the "lame duck amendment" because a president who was leaving office did not have much power and was therefore considered a "lame duck."

Life After the Presidency

Hoover ran for reelection in 1932 but was handily defeated by Franklin Roosevelt. During the campaign, Hoover was derided for not alleviating the widespread poverty that resulted from the Great Depression. He retired to Palo Alto, California. He was a strong opponent of the New Deal after his defeat.

In 1946, Hoover was appointed to a job that particularly suited him: coordinator of the food supply for world famine. He was an excellent administrator, able to find ways to streamline government, and as such he was selected to be chairman of the commission on organization of the executive branch of the government, nicknamed the Hoover Commission (1947–1949). He was again chosen to be on the commission on government operations (1953–1955). Many changes in government operations resulted from these two commissions recommendations. Hoover died in New York City on October 20, 1964, of cancer at the age of ninety.

32

Franklin D. Roosevelt: The Squire of Hyde Park

Born: January 30, 1882
Died: April 12, 1945
First Lady: Anna Eleanor Roosevelt
Political Party: Democratic
Presidential Term: March 4, 1933 to April 12, 1945
Famous Quote: "This generation of Americans has a rendezvous with destiny."

Timeline

1904 .... Graduated from Harvard University
1905............ Married Anna Eleanor Roosevelt
1907............ Admitted to the bar
1910–1912....... New York state senator
1913–1918....... Assistant secretary of the navy
1929–1932 ...... Governor of New York
1933–1945 ...... Thirty-second president of the United States

Childhood and Education

Franklin Delano Roosevelt was born on January 30, 1882, in Hyde Park, New York. His father, James Roosevelt, was a wealthy businessman and financier. His mother, Sara "Sallie" Delano, was a strong-willed woman. She never wished for her son to enter politics.

Roosevelt grew up in a world of privilege and often traveled overseas with his parents. He was brought to meet Grover Cleveland at the White House when he was five and was a cousin of Theodore Roosevelt. He grew up with private tutors before attending Groton from 1896 to 1900. Roosevelt was an average student at Harvard, graduating in 1904. He then went to Columbia Law School (1904–1907), passed the bar, and decided not to stay on to graduate.

First Lady: Anna Eleanor Roosevelt

Eleanor Roosevelt was born on October 11, 1884, in New York City. She was Theodore Roosevelt's niece and a fifth cousin to her husband. Eleanor married Franklin Delano Roosevelt on March 17, 1905.

SCANDALS & GOSSIP

Franklin Roosevelt had a long-term affair with Eleanor's social secretary, Lucy Mercer. He even considered divorcing Eleanor, but his mother talked him out of it and he agreed not to see Lucy any more. Whether or not he continued his affair is uncertain. What is known is that Lucy was with Franklin the day he died in Warm Springs, Georgia.

Together, the Roosevelts had one daughter and four sons: Anna Eleanor, James, Elliott, Franklin Jr., and John Aspinwall. All four of their sons served in World War II. James became a U.S. representative from 1955 to 1966; Elliott was mayor of Miami Beach in the 1960s; and Franklin Jr. was appointed by John F. Kennedy to be his undersecretary of commerce. John was the only Roosevelt child to become a Republican, backing Eisenhower in 1952.

Eleanor was an important first lady because she used her platform to advance causes that she found significant. She was a huge proponent not only for the New Deal but also for civil rights and the rights of women.

Civil Rights Proponent

As a civil rights activist, Eleanor believed that a quality education and equal opportunities for all were the most important things to fight for. Her desire to help led to a huge outpouring of support from African Americans for her and her husband. However, Franklin Roosevelt realized the importance of keeping the peace with Southern senators and never put the full force of the White House behind her efforts.

In 1939, African American contralto Marian Anderson was scheduled to perform at Constitution Hall, but the Daughters of the American Revolution (DAR) refused to allow her to sing because of her race. As a result, Eleanor resigned from the organization. She wrote a column called "My Day," which she used as a platform to pressure radio stations to broadcast Anderson's performance from the Lincoln Memorial.

After Roosevelt's death, Eleanor became even more involved in civil rights, joining the board of directors for the National Association for the Advancement of Colored People (NAACP) and continuing to fight for integration and equal rights.

The United Nations

Eleanor led in the formation of the United Nations after World War II. She was instrumental in drafting the UN "Universal Declaration of Human Rights" and was the first chairman of the UN Human Rights Commission. She believed that the declaration was a truly significant document and helped to assure its acceptance by the general assembly.

Early Career

After quitting college, Roosevelt practiced law for a time and then decided to run for the New York State Senate, winning and serving in 1912. In 1913, at the age of thirty-one, he was appointed assistant secretary of the navy by

President Woodrow Wilson. He worked in this position until 1917 and spent much of his time expanding the navy. He sent the navy in to intervene in Central America and also created the Naval Reserve.

In 1920, Roosevelt ran as vice president to James M. Cox, but the ticket lost to Warren Harding. Upon their defeat, Roosevelt went back to his law practice until 1929, when he was elected the governor of New York. When the Depression hit, he used state funds to help with relief efforts. He served as governor until being elected president.

Four-Term President

In 1932, Roosevelt won the Democratic nomination for the presidency with John Nance Garner as his vice president. He was opposed by Republican incumbent Herbert Hoover. The Great Depression was both the backdrop and the main issue of the campaign. Hoover had lost the confidence of America, while Roosevelt, on the other hand, had gathered a brain trust to help him come up with effective public policy.

PRESIDENTIAL TRIVIA

Franklin Roosevelt seemed destined for great things. He was related to many important figures in American and British history including George Washington, John and John Quincy Adams, James Madison, Martin Van Buren, William Henry and Benjamin Harrison, Zachary Taylor, Ulysses S. Grant, Jefferson Davis, Robert E. Lee, Theodore Roosevelt, William Howard Taft, and Winston Churchill.

Roosevelt campaigned continuously and his confidence and plans made Hoover's meager campaign pale in comparison. In the end, he carried 57 percent of the popular vote and 472 electors versus Hoover's fifty-nine.

Reelection: 1936

In 1936, Roosevelt was again his party's nominee with Garner as his vice presidential running mate. The campaign centered on the New Deal while his opponent, progressive Republican Alf Landon, argued that the program was unconstitutional. Landon wanted any programs instituted to be run by the states. Roosevelt maintained his commitment to the New Deal and campaigned on the program's effectiveness, easily winning reelection with 532 of the possible 540 electoral votes. His landslide victory was assisted by support from the NAACP.

Unprecedented Third Term: 1940

Roosevelt did not publicly ask for a third term. However, when his name was placed on the ballot by his loyal followers, he was quickly nominated. The Republican nominee was Wendell Willkie. Willkie had been a Democrat. However, he switched parties as a protest to the creation of the Tennessee Valley Authority (TVA). The TVA created cheap electricity for the poor in the Tennessee Valley, directly competing against the existing power companies, one of which Willkie represented as legal council.

One of the major issues of the election dealt with the war in Europe and America's response to it. Hitler was quickly taking over countries and appeasement did not seem to be working. Roosevelt, however, pledged to keep America out of the war. Many Americans felt that the United States should not get involved, having lost so many men during World War I. On the other hand, Willkie was in favor of a draft and wanted to stop Hitler. He also campaigned against Roosevelt's right to have a third term. No other president in history had run for three terms in office and, while not unconstitutional, it was a break in the precedent begun by George Washington. Roosevelt easily won the election with 449 out of 531 electoral votes.

Last Term: 1944

When Roosevelt was nominated for a fourth term in office, America was heavily involved in World War II and there was a strong desire to keep him in office through the course of it. However, Roosevelt's health was declining and the Democrats spent some time deciding who would be his vice presidential nominee. They wanted to make sure that they chose someone who would be a good president, seeing that he would have a strong possibility of taking over during the term. Harry S. Truman was eventually picked to be second in charge because he was a moderate Democrat who appealed to the party center.

The Republicans chose Thomas Dewey as their candidate. Dewey used Roosevelt's declining health and campaigned against the waste created by the New Deal. Roosevelt won by a slim margin, getting 53 percent of the popular vote. However, because of the distribution of votes, he was able to carry 432 electoral votes versus ninety-nine for Dewey.

Presidential Administration

Franklin Roosevelt spent twelve years in office and had an enormous impact on America. He took office in the depths of the Great Depression, and during his first inaugural speech he said: "[F]irst of all, let me assert my firm belief that the only thing we have to fear is fear itself." His immediate action the day after his inauguration was to call Congress into a special session and declare a four-day banking holiday.

New Deal Legislation

Roosevelt began his first term in office full force. In fact, during his first "Hundred Days" as president, fifteen major laws were passed to get America back on its feet and moving forward. Roosevelt called his entire program of legislation and actions the New Deal. Roosevelt was the first to truly use the mass media to his benefit when he instituted fireside chats to gain support for his programs while reassuring the nation.

IN THEIR OWN WORDS...

Roosevelt said on the importance of finding work for Americans: "Not only our future economic soundness but the very soundness of our democratic institutions depends on the determination of our government to give employment to idle men. The people of America are in agreement in defending their liberties at any cost, and the first line of defense lies in the protection of economic security."

Also during Roosevelt's first year, the prohibition of alcohol created through the eighteenth amendment was repealed with the passage of the twenty-first amendment.

Some of the most important legislative acts of Roosevelt's New Deal included:

Civilian Conservation Corps (CCC)—hired more than three million men to work on various projects.

Tennessee Valley Authority (TVA)—used the Tennessee River to provide electricity for the depressed area.

National Industrial Recovery Act (NIRA)—created the Public Works Administration to provide aid to cities for construction and the National Recovery Administration to help businesses.

Federal Emergency Relief Administration (FERA)—gave the unemployed money while providing incentives for states to create local job programs.

Securities and Exchange Commission (SEC)—corrected the abuses that led to the stock market crash.

Works Progress Administration (WPA)—hired many people for a variety of projects including work in the arts.

Social Security Act (SSA)—created the Social Security System.

At first, the Supreme Court did not believe that the government should take such an active role in private business practices. For example, the NIRA used price and wage controls imposed by the government, and therefore was questioned on its constitutionality. It was found to be unconstitutional by the Supreme Court in *Schechter v. United States* (1935).

Because of this attitude by the Supreme Court, Roosevelt attempted to pack the court with a new law in 1937. His plan was that whenever a judge "reached the age of seventy and [did] not avail himself of the opportunity to retire on a pension, a new member [would] be appointed by the president then in office, with the approval, as required by the Constitution, of the Senate of the United States." His stated objective was to bring new blood into the court, but critics claimed that he was just trying to put individuals on the court who would rule favorably on his New Deal legislation. The act failed in Congress, but it did have the important effect of changing the way that the judges were deciding on New Deal court cases as they became more favorable to the programs.

World War II

Adolf Hitler rose to power in Germany after World War I. Over time he began invading surrounding countries. At first Great Britain, France, and other European powers attempted a policy of appeasement that allowed Hitler to keep the territories he captured to avoid war. However, when this strategy failed and Hitler invaded France, Britain declared war. The events of World War I had resulted in a deeper commitment by Americans to isolationism, but as Germany began a full force attack on Great Britain, Roosevelt realized that America could not remain neutral.

To circumvent the Neutrality Acts, Roosevelt created a lend-lease system in 1941. This system allowed the United States to help Britain by delivering old destroyers in exchange for military bases abroad. Roosevelt also met with Winston Churchill in 1941 to create the Atlantic Charter that set forward joint beliefs about the nature of fascism and the need to fight against any country who takes over other countries and territories by force.

America did not enter World War II until December 7, 1941, with the Japanese attack on Pearl Harbor. In July 1939, Roosevelt announced that the United States would no longer trade items such as gasoline and iron to the Japanese, who needed it for their war with China. In July 1941, the Rome-Berlin-Tokyo Axis was created with mutual defense agreements between Italy, Germany, and Japan. All Japanese assets were frozen in the United States. When the Japanese attacked Pearl Harbor, more than 2,000 people were killed and eight battleships were damaged or destroyed. At that point, America officially entered the war.

SCANDALS & GOSSIP

Is it possible that Roosevelt knew the Japanese were going to attack at Pearl Harbor, but didn't do anything about it to have a reason to declare war? That was the claim made soon after the attack. Thomas Dewey even used it in his 1944 campaign against Roosevelt. However, there is no evidence that Roosevelt had foreknowledge of the attack.

America declared war on Japan on December 8, 1941. Germany and Italy then declared war on America. The United States decided to fight a Europe First policy, focusing on stopping Nazi aggression. Important victories in Europe for the United States and the allies included the Battle of Midway, the North African campaign, the capture of Sicily, and the D-Day invasion.

With an inevitable Nazi defeat, Roosevelt met with Churchill and Joseph Stalin at Yalta in February, 1945. Roosevelt and Churchill promised concessions to Soviet Russia if the Soviets entered the war against Japan. Concessions given in this agreement would eventually set up the Cold War by giving the Soviet Union a buffer zone of countries occupied and controlled by the USSR.

On April 12, 1945, Roosevelt died of a cerebral hemorrhage. Upon his death, Vice President Harry Truman became president. Roosevelt is consistently considered by historians to be one of the greatest presidents in America's history. His aggressive and unprecedented leadership during the Great Depression and World War II left lasting marks on the American landscape and the world.

Harry S Truman:
The Buck Stops Here

Born:	May 8, 1884
Died:	December 26, 1972
First Lady:	Elizabeth "Bess" Virginia Wallace Truman
Political Party:	Democratic
Presidential Term:	April 12, 1945 to January 20, 1953
Famous Quote:	"If there is one basic element in our Constitution, it is civilian control of the military."

Timeline

1917–1919 . . . . Served in the army during World War I

1919 . . . . Married Elizabeth "Bess" Virginia Wallace

1922–1924 . . . . . Jackson County Judge

1926–1934 . . . . . Jackson County Judge

1935–1945 . . . . . U.S. senator from Missouri

1945 . . . . Vice president of the United States under President Franklin D. Roosevelt

1945–1953 . . . . . Thirty-third president of the United States

1950–1953 . . . . . Korean War

Childhood and Education

Harry S. Truman was born on May 8, 1884, in Lamar, Missouri. His middle name was actually just the letter S because his parents could not decide on an actual name. In 1890, his family settled in Independence, Missouri. He spent his childhood growing up on his family's farm. His father, John Anderson Truman, was not only a farmer and livestock trader but was also very active in the Democratic party.

Truman had bad eyesight from a youth, but his mother, Martha Ellen Young Truman, taught him how to read at a young age. He especially liked reading about history and government. He was also an excellent piano player and continued to play for the rest of his life—in fact, during his presidency he would wake up early to get his practicing in before his day began.

Truman went to local grade and high schools. He graduated from high school in 1901 but did not immediately go into college because he had to work to help his family make money. He spent ten years working on his family's farm before continuing his education at Kansas City Law School for two years beginning in 1923. He was never admitted to the bar, however, and instead decided to open a clothing store.

First Lady: Elizabeth "Bess" Virginia Wallace Truman

Elizabeth "Bess" Virginia Wallace was born on February 13, 1885. Her father, David Wallace, was a public official who committed suicide when she was eighteen. Bess grew up in Independence and was a childhood friend of Truman. She attended Miss Barstow's Finishing School in Kansas City. Truman and Bess did not start dating until 1913, and waited until after World War I to marry when he was thirty-five and she was thirty-four. They were wed on June 28, 1919. The Trumans had one daughter, Mary Margaret, a singer and a novelist, who wrote not only biographies of her parents, but also mysteries such as *Murder in the White House* and *Murder at the Kennedy Center.*

QUIRKS & ODDITIES

Truman defended his daughter against criticism. Once when a critic wrote of her singing that "Miss Truman . . . cannot sing very well [and] is flat a good deal of the time," Truman responded, "It seems to me that you are a frustrated old man who wishes he could have been successful. When you write such poppy-cock . . . it shows conclusively that you're off the beam and at least four of your ulcers are at work."

Bess Truman did not relish the role of first lady. While Truman was president, the White House was being completely refurbished—it had been discovered that the building was in danger of actually falling down—and so their family lived in the Blair House nearby. Bess spent as little time in Washington as possible, only living there during the yearly social season that comprises the warmer summer months. The rest of her time was spent in Independence.

Early Career

Truman left high school to help out his family. He worked at odd jobs before moving back to his father's farm, where he worked until he was called to fight in World War I.

Truman had joined the Missouri National Guard in 1905. He helped organize the Second Regiment of Missouri Field Artillery, which was called into regular service when America entered the war. Truman served from August 1917 until May 1919. He was commissioned as a commander of a field artillery unit in France, where his unit fought in various campaigns including the Meuse-Argonne offensive in 1918, which was the biggest operation and victory for American forces in the war. Truman rose to the rank of colonel before the war's end.

Politics

After the war, Truman at first tried his hand at owning a men's clothing store, but this ultimately failed in 1922. Later in that year, Truman was appointed as a "judge" of Jackson County, Missouri, but the position was administrative rather than judicial and his role was similar to a county commissioner. From 1926 until 1934, Truman was the head judge of the county.

In 1935, Truman was elected as the Democratic senator representing Missouri, and he served throughout World War II. During his time as a senator, he led a committee that eventually bore his name: the Truman Committee. The committee's job was to look into military wastefulness and was able to save billions by exposing waste and fraud. Truman's leadership gained him national recognition that led to his being nominated as Roosevelt's vice president in 1945.

Becoming the President

Franklin D. Roosevelt died on April 12, 1945, and Truman took over the presidency. He had no real clue that Roosevelt was so close to death and his succession came as a bit of a shock. As he told reporters the day after his inauguration, "[W]hen they told me what had happened, I felt like the moon, the stars, and all the planets had fallen on me."

When the 1948 election year came around, the Democratic party was not sure that Truman could win reelection because in the 1946 midterm elections the Republican party had taken control of both houses of Congress, reflecting the public's opinions of his administration. However, in the end they did put their support behind him and nominated him to run with Alben Barkley as his vice president. He was opposed by Republican Thomas E. Dewey, Dixiecrat Strom Thurmond, and Progressive Henry Wallace. Thurmond and Wallace both had split from the Democratic party, so there was concern that they would each take votes away from Truman.

PRESIDENTIAL

TRIVIA

Throughout the campaign, it seemed assured that Thomas Dewey would beat Truman. In fact, the editors at the *Chicago Tribune* were so sure that Dewey was going to win that on election night they printed the headline, "Dewey Beats Truman" on their front page. Truman found humor in this and a famous photograph shows him holding up the paper while wearing a huge smile.

Truman campaigned vigorously, giving many "whistlestop" speeches from the back of a train car. His efforts paid off when, in the end, Truman won with 49 percent of the popular vote and 57 percent of the electoral vote.

Presidential Administration

One month after taking office, the war in Europe ended with Russia invading Germany from the east while the allies moved in from the west. Truman participated in the Potsdam Conference with British Prime Minister Winston Churchill and Soviet Premier Josef Stalin. At this meeting, the division of Europe was finalized including the dividing of Berlin into four separate occupation zones. This division of Europe would reinforce the coming issues of the Cold War as the Soviets would consolidate their control and holdings in Eastern Europe.

Hiroshima and Nagasaki

America was still at war with Japan when the war with Europe ended. The Japanese indicated that they were willing to make peace, but the United States and its allies were not willing to accept anything less than unconditional surrender. It appeared that the only way to get this was to invade the mainland. The military estimated that this type of invasion would cost the lives of thousands of troops. However, there was an alternative to conventional warfare.

Truman discovered soon after taking office that President Roosevelt had authorized the creation of a weapon of mass destruction—the atomic bomb. The Manhattan Project had resulted in two bombs, neither of which they were sure would work correctly. Faced with the estimate of troop losses, along with the specter of a postwar Soviet Union that was also busy developing atomic bombs, Truman decided to use the bombs on Japan. On August 6, 1945, the Enola Gay dropped an atomic bomb nicknamed "Little Boy" on the city of Hiroshima. On August 9, 1945, a second bomb nicknamed "Big Man" was dropped on Nagasaki.

In the end more than 200,000 Japanese were killed by the two bombs. Japan sued for peace on August 10 and formally surrendered on September 2, 1945, finally ending World War II.

On August 6, 1945, Truman issued this statement: "Sixteen hours ago an American airplane dropped one bomb on Hiroshima. The Japanese began the war from the air at Pearl Harbor. They have been repaid many fold. . . . The force from which the sun draws its power has been loosed against those who brought war to the Far East."

Aftermath of World War II

Adolf Hitler and the Nazis had systematically killed millions of Jews in the Holocaust. At the end of the war, twenty-four Nazi leaders were brought before a tribunal at Nuremberg and accused of various crimes, including crimes against humanity for their role in the Holocaust. Nineteen of these men were found guilty and twelve were executed.

Many Jewish people around Europe had been stripped of their homes and properties. They fought for their own new homeland. In 1948, the Jewish people created the state of Israel in Palestine. The United States was among the first to recognize the new nation. This set up the conflict that still rages today between the Palestinians who were living in the region and the new Jewish state.

Truman agreed to help rebuild Europe in what was called the Marshall Plan, named after its creator, Secretary of State George Marshall. America spent more than $13 billion dollars to help get Europe back on its feet. At the same time, America set up permanent military bases throughout the region.

Additionally, Japan was occupied after World War II from 1945 until 1952. Led by General Douglas MacArthur, American forces helped ensure that Japanese war criminals were tried, the military establishments were destroyed, the economic infrastructure was rebuilt, and a new Democratic government was put in place.

At the end of the war, the United Nations was established with strong support from Truman. Representatives from fifty countries met in San Francisco to draw up the UN's charter. The purpose of the UN was to help the worldwide community settle conflicts peacefully so as to avoid another world war.

Cold War and Fighting Communism

At the end of World War II, the Soviet Union and the United States began what has been called the Cold War. No open fighting between the two countries ever occurred, but many conflicts over the years resulted from America's fighting the incursion of Soviet-backed communism around the world. Truman created the Truman Doctrine that stated that it was the duty of the United States to "support free peoples who are resisting attempted subjugation by armed minorities or outside pressures." The outside pressure he was speaking of was in fact the Soviet Union.

Moreover, Berlin had been divided between the Allies and the Soviets. By 1948, the Soviet Union tried to gain all of Berlin for itself by blockading the city. America joined with Great Britain to fight against this Soviet blockade by airlifting more than 2 million tons of supplies to the city until the USSR lifted the blockade. Due in part to this, the North Atlantic Treaty Organization (NATO) was formed on April 4, 1949. Its purpose was collective security for the treaty members. By 1952, there were fourteen members including the United States, Great Britain, France, Canada, Italy, and Belgium.

From 1950 to 1953, America participated in the Korean Conflict. North Korean communist forces had invaded South Korea. Truman got the United Nations to agree that the United States could expel the North Koreans out of the South according to the Truman Doctrine. MacArthur called for America to go to war with China, which was backing many of the activities of the North. Truman would not agree, fearing this would set off another massive war. MacArthur publicly disagreed with and criticized Truman and therefore was removed from his post. This caused a huge drop in popularity for Truman. The Korean Conflict remained a stalemate until President Eisenhower managed to get a cease-fire from the Chinese.

At home, America started purging communist influences from government. Individuals with ties to communist parties were brought before the House Un-American Activities Committee (HUAC). During this time, state department official Alger Hiss was brought to trial for alleged espionage for the Soviet Union. He was convicted of perjury during his trial. The important aftermath of this, however, was the rise of Senator Joseph McCarthy and his claims that communist elements had infiltrated all levels of government.

Domestic Issues

Other important events that occurred during Truman's administration included:

- The passage of the twenty-second amendment, which limited a president to two terms.
- The Taft-Hartley Act, which restricted the power of labor unions.
- Attempts to get Truman's Fair Deal programs for social improvements passed.

Very few of Truman's Fair Deal programs actually became law because of lack of congressional support. On November 1, 1950, an assassination attempt was made on President Truman's life. The Trumans were living in the Blair House at the time when two Puerto Rican nationals, Oscar Collazo and Griselio Torresola, tried to storm their home. They were attempting to bring attention to the case for Puerto Rican independence. One policeman and Torresola died in the gunfight. Two other policemen were wounded, and Collazo was arrested and sentenced to death. However, Truman commuted his sentence to life in prison. In 1979, President Carter freed Collazo from prison.

Life After the Presidency

When it became apparent that public opinion still had not turned in favor of Truman, he decided not to seek reelection in 1952. Instead, he retired to his home in Independence, Missouri.

While he never returned to public office, he did remain active in the Democratic party. On December 26, 1972, Truman died of multiple organ failure after having suffered from pneumonia.

Dwight David Eisenhower: Supreme Commander

Born:	October 14, 1890
Died:	March 28, 1969
First Lady:	Mamie Geneva Doud Eisenhower
Political Party:	Republican
Presidential Term:	January 20, 1953 to January 20, 1961
Famous Quote:	"Whatever America hopes to bring to pass in this world must first come to pass in the heart of America."

Timeline

1915	Graduated from West Point
1916	Married Mamie Geneva Doud
1933–1935	Aide to General Douglas MacArthur
1935–1939	Assistant military adviser to the Philippines
1944	Supreme allied commander
1950	Supreme commander of NATO
1953–1961	Thirty-fourth president of the United States
1959	Alaska and Hawaii admitted to the Union

Childhood and Education

Eisenhower was born on October 14, 1890, in Denison, Texas. His given name was David Dwight, but he was always called Dwight. At some point, probably when he went to West Point, the order of his first two names was reversed. His nickname was Ike.

As an infant, Eisenhower moved to Abilene, Kansas. His father, David Jacob Eisenhower, was a mechanic. His family was poor and he helped out by working odd jobs to make extra money. He attended local public schools and graduated from high school in 1909.

Despite the fact that his mother, Ida Elizabeth Stover, was a deeply religious pacifist, Eisenhower decided to join the military to gain a free college education. He went to West Point from 1911 to 1915. He was commissioned a second lieutenant but continued his education in the military, eventually attending the Army War College.

First Lady: Mamie Geneva Doud Eisenhower

Marie "Mamie" Geneva Doud was born on November 14, 1896, in Boone, Iowa. Her family was extremely wealthy, and her father did well enough in the meat-packing industry to retire at the age of thirty-six. She met Eisenhower while visiting Texas in 1915, and they got married on July 1, 1916. She became an army wife, moving with her husband more than twenty times. Together, the Eisenhowers had one child who lived to maturity, John Sheldon Doud Eisenhower. John followed in his father's footsteps and went to West Point, served in the Korean War, and was appointed by Nixon to be ambassador to Belgium.

SCANDALS & GOSSIP

During World War II, Eisenhower had a woman driver named Kay Summersby. In 1975, after Kay's death, an "autobiography" written by a ghostwriter detailed an alleged affair between Eisenhower and Summersby. The book was entitled *Past Forgetting: My Love Affair with Dwight D. Eisenhower.* Historians today question whether the two of them actually ever had an intimate relationship.

Mamie was a very popular first lady. She was an accomplished hostess who dressed with style. She arranged for important state dinners for an unprecedented number of heads of state, partly because of the proliferation of air travel. She and her husband did not own their own permanent home until after Eisenhower retired from the presidency.

Career in the Military

Upon graduating from West Point, Eisenhower was assigned to be a second lieutenant in the infantry. During World War I, he was a training instructor and commander of a training center before joining General MacArthur's staff. He took part in the removal of the Bonus Marchers from Washington, D.C. These World War I veterans had marched on Washington during the Great Depression to ask the government to pay off their awarded insurance payments early. When they were denied, they had no place to go and set up shantytowns. The military was sent in and forcibly ejected the veterans.

QUIRKS & ODDITIES

Amazingly, Eisenhower never once saw active combat during his thirty-five years in the military. He was stuck in lower level positions until General George C. Marshall recognized his superior organizational skills and helped him move up the ranks until he eventually became the supreme commander during the war.

In 1935, Eisenhower was sent to the Philippines with General MacArthur. Eisenhower served as the assistant military adviser to the Philippine government. He returned to America in 1939 when Europe had become embroiled in war. By June 1941, he was appointed to be General Walter Krueger's chief of staff.

World War II

Three months before the Japanese bombing of Pearl Harbor, Eisenhower was made a brigadier general. He continued in positions within the general staff in the United States before being appointed to senior command positions.

In June 1942, Eisenhower was appointed commander of all U.S. forces in Europe. He commanded the troops as they invaded North Africa, landed in Sicily, and retook Italy from the German occupiers. To reward his valor and leadership, he was named supreme allied commander in February 1944. In this position, he was responsible for the successful D-Day Invasion at Normandy with Operation Overlord.

By December 1944, he had been made a five-star general due to his successes. He went on to lead the Allies in their liberation of Europe and invasion of Germany, accepting that country's surrender on May 7, 1945.

Supreme Commander of NATO

Eisenhower served as chief of staff of the U.S. Army until 1948, when he became the president of Columbia University. Eisenhower returned to active military duty when he was appointed by Truman to be the supreme commander of NATO. NATO, or the North Atlantic Treaty Organization, was established in 1949. The purpose of this organization was for allies to join together so that if the USSR or its allies launched an attack on any one NATO member, then all of the other members would come to that country's defense. Eisenhower served as the supreme commander until 1952 when he began his political career.

IN THEIR OWN WORDS...

Eisenhower made this statement before the storming of the beaches in Normandy: "You are about to embark upon the Great Crusade, toward which we have striven these many months. The eyes of the world are upon you. The hopes and prayers of liberty-loving people everywhere march with you. . . . I have full confidence in your courage, devotion to duty and skill in battle. We will accept nothing less than full victory!"

Nomination and Election

Both parties courted Eisenhower, who had not made his politics known. In 1952, he accepted the Republican nomination to run with Richard Nixon as his vice president. They were opposed by Democrat Adlai Stevenson. Both Eisenhower and Stevenson ran vigorous campaigns. The main issues were how to deal with communism at home and abroad and how to cut governmental waste. War hero Eisenhower ended up winning with 55 percent of the popular vote and 83 percent of the electoral vote.

In 1956, Eisenhower was easily nominated to run again, and again he was opposed by Stevenson. Prior to the campaign, Eisenhower had suffered a heart attack, and this health concern was one of the main issues that Stevenson used against him. Also at issue was whether or not to end the draft. Eisenhower felt that maintaining the draft was important for national security. In the end Eisenhower proved to be even more popular, winning 57 percent of the popular vote.

Presidential Administration

Eisenhower was president during a crucial period in American history. The Cold War was truly getting started and the United States and the Soviet Union were calling each other out as the two major players in the world. Actions and events during his administration were significant for future Cold War developments. The creation of the interstate highway system that Eisenhower signed into law in 1956 was necessary, in his eyes, for national defense. The roads provided easy means for the military to move about the country if necessary.

Part of Eisenhower's initial campaign was his promise to bring the Korean Conflict to an end. Once elected, but before he took office, Eisenhower traveled to Korea to help conclude peace talks that had been dragging on. By July 1953, an armistice was signed that separated Korea into two nations with a demilitarized zone at the 38th parallel. American troops were stationed along the demilitarized zone to ensure that this peace was honored.

Eisenhower Doctrine

Eisenhower came into office with the Cold War in full bloom. He believed that it was important to build up an arsenal of nuclear weapons as deterrence. This arsenal's purpose was to warn the Soviet Union that the United States would retaliate if fired upon.

In 1959, Fidel Castro took over in Cuba and became friendly with the Soviet Union. In return, Eisenhower placed an embargo on Cuba and ended all diplomatic relations.

Eisenhower was also concerned about the Soviet involvement in Vietnam. At the time, North Vietnam was under the influence of the Soviet Union and there was fear that the North would soon take over the democratic Southern portion of the country. Eisenhower believed in something that has come to be called the "Domino Theory." In a 1954 press conference, Eisenhower said that if communist powers gained control in one region (like Vietnam), then those powers would find it easier and easier to topple further regimes. He feared that all of Southeast Asia could eventually fall to communist forces if left unchecked. Therefore, Eisenhower felt that it was important for America to become involved in some fashion in protecting South Vietnam. He was the first to send advisers to the region. This action went hand in hand with his Eisenhower Doctrine, with which he asserted that America had the right to aid any country threatened by communist aggression.

End of McCarthy

After the Alger Hiss espionage trial during Truman's time in office, a senator from Wisconsin, Joseph McCarthy, began to make a name for himself by accusing various government employees of being communist sympathizers. Eisenhower did not agree with McCarthy or his methods. McCarthy began investigating the military in 1953 and made enemies by degrading a World War II battlefield general. When the army brought charges against McCarthy that he had asked for special treatment for a friend, Congress began the televised Army-McCarthy hearings to look into the matter. McCarthy's actions and words caused the public to turn against him and led to his fall from power. He was charged with improper conduct and censured by the Senate in December 1954.

Desegregating Schools

In 1954, the landmark Supreme Court decision for *Brown v. Board of Education of Topeka* was delivered, stating that schools had to be desegregated. Some public officials were resisting this order. In 1957, the local government of Little Rock, Arkansas, was standing in the way of allowing black students to enroll at a previously all-white school, so Eisenhower used his presidential powers to send in federal troops.

Likewise, many African Americans were being prevented from voting by various means. In 1960, the Civil Rights Act was passed, sanctioning local officials who blocked blacks from voting.

The U-2 Spy Plane Incident

On May 1, 1960, a U-2 spy plane piloted by Francis Gary Powers was brought down near Svedlovsk in the Soviet Union. Powers was captured and taken prisoner by the Soviets. Eisenhower, however, defended the need for reconnaissance flights as necessary for national security. The details surrounding this event remain shrouded in mystery to this day. However, Powers was eventually exchanged for a Soviet prisoner held by the United States. This event had a lasting negative impact on U.S.-Soviet relations.

Life After the Presidency

Eisenhower retired after his second term on January 20, 1961. He and his wife, Mamie, moved to a farm in Gettysburg, Pennsylvania. He spent the next eight years working on his autobiography and memoirs. Some of his most popular books include *Crusade in Europe* and *Waging Peace: The White House Years*. Eisenhower never held another public position. He died on March 28, 1969, of congestive heart failure.

35

John Fitzgerald Kennedy:
The King of Camelot

Born:	May 29, 1917
Died:	November 22, 1963
First Lady:	Jacqueline "Jackie" Lee Bouvier Kennedy
Political Party:	Democratic
Presidential Term:	January 20, 1961 to November 22, 1963
Famous Quote:	"We stand today on the edge of a new frontier—the frontier of the 1960s—a frontier of unknown opportunities and perils—a frontier of unfulfilled hopes and threats."

Timeline

1940 . . . . .Graduated from Harvard University

1941–1945 . . . . . .Served in the navy during World War II

1947–1953. . . . . .Member of the U.S. House of Representatives

1953–1960 . . . . . .U.S. senator from Massachusetts

1961–1963 . . . . . .Thirty-fifth president of the United States

Childhood and Education

Kennedy was born on May 29, 1917, the first president to be born in the twentieth century. His father, Joseph Kennedy, was an extremely powerful businessman who had made his fortune on the stock market. Some of his deals were questionable, and it was somewhat fitting that he was appointed to be the head of the SEC—the U.S. Securities and Exchange Commission—by Franklin Roosevelt. As such, he would be responsible for making rules for others concerning the exchange of securities like stocks.

Joseph Kennedy was sent to Great Britain as an ambassador in 1938. The whole family traveled with him and lived in England while he was in his post there. John Kennedy's mother, Rose Fitzgerald, was the daughter of the mayor of Boston and a Boston socialite. As such, the Kennedy clan grew up surrounded by wealth and privilege.

Famous Siblings

Kennedy was one of nine children, and many of his siblings also went on to public life. Kennedy appointed his brother Robert to be his attorney general. When Robert was running for president in his own right in 1968, he was assassinated by Sirhan Sirhan.

PRESIDENTIAL TRIVIA

The Kennedy clan was very competitive and enjoyed playing sports with each other. Sailing was a common pastime, but the family football games were legendary. Once in office, President John F. Kennedy appointed a staff member named Dave Powers to be his unofficial "undersecretary of baseball."

Kennedy's brother Edward "Ted" Kennedy is a senator from Massachusetts who has been serving since 1962. His sister Eunice founded the Special Olympics and her husband, Robert Sargent Shriver, was instrumental in founding the Peace Corps.

Health

Kennedy was a sickly child and he continued to have health problems for the rest of his life, including Addison's disease, which occurs when the body does not produce enough cortisol. It leads to chronic fatigue, muscle weakness, darkened skin, depression, and more. Kennedy and his family kept this a secret throughout his presidency. Further, he developed osteoporosis in his lower spine and was plagued by a bad back throughout his life and his time in office.

Education

Kennedy attended private schools his whole life, including the famous prep school Choate Rosemary Hall, located in Connecticut. He went to Harvard from 1936 until 1940 and majored in political science. He was an active undergraduate who enjoyed sports, especially swimming. Kennedy graduated cum laude and turned his graduate thesis—on Britain and their response to Germany's early aggression—into a bestselling book entitled *Why England Slept*.

First Lady: Jacqueline "Jackie" Lee Bouvier Kennedy

Jacqueline "Jackie" Lee Bouvier was also born into a wealthy family on July 28, 1929. Her father was a New York stockbroker and her parents divorced when she was quite young. Jackie spent three years of college at Vassar in New York before transferring to George Washington University in her senior year. She graduated with a degree in French literature and then went to work as a journalist for the *Washington Times-Herald*.

Jackie first met Kennedy at a dinner party in 1952. They began dating early in 1953 and were married on September 12, 1953. The Kennedys had two children who lived to maturity: Caroline and John F. Kennedy Jr. Their son John and his wife died in a plane accident on July 16, 1999.

SCANDALS & GOSSIP

John F. Kennedy allegedly had an affair with movie actress Marilyn Monroe. She famously sang "Happy Birthday Mr. President" to him during his birthday celebration at Madison Square Garden on May 19, 1962. Kennedy's response to the sultry song was, "I can now retire from politics after having had 'Happy Birthday' sung to me in such a sweet, wholesome way."

As first lady, Jackie was revered for her fashion sense and poise. She spent much time while living in the White House working on its restoration. She worked tirelessly to bring furnishings and items of historical significance to the White House. Then, in 1962, she allowed America to see the interior of the White House through a television tour on CBS. Jackie Kennedy handled the assassination and funeral of President Kennedy with dignity and poise. She removed herself from public life for a time to mourn her husband. In 1968, she married Greek shipping tycoon Aristotle Onassis. In later years she worked as an editor for Doubleday. She died on May 18, 1994, from non-Hodgkins Lymphoma.

Early Career

In 1941, Kennedy joined the navy to fight in World War II. He was eventually given command of a boat called PT-109. When the boat was rammed by a Japanese destroyer, he and his crew were thrown into the water. He was able to swim for four hours, saving himself and a crewman. However, the ordeal aggravated his back. For his valor and bravery he received the Purple Heart and Navy and Marine Corps Medal, and returned at the end of the war as a hero.

After the war, Kennedy worked for a time as a journalist until he decided to run for the House of Representatives. He won in 1947 and was reelected twice. While in Congress he showed himself to be an independent thinker, not always following the Democratic party line. In 1953, Kennedy was elected as a senator from Massachusetts. Critics were upset that he would not stand up to Senator Joe McCarthy who was conducting his witch hunt for communist sympathizers in the government.

Before becoming president, Kennedy won a Pulitzer Prize for his book *Profiles in Courage*. This book discussed eight senators over the years who were willing to go against public opinion, often to the detriment of their careers, to do what was right. Some questioned at the time how much of the book he truly wrote himself and how much was done by his research assistants. However, both he and his research assistant Theodore Sorensen denied this rumor.

Becoming the President

In 1960, Kennedy was nominated to run for the presidency against Richard Nixon, Eisenhower's vice president.

One issue of the campaign was Kennedy's Catholicism. Kennedy met critics head on when he proclaimed that he would not be influenced by Rome. As he said, "I am not the Catholic candidate for President. I am the Democratic Party's candidate for President who also happens to be a Catholic. I do not speak for my Church on public matters—and the Church does not speak for me."

IN THEIR OWN WORDS...

During Kennedy's acceptance speech at the Democratic nominating convention, he said: "We stand at the edge of a New Frontier—the frontier of unfulfilled hopes and dreams. It will deal with unsolved problems of peace and war, unconquered pockets of ignorance and prejudice, unanswered questions of poverty and surplus." The term New Frontier was then used for his domestic and foreign policies.

During the campaign, Nixon made the mistake of meeting Kennedy in televised debates. Kennedy came off as young and vital, while Nixon, who was recovering from a bout of food poisoning and refused to wear makeup, looked older and somber. These debates are believed to have had a huge impact on the eventual outcome of the campaign. Kennedy won by the smallest margin of popular votes since 1888, winning by only 118,574 votes. However, he received 303 electoral votes—more than enough to win.

Presidential Administration

Kennedy's New Frontier was a package of programs to help Americans that included funding for education, housing, medical care for the elderly, and more. However, he had a tough time getting many of his domestic programs through Congress because of the narrowness of his victory margin. He was able to get an increase in the minimum wage passed, along with better Social Security benefits and an urban renewal package. He also created the Peace Corp.

Kennedy was an iconic figure and an excellent speaker who set forth ambitious goals. Probably his most ambitious goal was when he set the agenda that America was to get to the moon by the end of the 1960s. His goal found overwhelming support and NASA was created to come up with a means to the moon before the end of 1969.

Civil Rights

In the beginning of Kennedy's presidency, he was not willing to openly challenge Southern Democrats concerning the treatment of blacks in the South and the burgeoning civil rights movement. However, as the peaceful demonstrations espoused by Reverend Martin Luther King Jr. revealed daily the true nature of how blacks were treated in the South, public opinion began to change. Images of the atrocities committed against those involved in nonviolent protests and reports of civil rights activists being killed led Kennedy to use executive orders and personal appeals to help aid the movement. He proposed legislative programs to help, including civil rights bills, although they would not pass until after his death.

Bay of Pigs and the Cuban Missile Crisis

In 1961, Kennedy had a huge failure with the Bay of Pigs debacle. A small group of Cuban exiles were backed by the United States as they tried to lead a revolt in Cuba against the Soviet-backed Fidel Castro, but they were captured instead. The reputation of the United States was harmed around the world.

Khrushchev, the leader of the USSR, began building nuclear missile bases in Cuba after the failed Bay of Pigs invasion. Their purpose was to protect Cuba from further planned attacks by the United States. In response, Kennedy ordered a "quarantine" of Cuba. He warned the USSR that any attack on the United States from Cuba would be seen as an act of war by the Soviet Union. This standoff was known as the Cuban Missile Crisis and led to the dismantling of the missile silos in exchange for promises that the United States would not invade Cuba.

Vietnam

Communist North Vietnam was sending troops through the country of Laos to fight in South Vietnam. Diem, the leader of South Vietnam, was ineffective at leading a defense of his country. To help out, Kennedy increased the number of military advisers that Eisenhower had sent in from 2,000 to 16,000. This would presage events that would unfold under Kennedy's successor, Lyndon B. Johnson, concerning American escalation in Vietnam.

Assassination

On November 22, 1963, John F. Kennedy was visiting Dallas, Texas. He was riding in a convertible during a motorcade through Dallas when he was shot in the head. His apparent assassin, Lee Harvey Oswald, was located in the Texas Book Depository and fled the scene but was captured in a movie theater and brought to jail. Oswald was shot and killed two days later by Jack Ruby before he could stand trial.

QUIRKS & ODDITIES

Kennedy and Lincoln buffs have noted odd coincidences between the two assassinations. For example, each of them was succeeded by a president whose last name was Johnson; both were shot on a Friday, in the head, in the presence of their wives; both assassins were killed before they came to trial; and Booth shot Lincoln in a theater and ran to a warehouse, while Oswald did the opposite with Kennedy.

So many controversies and theories surrounded Kennedy's assassination that the Warren Commission was called to investigate his death. After ten months of investigation, the committee found that Oswald had acted alone to kill Kennedy. Many argued, however, that there was more than one gunman, a theory that was upheld by a 1979 House Committee investigation. The Federal Bureau of Investigation (FBI) and a 1982 study disagreed. Speculation continues to this day about the truth behind the assassination.

While Kennedy was president, the hit musical *Camelot* was playing on Broadway. It happened to have been a favorite of the president. The play told the story of King Arthur and its title song was a huge success. When Jackie Kennedy was interviewed a few days after her husband's assassination, she brought this up, linking the play and the song with Kennedy's time in office. She stated: "There'll be great presidents again . . . but there'll never be another Camelot."

36

Lyndon Baines Johnson: All the Way with LBJ

Born:	August 27, 1908
Died:	January 22, 1973
First Lady:	Claudia Alta Taylor "Lady Bird" Johnson
Political Party:	Democratic
Presidential Term:	November 22, 1963 to January 20, 1969
Famous Quote:	"The Great Society is a place where every child can find knowledge to enrich his mind and to enlarge his talents.... It is a place where men are more concerned with the quality of their goals than the quantity of their goods."

Timeline

1930...........Graduated from Southwest Texas State Teacher's College
1934...........Married Claudia Alta Taylor
1935–1937.......Head of Texas National Youth Administration
1937–1949 ......Member of the U.S. House of Representatives
1949–1961 ......U.S. senator from Texas
1961–1963 ......Vice president of the United States under President Kennedy
1963–1969 ......Thirty-sixth president of the United States

Childhood and Education

Lyndon B. Johnson was born on August 27, 1908, in Texas. Johnson grew up the son of a politician, Sam Ealy Johnson Jr., who was the member of the Texas legislature for eleven years. Despite being a politician, his father struggled to make enough money to support his family. Johnson worked throughout his youth to earn money for the family. His mother, Rebekah Baines Johnson, taught him to read at an early age. She was a journalist who had graduated from Baylor University.

Johnson went to local public schools and graduated from high school in 1924. He spent three years traveling around and working at odd jobs before going to college at the Southwest Texas State Teachers College. He graduated in 1930 and attended Georgetown University to study law from 1934 to 1935. However, he left the school without his law degree to pursue a career in politics.

First Lady: Claudia Alta Taylor "Lady Bird" Johnson

Claudia Alta "Lady Bird" Taylor was born on December 22, 1912, the daughter of T. J. Taylor and Minnie Patillo-Taylor. Lady Bird—as she was called from her youth—was a savvy businesswoman.

PRESIDENTIAL TRIVIA

Lyndon Johnson met Lady Bird at the home of a mutual friend in 1934. Johnson asked her to meet him for breakfast the next morning. While they were eating, he asked her to marry him. She took some time to consider his proposal before agreeing to be wed. They were married on November 17, 1934, in San Antonio, Texas.

As first lady, Lady Bird worked to improve the way America looked through what was known as the beautification program. Part of her accomplishment included supporting the Highway Beautification Act, which limited billboards and increased funding for roadside landscaping. Together, the Johnsons had two daughters: Lynda Bird and Luci Baines. All four members of the Johnson family had the same initials, LBJ. Both of Johnson's daughters got married while he was president. Lynda's ceremony was in the White House, while Luci had her reception there.

Early Career

Because Johnson's father was involved in Democratic politics in Texas, he made connections that helped his son gain political influence in the state. In 1935, Johnson was named the director of the National Youth Administration in Texas. This was part of Franklin Roosevelt's New Deal. In 1937, Johnson was elected to be a U.S. representative where he served until 1949. During his term as a congressman, he joined the navy to fight in World War II. At that time, a dispensation was made so that congressmen could hold their seat while serving in the military. Johnson was awarded the Silver Star by MacArthur for gallantry in battle.

SCANDALS & GOSSIP

Many historians called Johnson's Silver Star one of the most undeserved in history. Johnson went on one bombing mission as an observer. The plane's generator went out so they turned around and headed home. One account said his plane came under attack while another said it never saw combat.

In 1949, Johnson was elected to the U.S. Senate. He rose in power to become the youngest Democratic majority leader up to that time at age forty-six in 1955. He was part of some of the most powerful committees including appropriations, finance, and armed services. He was responsible for getting crucial Southern support for the Civil Rights Acts of 1957 and 1960. He remained a member of the Senate until 1961, when he won the vice presidency under John F. Kennedy.

Succession and Election

When John F. Kennedy was assassinated on November 22, 1963, Johnson took over as president. He was actually given the oath of office on Air Force One. He served out the rest of Kennedy's term in office before running for election in his own right in 1964. At that time, Hubert Humphrey was selected as his vice president. Johnson was opposed by Barry Goldwater. Johnson was able to make Goldwater look like an extreme conservative while he painted himself as a moderate. Throughout the campaign, Johnson refused to debate Goldwater. In the end, America went "all the way with LBJ" as he won with a huge majority—61 percent of the popular vote and 486 of the electoral votes.

Presidential Administration

Johnson took over the presidency as the nation was in mourning. He called for an investigation into Kennedy's death with the creation of the Warren Commission. At first, he had a hard time gaining backing for his programs, so he used many strong-arm tactics to get his legislation pushed through Congress.

IN THEIR OWN WORDS...

Johnson was known as a womanizer. Johnson once told the press: "I may go into a strange bedroom every now and then that I don't want you to write about, but otherwise you can write everything." He had a long-term affair with Alice Glass, who also happened to be his friend's mistress. According to biographer Robert Caro, Johnson considered divorcing his wife and ending his political career to be with Alice.

Great Society

Johnson espoused a group of programs that he called the "Great Society." The point of these programs was to help the poor and provide important protections for Americans. The significant elements of Johnson's Great Society were:

- Antipoverty programs
- Civil rights legislation
- Medicare and Medicaid
- Environmental protection acts
- Consumer protection acts

Although the Great Society did not accomplish all of Johnson's goals, it has had far-reaching effects to this day.

Civil Rights

Three significant civil rights acts were passed during the Johnson administration.

Civil Rights Act of 1964—No discrimination for employment or the use of public facilities.
Voting Rights Act of 1965—Discriminatory practices like literacy tests, which had kept minorities from voting, were outlawed.
Civil Rights Act of 1968—No discrimination for housing.

Further, in 1964, the twenty-fourth amendment was passed, outlawing the charging of a poll tax before individuals could vote. Poll taxes were targeted at keeping blacks from voting in certain areas in the South.

In 1968, Martin Luther King Jr. was assassinated by James Earl Ray.

PRESIDENTIAL TRIVIA

Literacy tests were used in the South to keep the poor and African Americans from voting. They included questions that were confusing and difficult—if not impossible—to answer. For example, one question from the Alabama literacy test was: "A U.S. Senator elected at the general election in November takes office the following year on what date? A. March 17th, B. January 3rd, C. January 1st."

Vietnam

When Johnson took over the presidency from Kennedy, 16,000 advisers were in Vietnam but no official military action was being taken. However, during Johnson's presidency, America became deeply embroiled in the conflict. America continued to commit more troops to the region. In fact, troop levels, which had started at 3,500 in 1965, reached 550,000 by 1968.

America was deeply divided about the war. Many felt that American lives were being needlessly lost. In the end, America did not have a chance of winning due to the guerrilla fighting methods used by the Vietnamese and the fact that the administration did not want the war to escalate and involve other countries like China and the Soviet Union. In 1968, Johnson announced that he would not run for reelection. He said that he was going to spend his last months in office trying to get peace in Vietnam. However, peace would not be achieved until President Nixon's administration.

Life After the Presidency

Johnson retired on January 20, 1969, to his ranch in Johnson City, Texas. He did not return to politics. In 1971, he published his memoirs as a work entitled *The Vantage Point*. That same year, the University of Texas at Austin opened its Lyndon Baines Johnson memorial library in his honor; it has since become the most visited presidential library in the country. His health having been injured by many years of heavy smoking and stress, Johnson died on January 22, 1973, from a third heart attack when he was sixty-four years old. Johnson was found in his bed reaching for the phone.

In his will Johnson donated his ranch to the public under the stipulation that it remain an active ranch and not become a "sterile relic of the past." Johnson was posthumously awarded the presidential Medal of Freedom in 1980.

37

Richard M. Nixon: Fallen President

Born:	January 9, 1913
Died:	April 22, 1994
First Lady:	Thelma Catherine Patricia "Pat" Ryan Nixon
Political Party:	Republican
Presidential Term:	January 20, 1969 to August 9, 1974
Famous Quote:	"This office is a sacred trust and I am determined to be worthy of that trust."

Timeline

1934 . . . . .Graduated from Whittier College
1937 . . . . .Graduated from Duke University Law School
1940 . . . . .Married Thelma Catherine Patricia Ryan
1942–1946 . . . . . .Served in the navy during World War II
1947–1950 . . . . . .Member of the U.S. House of Representatives
1951–1953 . . . . . .U.S. senator from California
1953–1961 . . . . . .Vice president of the United States under President Johnson
1969–1974 . . . . . .Thirty-seventh president of the United States

Childhood and Education

Richard Nixon was born on January 9, 1913, in Yorba Linda, California, to a poor family. He grew up in California, helping out his father, Francis "Frank" Anthony Nixon, at the family's grocery store. Nixon's mother, Hannah Milhous Nixon, was a devout Quaker and Nixon was raised in the religion. He had two brothers die of tuberculosis, which seriously affected him.

QUIRKS & ODDITIES

Richard Nixon loved sports—both watching and playing them. While president he supported the Washington Redskins and even gave the team a pep talk after they lost a game. During the 1971 playoff game, Redskins coach George Allen told his team that they were running a play designed by Richard Nixon in an effort to motivate them, even though Nixon did not actually design the play.

Nixon attended local public schools. He was valedictorian of his high school class in 1930. He then went to Whittier College from 1930 to 1934 and graduated with a history degree. He enrolled at Duke University Law School and graduated in 1937. He was admitted to the California bar that year.

First Lady: Thelma Catherine Patricia "Pat" Ryan Nixon

Thelma Catherine "Pat" Ryan was born on March 16, 1912, in Ely, Nevada. When she was young, her family moved to a small farm outside of Los Angeles. She was a business teacher, teaching typing and shorthand. Her mother, Katherine Halberstadt Ryan, died when Pat was only thirteen. She met Richard Nixon while she was at Whittier College and he had just graduated from law school. They married on June 21, 1940. Together, the Nixons had two daughters: Patricia and Julie.

As first lady, Pat Nixon took up volunteerism as her cause. She spoke about the importance of Americans volunteering in their communities. She continued with Jackie Kennedy's attempts to add important historical artifacts to the White House, accompanied her husband on his historic trips to China and the Soviet Union, and also traveled on her own as the president's personal representative to Peru, Africa, and South America.

Early Career

Nixon began practicing law in 1937. In 1940, he went in on a business to open a frozen orange juice manufacturing business, but this venture failed within two years.

Nixon joined the navy to serve in World War II in June 1942. He was first an aide to the executive officer at the Naval Reserve air base in Iowa before going overseas. He was made the officer in charge of the South Pacific Combat Air Transport Command until June 1944. As an administrator, he was cited for his efficiency. He resigned from the military in 1946, having achieved the rank of lieutenant commander.

House Un-American Activities Committee

In 1947, Nixon was elected a U.S. representative. In the House, he was a member of the House Un-American Activities Committee, which investigated communist involvement in America. He was the chairman of the committee when Alger Hiss, a former state department official, was identified as a communist spy during the 1930s. Hiss was indicted and convicted of perjury for lying to the committee about his espionage.

Checkers Speech

In 1950, Nixon was elected as a U.S. senator. He served in that capacity until being chosen as Dwight Eisenhower's vice presidential nominee. However, during the campaign, Nixon was accused of having an $18,000 secret fund that contributors had given him. Eisenhower was considering dropping Nixon from the ticket when Nixon delivered a televised speech that has been dubbed the Checkers speech. In this speech, he admitted that he had a fund but it went to pay for political expenses, not for his own use. However, he admitted that he had been given a dog, which his daughter had named Checkers, and stated that they were going to keep the dog. Viewers supported him overwhelmingly and Eisenhower kept him on the ticket. Eisenhower and Nixon were elected in 1953.

Nixon ran for president in his own right in 1960 but lost to John F. Kennedy. He also unsuccessfully ran for the governorship of California in 1962.

Nomination and Elections

In 1968, Richard Nixon was chosen on the first ballot as the Republican candidate for president with Spiro Agnew as his vice president. The campaign centered on ending the war in Vietnam and dealing with taxes and inflation at home. Nixon defeated both Democrat Hubert Humphrey and American Independent George Wallace with 43 percent of the popular vote and 301 electoral votes.

In 1972, President Nixon was the obvious choice for nomination by the Republicans with Agnew as his running mate again. This time, he was opposed by Democrat George McGovern, who was seen as representing the far left. Nixon did not spend much time campaigning yet he easily won with 61 percent of the popular vote and 520 out of 531 electoral votes.

Presidential Administration

When Nixon took over the office, America was deeply divided over the war in Vietnam. During his tenure, he would cut the number of soldiers in Vietnam from more than 540,000 troops down to 25,000, eventually withdrawing all ground troops.

At first, Nixon had the troops work with the South Vietnamese to train them for their own defense before withdrawal. On April 30, 1970, the U.S. and South Vietnamese troops joined to raid and attempt to capture the communist headquarters in Cambodia. This caused a string of protests around the United States. At Kent State University, a group of students gathered to protest the invasion and were fired upon by the Ohio National Guard. Four students were killed and nine were injured, resulting in a lot of bad publicity for the administration.

One of the many arguments that were being used by those who disagreed with the war was that young men under the age of twenty-one were being sent to Vietnam through the draft but were not even able to vote. This situation resulted in the ratification of the twenty-sixth amendment in 1971 which lowered the voting age from 21 to 18.

By January 1973, a peace treaty was signed between North and South Vietnam. The United States agreed to withdraw all forces in exchange for the release of all prisoners of war. Soon after the agreement, fighting between the North and South resumed and eventually the communists won.

Going Where No One Has Gone

On July 20, 1969, President Nixon fulfilled Kennedy's dream of putting a man on the moon by the end of the decade. The lunar module from Apollo 11 landed on the moon, allowing Neil Armstrong to become the first man to take a step off the Earth. The landing was televised and a plaque was placed on the moon proclaiming the landing with Nixon's name attached as president.

PRESIDENTIAL TRIVIA

Richard Nixon is the only president who has his name on the moon. A plaque was left behind on the moon's surface with each lunar landing. The one left by the Apollo 11 astronauts said, "Here men from the planet Earth first set foot upon the moon." It was signed by the three astronauts and Richard Nixon.

Nixon also traveled to a place where no president had gone before—communist China. He supported China's admission to the United Nations in 1971 and then went on a trip to China in February 1972 to encourage peace. He met with China's leader and they discussed cultural exchanges. This visit was also significant because America had no formal diplomatic ties with the country.

Environmental Policies

During Nixon's time in office, a number of acts were passed to help protect the environment. The bills included the creation of the Environmental

Protection Agency in 1970. Further, the National Air Quality Standards Act of 1970 restricted auto emissions and established federal clean air standards to be met by states.

Watergate

On June 17, 1972, five individuals from the Committee to Reelect the President (CREEP) were caught breaking into the Democratic National Headquarters at the Watergate business complex. Two reporters for the *Washington Post*, Bob Woodward and Carl Bernstein, uncovered a massive cover-up of the break-in. The investigation found, among other things, that eavesdropping devices had been installed in the Democratic headquarters and that White House officials paid hush money to Watergate defendants.

Further, the Administration had a list of enemies that they intended to stop using federal means, including people ranging from a U.S. representative to actors like Bill Cosby and Paul Newman.

Nixon's involvement was determined through subpoenaed tapes that had him speaking with top aides about the events. In fact, Nixon himself had installed a White House taping system that he was going to use to help write his memoirs. When the Senate asked for the tapes recorded during his time in office, Nixon refused to hand them over citing executive privilege.

IN THEIR OWN WORDS...

Here is what Nixon had to say about executive privilege and why he should not be required to provide the tapes to the Senate: "Under the doctrine of separation of powers, the manner in which the president personally exercises his assigned executive powers is not subject to questioning by another branch of government."

The case went before the Supreme Court, which forced him to produce the tapes. The tapes showed that while Nixon was not involved in planning the break-in, he was part of the cover-up. In the end, Nixon was sure to be impeached and preemptively resigned his office on August 9, 1974. Faith in the office of the presidency would never be the same after Watergate. It would change the public's view and the way that the press dealt with the office forever.

Life After the Presidency

After Richard Nixon resigned, he retired to San Clemente, California. One month later, he was pardoned by his successor, President Gerald Ford. He worked on writing a number of books about his experiences and about foreign policy while traveling extensively. In 1985, he mediated a dispute between major league baseball and the umpire association. He provided advice about foreign affairs to presidents of both parties. Nixon died on April 22, 1994, after suffering a stroke four days earlier.

Gerald R. Ford: President by Succession

Born:	July 14, 1913
Died:	December 24, 2006
First Lady:	Elizabeth "Betty" Ann Bloomer Warren Ford
Political Party:	Republican
Presidential Term:	August 9, 1974 to January 20, 1977
Famous Quote:	"A government big enough to give you everything you want is a government big enough to take from you everything you have."

Timeline

1935 . . . . Graduated from University of Michigan

1941 . . . . Graduated from Yale Law School

1942–1946 . . . . . . Served in the navy during World War II

1948 . . . . Married Elizabeth "Betty" Ann Bloomer Warren

1949–1973 . . . . . . Member of the U.S. House of Representatives

1963–1964 . . . . . . Member of the Warren Commission

1973–1974 . . . . Vice president of the United States under President Nixon

1974–1977 . . . . Thirty-eighth president of the United States

Childhood and Education

Gerald Rudolph Ford Jr. was born on July 14, 1913, in Omaha, Nebraska, but grew up in Grand Rapids, Michigan. He found out when he was about twelve years old that the man he thought was his biological father was actually his adoptive father. His biological father, Leslie Lynch King, had nothing to do with his son over the years. Ford was actually named after his father at birth, but his mother, Dorothy Ayer Gardner, changed his name once she married her second husband, Gerald Rudolph Ford Sr.

Ford attended local public schools before going to the University of Michigan. He played on the school's football team and could have played for either the Detroit Lions or the Green Bay Packers after college but instead decided to go to law school. Ford worked his way through Yale Law School and received his degree in 1941. He was admitted to the bar that same year.

First Lady: Elizabeth "Betty" Anne Bloomer Ford

Elizabeth "Betty" Anne Bloomer was born in Chicago, Illinois, on April 8, 1918. Her parents, Hortense Neahr and William Stephenson Bloomer, moved to Grand Rapids, Michigan, when she was only three. She took dance throughout her youth and used it to help earn money for the family during the Great Depression. As she grew older, she studied under Martha Graham and then moved to Manhattan to become a model before coming back home to become a fashion buyer at a department store.

Betty Bloomer married a childhood sweetheart named William G. Warren in 1942. They divorced in 1947. She then began dating Ford, and the couple was married on October 15, 1948.

Together they had three sons—Michael Gerald, John Gardner, and Steven Meigs—and one daughter named Susan Elizabeth.

As first lady, Betty Ford was very open about her private life. She spoke openly about undergoing psychiatric treatment. She was a huge advocate for women's rights, including the Equal Rights Amendment and the legalization of abortion. She spoke out about breast cancer awareness after her own mastectomy.

PRESIDENTIAL TRIVIA

Susan Elizabeth was a high school student while her father was president. In fact, her senior class prom took place in the East room at the White House on May 31, 1975. Two bands played until 1:00 A.M., and food was served in the state dining room.

After Ford's retirement, it came out that Betty Ford was an alcoholic and was addicted to pain relievers. She recovered and opened the Betty Ford Center in 1982 to help others who are addicted to alcohol or drugs. She is still on the Center's Board of Directors.

Early Career

Ford briefly practiced law in 1941 to 1942 before joining the navy to fight in World War II. In 1943, he was sent to sea on the USS *Monterey* in the South Pacific where he took part in the recapture of the Philippines. He left the navy as a lieutenant commander in 1946. After the war he went back to practicing law. In 1949, Ford became a U.S. representative and was chosen to be a member of the Warren Commission to determine the facts behind Kennedy's assassination. He was reelected twelve times until 1973 when he became the vice president under Richard Nixon.

Vice Presidential Appointment

In 1973, Vice President Spiro Agnew resigned from office to avoid criminal charges for bribery. According to the twenty-fifth amendment, when there was a vacancy in the vice presidency the president would nominate, and the Senate and House would confirm, a new vice president. Ford was chosen as a moderate and was confirmed by both the House and Senate. He took office on December 6, 1973. When Nixon resigned on August 9, 1974, Ford became the first president who had not been elected to either the presidency or the vice presidency.

Presidential Administration

One month after taking over the presidency, Ford pardoned Nixon. This caused a lot of controversy but Ford claimed he did it to save the nation from the prospect of a long, messy, and divisive trial.

IN THEIR OWN WORDS...

Ford on Nixon's pardon: "After years of bitter controversy . . . I am compelled to conclude that many months and perhaps more years will have to pass before Richard Nixon could obtain a fair trial. . . . But it is not the ultimate fate of [Nixon] that most concerns me. . . . My concern is the immediate future of this great country."

This action, however, cost him support throughout his presidency and possibly the 1976 election. In 2001, Ford was awarded the John F. Kennedy Profiles in Courage award for this action.

Clemency for Draft Dodgers

In 1974, President Ford offered clemency to those who had evaded the draft during the Vietnam War if they would swear allegiance and perform two years of public service. Similarly, those who deserted during the war could return to the branch they left for two years to achieve clemency. Ford was criticized by both sides for this action. On one hand, he was seen as being too easy on those who evaded the draft; on the other hand, those who had avoided the service felt they were in the right and should not have to perform any public service.

Foreign Affairs

At the beginning of Ford's administration, the rest of the American troops left Vietnam. Ford actually asked for aid to be sent to South Vietnam in 1974, as fighting had resumed. With American opinion completely against any further intervention, Congress would not agree. In April 1975, Saigon fell to the North and by 1976, North and South Vietnam were united into one country.

PRESIDENTIAL TRIVIA

Ford not only pardoned Nixon, but he also pardoned Robert E. Lee. In 1970, a researcher found an old signed Pledge of Allegiance by Lee dated 1865. Senator Harry Byrd from Virginia offered a resolution asking for him to be pardoned posthumously. It passed through Congress and Ford signed it into law on August 5, 1975, at General Lee's family home.

Ford continued with Nixon's goal of building better relationships with China and the Soviet Union, visiting China again in December 1975. He also entered into the Helsinki Accords with the Soviet Union and thirty-three other countries. The goal of the accords was to mutually agree upon certain natural rights, including the right to sovereignty, territorial integrity of states, respect for human rights, and others.

Assassination Attempts

Ford escaped two assassination attempts in the year 1975, both of which were carried out by women. On September 5, 1975, Lynette Fromme, a follower of Charles Manson, pointed a gun at Ford but did not fire. She was supposedly trying to talk to him about the plight of California redwoods. She was convicted of attempting to assassinate the president and sentenced to life in prison.

The second attempt on Ford's life occurred on September 22, 1975, outside the St. Francis Hotel in San Francisco. Sara Jane Moore fired one shot that was deflected by bystander Oliver Sipple. Moore was trying to prove herself to some radical friends by assassinating the president. She was convicted of attempted assassination and sentenced to life in prison.

Life After the Presidency

Ford ran for reelection in 1976 but lost to Jimmy Carter. He then retired to his home in California. Ford joined the lecture circuit and spent time writing his memoirs. He has also served on the boards of numerous corporations. In 1999, Ford was awarded the Presidential Medal of Freedom by President Clinton. Ford died on December 26, 2006; he was ninety-three years old.

39

James Earl "Jimmy" Carter: Southern Legacy

Born: October 1, 1924
First Lady: Eleanor Rosalynn Smith Carter
Political Party: Democratic
Presidential Term: January 20, 1977 to January 20, 1981
Famous Quote: "If the misery of others leaves you indifferent and with no feeling of sorrow, then you cannot be called a human being."

Timeline

1946 . . . . Graduated from the U.S. Naval Academy
1946 . . . . Married Eleanor Rosalynn Smith
1963–1967 . . . . . .Georgia state senator
1971–1975 . . . . . . .Governor of Georgia
1977–1981 . . . . . . .Thirty-ninth president of the United States
2002 . . . . .Nobel Peace Prize winner

Childhood and Education

James Earl Carter was born on October 1, 1924, in Plains, Georgia. His father, James Carter Sr., was a farmer and a local public official. His mother was a Peace Corps volunteer. Jimmy grew up working in the fields to help bring in money and attended public schools in Plains, Georgia. After high school, he attended the Georgia Institute of Technology before being accepted into the U.S. Naval Academy in 1943. He graduated from the academy in 1946.

First Lady: Eleanor Rosalynn Smith Carter

Eleanor Rosalynn Smith was born on August 18, 1927, in Plains, Georgia, the daughter of Edgar Smith and Frances Allethea Murray. Her father died when she was thirteen, and Rosalynn worked to financially help her mother and family.

Rosalynn was Carter's sister Ruth's best friend, so the pair had known each other for some time before they began dating. They married on July 7, 1946, after Carter graduated from the Academy. Together, the Carters had three sons and one daughter: John William, James Earl III, Donnel Jeffrey, and Amy Lynn, respectively. Their daughter, Amy, was a child while Carter was president and lived in the White House from age nine until thirteen.

QUIRKS & ODDITIES

Jimmy Carter made a mistake during a 1980 televised debate against Ronald Reagan when he mentioned that he asked his thirteen-year-old daughter, Amy, about the problems facing the world. "I had a discussion with my daughter, Amy, the other day before I came here to ask her what the most important issue was, she said she thought nuclear weaponry." The Republicans capitalized on this throughout the campaign.

As first lady, Rosalynn was very close to her husband and was one of his closest advisers. In fact, she sat in on many cabinet meetings. She worked hard on behalf of those with mental health issues and was named the honorary chair of the president's Commission on Mental Health. Since leaving the

White House, Rosalynn has received many honors, including being placed on the board of advisers for Habitat for Humanity.

Early Career

Carter served in the navy from 1946 to 1953. He loved the navy and wanted to make it his career, but he resigned upon his father's death to take over the family peanut farming business.

Nuclear Submarines

After attending submarine school, Carter gained his first assignment aboard the submarine *Pomfret*. He was then assigned to an antisubmarine vessel in 1950. Carter served on one of the first nuclear submarines in the navy as an engineering officer until he resigned.

Successful Peanut Farmer

Carter went home to Plains, Georgia, and entered into the family business as a peanut farmer. His efforts on the family farm led to expansion of the business and eventually made him a very wealthy man. At this point, he turned his eye toward politics.

IN THEIR OWN WORDS...

Jimmy Carter was always a huge proponent of equal opportunities for everyone. During Jimmy Carter's inaugural address as governor of the state of Georgia, he said: "The test of a government is not how popular it is with the powerful and privileged few, but how honestly and fairly it deals with the many who must depend on it."

He ran and won a seat in the Georgia State Senate where he served from 1963 to 1967. His success as a politician led him to the governor's mansion in 1971, where he was responsible for massively restructuring Georgia's bureaucracy.

Nomination and Election

In 1974, Jimmy Carter declared his candidacy as dark horse candidate for the 1976 Democratic presidential nomination. He was not a nationally known figure, but by the time the presidential campaign began he led in the polls by thirty points. His platform was one of restoring trust after Watergate. He ran against President Gerald Ford; one of the main campaign issues was Ford's pardon of Nixon.

The vote was very close, with Carter winning 50 percent of the popular vote and 297 out of 538 electoral votes.

SCANDALS & GOSSIP

Carter committed a faux pas in November 1976 when, during a *Playboy* interview, he made the following comment: "I've looked on a lot of women with lust. I've committed adultery in my heart many times." His words were widely discussed and, during the third debate between Carter and Ford, he was asked about it. He stated that he would not do the interview again if given the chance.

Presidential Administration

Carter began his presidency in a fairly controversial way. One of his first actions as president was to pardon all those who had illegally avoided the draft during the Vietnam War, angering veterans's groups around the nation. Carter did not extend the pardon to deserters.

Energy

Energy policy was a major initiative of Carter's and ironically was one of the areas in which his presidency really suffered. His robust energy plans consisted of many points, including reducing the national growth rate for energy consumption, reducing gasoline use, cutting the amount of oil that America imported, increasing coal production, and using more solar energy, among other things.

QUIRKS & ODDITIES

Carter was not one to give compliments. Staffers and the press found him hard to relate to. According to Bob Woodward in his book *Shadow*, one time Carter agreed to play tennis with some congressmen, but after the match he simply said goodbye. He did not see the importance of sitting down with them for drinks or building relationships in this way.

Carter's measures were severely curtailed in Congress, although he did manage to create the Department of Energy with James Schlesinger as its first secretary.

In March 1979, the most serious accident in a nuclear power plant in America occurred at Three Mile Island near Middletown, Pennsylvania. Even though no deaths or injuries resulted, the incident brought about sweeping changes to regulations, planning, and operations at nuclear power plants.

Panama Canal

During the Carter presidency, a treaty was created in which the Panama Canal would be ceded back to the nation of Panama. The treaty was necessary because of Panamanian unrest toward the U.S. presence in Panama over the canal zone. To keep the canal safe, Carter deemed it necessary to negotiate this very controversial treaty that relinquished control of the canal to Panama in 2000. The treaty barely passed ratification in the Senate.

Camp David Accords

When Carter took over the presidency, Egypt and Israel had been at war for some time. The Egyptian president had made overtures for peace but talks had stalled. In 1978, President Carter invited Egyptian President Anwar Sadat and Israeli Prime Minister Menachem Begin to Camp David to help them forge a peace agreement. The Camp David Accords eventually led to a formal peace treaty in 1979. However, the fallout for Egypt was huge. The accords meant that there was no longer a united Arab front against Israel, and Anwar Sadat was later assassinated in 1981.

Iran Hostage Crisis

On November 4, 1979, the U.S. embassy in Tehran, Iran, was seized and sixty Americans were taken hostage. Iran's leader, the Ayatollah Khomeini, demanded the return of the Reza Shah to Iran to stand trial in exchange for the hostages. America did not comply and fifty-two of the hostages were held for more than a year. Carter suspended oil imports from Iran and froze all Iranian assets. Further, the UN security council called for the release of the hostages to no avail.

In 1980, Carter attempted to rescue the hostages. Ironically, three helicopters malfunctioned and the military was unable to follow through with the rescue. When Iran entered war with Iraq, the economic sanctions placed upon the country by the United States began to take a toll. The Ayatollah Khomeini finally agreed to release the hostages in exchange for the unfreezing of Iranian assets in the United States. The hostages, however, were not released until Reagan was officially president. The hostage crisis was a large part of the reason that Carter did not win reelection.

Life After the Presidency

Carter left the presidency on January 20, 1981, after losing to Ronald Reagan. He retired to Plains, Georgia. Since that time, he has been an important and influential figure in America. He became a leader of Habitat for Humanity, an organization that builds homes for needy families. Carter has also been involved in both official and personal diplomatic endeavors, including helping to forge an agreement with North Korea. In 2002, Carter was awarded the Nobel Peace Prize "for his decades of untiring effort to find peaceful solutions to international conflicts, to advance democracy and human rights, and to promote economic and social development."

40

Ronald Reagan: The Great Communicator

Born:	February 6, 1911
Died:	June 5, 2004
First Lady:	Nancy Davis Reagan
Political Party:	Republican
Presidential Term:	January 20, 1981 to January 20, 1989
Famous Quote:	"What I'd really like to do is go down in history as the President who made Americans believe in themselves again."

Timeline

1932 . . . . Graduated from Eureka College

1940 . . . . Married Jane Wyman

1942–1945 . . . . . . Served in the army during World War II

1947–1952 . . . . President of the Screen Actors Guild

1948 . . . . Divorced Jane Wyman

1952 . . . . Married Nancy Davis

1959–1960 . . . . . . President of the Screen Actors Guild

1967–1975 . . . . Governor of California

1981–1989 . . . . . . Fortieth president of the United States

Childhood and Education

Ronald Reagan was born on February 6, 1911, in Tampico, Illinois. He had a happy childhood. His father, John Edward "Jack" Reagan, was a shoe salesman. His mother, Nelle Wilson Reagan, taught her son how to read when he was five years old. Reagan worked at various jobs while growing up and attending local public schools. He then enrolled at Eureka College in Illinois where he played football and made average grades, graduating in 1932.

Marriages: Jane Wyman and Nancy Davis Reagan

Ronald Reagan was the only president to have been divorced. His first wife, Jane Wyman, was a well-known actress who starred in movies such as *The Lost Weekend* and *The Yearling*. She would later star in the television series *Falcon Crest*. The pair was married on January 26, 1940. Together, Reagan and Wyman had three children: Maureen Reagan, who died in 2001; Michael Reagan, who they adopted; and Christine Reagan, who died the day she was born in 1947. Reagan and Wyman divorced on June 28, 1948.

First Lady: Nancy Davis Reagan

Reagan's second wife was also an actress, although she was not as well known as his first wife. Nancy Davis met her husband when he was president of the Screen Actors Guild in 1951. They were married on March 4, 1952. Together, they had two children: Patti Davis and Ronald Prescott Reagan Jr.

Nancy Reagan caused controversy as first lady when she purchased new china for the White House while the country was experiencing a recession. She espoused the "Just Say No" campaign, which was aimed at helping kids say no to drugs. She was also known for using astrology throughout Reagan's time as president.

Reagan's chief of staff, Donald Regan, eventually resigned after a power struggle with Nancy over her use of astrology to influence the schedule.

**QUIRKS &
ODDITIES**

Nancy Reagan hired astrologist Joan Quigley as a confidante after Reagan was almost assassinated. Quigley used astrology to affect the president's daily schedule. She had some of the most important events of the presidency timed down to the second. When Joan's influence was revealed, she was forced to leave. The whole situation became the source of jokes across the nation.

Early Career

After graduating from Eureka College in 1932, Reagan began his career as a radio announcer and became the voice of the Chicago Cubs. In 1937, he became an actor with a seven-year contract with Warner Brothers. As such, he was given many roles and ended up making about fifty movies. Some of his most famous included *Kings Row*, *Hellcats in the Navy*, *Knute Rockne, All American*, and *Bedtime for Bonzo*.

PRESIDENTIAL

TRIVIA

Reagan played Notre Dame football player, George Gipp, in the movie *Knute Rockne, All American*. During "The Gipper's" death scene, Reagan delivered the line, "[T]ell them to go in there . . . and win just one for the Gipper." Reagan was nicknamed "the Gipper" and even referenced this line during a speech, when he told presidential nominee George H. W. Bush to "win one for the Gipper."

World War II

In 1935, Reagan had become part of the U.S. Army Reserve. He was called to active duty after the attack on Pearl Harbor. He served in the army from 1942 to 1945. He remained in Hollywood throughout the war, working for the Army Air Forces First Picture Unit. He narrated training films and rose to the level of captain before the war's end.

Burgeoning Political Career

Reagan was elected president of the Screen Actors Guild in 1947 and served until 1952, and again from 1959 to 1960. While he was president of the organization, Reagan testified before the House Un-American Activities Committee about communist influences in Hollywood. He gave names of individuals who he felt had communist ties and leanings to the FBI.

While Reagan had begun his adult life as a Democrat, by 1967 he was a Republican and won the governor's seat in California. He was reelected for a second term and served until 1975. He attempted to run for president in 1968 and 1976 but was not chosen either time by the Republican party. However, he had an extremely strong showing against incumbent Gerald Ford, setting up his nomination in 1980.

Becoming the Oldest President

Reagan was the obvious choice for the Republican nomination in 1980, having won most of the primaries leading up to the nominating convention. George Bush was chosen to run as his vice president. Reagan was opposed by incumbent President Jimmy Carter. The campaign centered on inflation, high unemployment rates, the gasoline shortage, and the Iran hostage situation.

IN THEIR OWN WORDS...

Reagan was known for his quick wit and public speaking abilities, which earned him the nickname "the Great Communicator." Here is what he had to say during his campaign against Jimmy Carter: "A recession is when your neighbor loses his job; depression is when you lose your job. Recovery is when Jimmy Carter loses his."

Reagan won with 51 percent of the popular vote. Carter only gained 41 percent of the vote. In the end, forty-four out of the fifty states went to Reagan, giving him 489 out of 538 electoral votes.

In 1984, Reagan chose to run for reelection. He ran against former Democratic vice president Walter Mondale. The economy was recovering during the campaign and Reagan was hugely popular. He ended up winning 59 percent of the popular vote and 525 out of 538 electoral votes. He carried forty-nine of the fifty states, with Mondale receiving electoral votes only from his home state of Minnesota and from Washington, D.C.

Presidential Administration

Two months after taking office, an assassination attempt was made on Reagan's life. On March 30, 1981, John Hinckley Jr. shot six rounds at Reagan. He was hit by one of the bullets, which caused a collapsed lung. His press secretary James Brady, policeman Thomas Delahanty, and secret service agent Timothy McCarthy were also seriously wounded. Hinckley claimed he did it to impress actress Jodie Foster. He was later found not guilty by reason of insanity and was committed to a mental institution. Reagan's words before going into surgery—"I forgot to duck"—were typical of his quick wit.

Reaganomics

When Reagan took over as president, the United States was experiencing double-digit inflation. To combat this, interest rates were increased to push people to begin to save more money. This led to a reduction in inflation but also to higher unemployment and a huge recession. Reagan adopted supply-side economic policies, sometimes called Reaganomics, to try and rectify the situation. This was the idea that money given to people through tax cuts would cause them to spend and invest more, in the end leading to more jobs. This idea of economic prosperity "trickling down" through society was controversial.

His vice president had previously called Reagan's ideas about economics "voodoo economics." Nonetheless, inflation did go down and so eventually did unemployment. America entered a period of prosperity but at the same time incurred a huge budget deficit.

**QUIRKS &
ODDITIES**

Reagan was widely known for his love of jelly beans. He had a huge impact on the jelly bean industry, especially the Jelly Belly Candy Company. Jelly Belly created the blueberry flavor just for his 1981 inauguration. Further, a portrait of Reagan made from 10,000 Jelly Belly jelly beans hangs in his Presidential Library in Simi Valley, California.

Terrorism and Military Action

When Reagan took over the presidency from Jimmy Carter, the United States had just come through a long period of trouble with Iran holding fifty-two hostages for more than a year. Reagan took a strong stance against terrorists, claiming that America would never negotiate. America's resolve was put to the test throughout Reagan's administration as many terrorist acts occurred. For example, in April 1983 an explosion occurred at the U.S. embassy in Beirut. In June 1985, a TWA jetliner was hijacked by Shiite Moslems with 104 Americans on board. One American was killed before the hostages were released. In April 1986, a bomb exploded in a West Berlin disco killing one American and wounding sixty people. In December 1988, Pan Am Flight 103 was blown up over Lockerbie, Scotland, killing everyone on board and many on the ground.

Reagan singled out Mu'ammar al-Qadhdhafi of Libya as the primary terrorist in the world with five countries typically harboring terrorists: Cuba, Iran, Libya, North Korea, and Nicaragua. In 1983, the United States invaded Grenada to rescue threatened Americans. They were rescued and the leftists were overthrown.

Iran-Contra Scandal

One of the major issues of Reagan's second administration was the Iran-Contra scandal, in which several individuals within his administration were implicated. In exchange for secretly selling arms to Iran, money would be given to the revolutionary Contras in Nicaragua. The hope was that by selling arms to Iran, terrorist organizations would be willing to give up hostages. This was contrary to Reagan's assertion that America would never negotiate with terrorists. The revelations of the Iran-Contra scandal resulted in one of the major scandals of the 1980s.

Glasnost

One of the most important events that occurred during Reagan's administration was the growing relationship between the United States and the Soviet Union. Reagan created a relationship with Soviet leader Mikhail Gorbachev, who instituted a new spirit of openness or "glasnost." As the 1980s progressed, countries controlled by the USSR began claiming their independence. Then on November 9, 1989, the Berlin Wall fell, marking the end of communist suppression in East Berlin. All of these events would eventually lead to the downfall of the Soviet Union during President George H. W. Bush's term in office.

Life After the Presidency

Reagan retired to his ranch after his second term in office. In 1994, Reagan announced that he had Alzheimer's disease and left public life for good. He died of pneumonia on June 5, 2004.

George Herbert Walker Bush: Bush the Elder

41

Born: June 12, 1924
First Lady: Barbara Pierce Bush
Political Party: Republican
Presidential Term: January 20, 1989 to January 20, 1993
Famous Quote: "We know what works: Freedom works. We know what's right: Freedom is right. We know how to secure a more just and prosperous life for man on Earth: through free markets, free speech, free elections, and the exercise of free will unhampered by the state."

Timeline

1942–1945.......Fought in World War II
1945...........Married Barbara Pierce
1948............Graduated from Yale
1967–1971.......Member of the U.S. House of Representatives
1971–1973.......U.S. ambassador to the United Nations
1973–1974.......Chairman of the Republican National Committee
1976–1977.......Director of the Central Intelligence Agency
1981–1989.......Vice president of the United States under President Reagan
1989–1993......Forty-first president of the United States

Childhood and Education

George Herbert Walker Bush was born on June 12, 1924, in Milton, Massachusetts. He was the son of Prescott S. Bush and Dorothy Walker Bush. His family moved to a suburb of New York City where he was raised and where his father was a successful businessman and a senator. His family was very wealthy and had numerous servants including a chauffer. Bush attended private schools including Greenwich Country Day School and the Phillips Academy.

World War II

After graduating from the Phillips Academy, Bush joined the military at the age of eighteen to fight in World War II. He was trained as a naval aviator and stationed in the Pacific. In June 1944, he had a forced water landing in which the navigator was killed and he was picked up by a submarine. In July, he helped sink a cargo ship. In September 1944, he was attacking Japanese installations when his aircraft was hit. He completed his mission and then bailed out of the plane. In the end, three of the four-man crew were killed, and Bush was again rescued by a submarine. He received the Distinguished Flying Cross for this. Bush then trained for a new torpedo squadron but when the Japanese surrendered, he was discharged from the military.

Yale University

Bush enrolled in Yale University at the end of the war. During his time at Yale he was very active—he was president of his fraternity and on the Yale baseball team.

In 1948, Bush graduated with honors with a degree in economics.

QUIRKS & ODDITIES

George H. W. Bush was a member of the secret Skull and Bones Society at Yale University. The society is limited to fifteen members each year with outgoing Seniors choosing from the juniors. President Taft's father, Alphonso, was one of the original creators of the society. Other well-known members of the society include William Howard Taft, George W. Bush, and John Kerry.

First Lady: Barbara Pierce Bush

Barbara Pierce was born on June 8, 1925. Her father was the president of the McCall Corporation and she was raised in a wealthy family. Barbara met her future husband when she was a teenager. They became engaged before Bush joined the navy to fight in World War II. While he was serving, Barbara was enrolled at Smith College. However, she dropped out of Smith at the end of 1944 and was married to Bush on January 6, 1945.

Children

The Bushes had six children, but their daughter Robin died at the age of four of leukemia. Their other children are George W. Bush, forty-third president of the United States; John F. "Jeb" Bush, governor of Florida; Neil M. Bush; Marvin P. Bush, venture capitalist; and Dorothy W. "Doro" Bush.

Life as First Lady

Barbara Bush was a well-loved and respected first lady. While she was the first lady, she tried to avoid controversy. She worked hard on many causes including AIDS and homelessness, but her true passion was promoting literacy.

IN THEIR OWN WORDS...

Barbara Bush on learning disabilities: "George Bush and I know the frustration of living with an undiagnosed or untreated learning problem, and we know the great joy and relief that comes when help is finally found. I foresee the day when no American—neither child nor adult—will ever need to be limited in learning."

She established the Barbara Bush Foundation for Family Literacy in 1989 and currently serves as its honorary chairman.

Early Career

Bush began working in the oil industry in Texas in 1948 and created a lucrative career for himself. He became active in the Republican party, winning a seat in the U.S. House of Representatives in 1966. In the House, he was appointed to the powerful House Ways and Means committee. He ran unopposed again and was reelected to his congressional seat in 1968.

Bush attempted to run for Senate in 1970 but was defeated. President Nixon then appointed Bush as U.S. ambassador to the United Nations, where he served until 1973. He was then named chairman of the Republican National Committee and served in this capacity during the Watergate Scandal and its fallout.

PRESIDENTIAL TRIVIA

Bush became the first vice president to ever serve as "acting president" when Reagan had surgery to remove polyps on his colon on July 13, 1985. Before his surgery, Reagan sent a letter to the speaker of the House handing power to Bush while he was under anesthesia. Bush was acting president for eight hours.

In 1974, after Nixon's resignation, Ford appointed Bush to be the unofficial ambassador to China. It was an unofficial position because America did not have an official embassy in China at the time. In 1976, Ford appointed him to be the director of the CIA. When Carter won the presidency, Bush was replaced in this position and went into private business for a time, including a period as an adjunct professor at Rice University.

Bush ran against Reagan in the primaries to attempt to get the Republican nomination for president in 1980. When Reagan, the more conservative of the two, won the nomination he chose Bush as his vice president.

From 1981 to 1989, he served as vice president under Reagan.

Becoming the President

Bush gained the nomination in 1988 to run for president. Notably, in Bush's acceptance speech at the Republican Nominating Convention, he made a statement that would come back to haunt him when he became president: "Read my lips: no new taxes." Bush chose Dan Quayle to run as vice president. He was opposed by Democrat Michael Dukakis. The campaign was extremely negative and centered on personal attacks instead of plans for the future. In the end, Bush won with 54 percent of the popular vote and 426 out of 537 electoral votes.

Presidential Administration

Much of George Bush's attention during the four years of his administration was focused on foreign policy. Reagan's presidency had ended with the downfall of the Soviet regime in sight. As Bush said in his inaugural address, "For in man's heart, if not in fact, the day of the dictator is over."

Deposing Noriega

In December 1989, Bush sent troops into Panama to depose General Manuel Noriega in an action code named Operation Just Cause. Noriega was heavily involved in drug trafficking. The invasion only lasted fourteen days and resulted in a decisive victory with Noriega removed from power. He was brought to the United States and sent to prison for drug and racketeering violations.

Operation Desert Storm

From 1990 to 1991, the United States led a United Nations coalition against Iraq in the First Persian Gulf War. Iraq, led by Saddam Hussein, had invaded Kuwait. At first the UN issued a resolution demanding that Iraq leave Kuwait by January 15, 1991. When this did not happen, the U.S.-led coalition moved against Iraq using precision air attacks. This action was given the name Desert Storm. When the Iraqi forces were removed from Kuwait, Bush stopped all military activity and left Hussein in power. His reasoning was, he later said, that it would have been a unilateral action against international law and beyond the stated mission.

Breakup of the Soviet Union

In 1985, while Reagan was President, Mikhail Gorbachev came to power. Over time, he introduced many new elements and democratizing forces into the Soviet Union including a sense of openness and multi-candidate elections. However, the unintended results of these and other Soviet reforms eventually led to the breakup of the Soviet Union. In July 1991, the Cold War officially ended when Bush and Gorbachev announced a partnership. By December 1991, the Soviet Union had dissolved into individual nations.

Economic Issues

Economically, Bush had boxed himself into a corner with his campaign promise not to institute new taxes. In 1985, the Gramm-Rudman-Hollings Balanced Budget and Emergency Deficit Control Act passed that required Congress to pay for tax cuts with spending cuts; if Congress or the President did not provide for spending cuts, they would automatically be made. The point of the bill was to reduce the deficit. To meet the terms of this law, Bush had to sign a bill into law that raised taxes. His failure to keep his promise was one of the key issues brought up in the 1992 election.

One other major economic issue that occurred during Bush's time in office was the Savings and Loan Scandal. Before the 1980s, savings and loans were highly regulated by the government in terms of the types of loans that they were able to give.

SCANDALS & GOSSIP

Neil Bush, President Bush's son, was the director of Silverado Banking, Savings and Loan when it crashed in 1988. For his part in the event, Neil Bush was required to pay a $50,000 fine and was banned from banking activities. The cost to taxpayers for bailing out this failed Savings and Loan was $1.3 billion.

However, during Carter's and Reagan's terms they were gradually dereg-ulated to the point where they had much more leeway in making risky loans. At the same time, they did not have to meet the same regulatory standards as other types of banks. When individuals and businesses began to default on their loans, many savings and loans had to take bankruptcy. By 1989, it was obvious that this was a crisis. President Bush signed into law a bail-out plan paid for by taxpayers that resulted in ever-increasing budget deficits; the estimated cost to taxpayers exceeded $125 billion.

Life After the Presidency

When Bush lost the 1992 election to Bill Clinton, he retired from public ser-vice. Since that time he has remained personally active. He has joined with Bill Clinton since the latter's retirement from office to raise money for victims of the tsunami that hit in Thailand (2004) and Hurricane Katrina (2005).

42

William Jefferson "Bill" Clinton: The Comeback Kid

Born: August 19, 1946

First Lady: Hilary Rodham Clinton

Political Party: Democratic

Presidential Term: January 20, 1993 to January 20, 2001

Famous Quote: "There is nothing wrong in America that can't be fixed with what is right in America."

Timeline

1968 . . . . Graduated from Georgetown University

1973 . . . . Graduated from Yale Law School

1975 . . . . Married Hillary Rodham

1976 . . . . Elected Arkansas attorney general

1979–1981 . . . . . . Governor of Arkansas

1983–1992 . . . . . . Governor of Arkansas

1993–2001 . . . . . . Forty-second president of the United States

Childhood and Education

William Jefferson Blythe III was born on August 19, 1946, in Hope, Arkansas. His father was a traveling salesman who died in a car accident three months before William was born. His mother, Virginia Dell Cassidy, remarried to Roger Clinton when her son was four years old. The future president took the Clinton name in high school. He excelled in school and became an accomplished saxophonist. Clinton decided to become a politician after an inspiring visit to the Kennedy White House as a Boys Nation delegate.

Clinton distinguished himself at Georgetown University where he earned his Bachelor's degree in foreign service. He received a Rhodes Scholarship to attend Oxford University and then went to Yale Law School where he graduated in 1973.

First Lady: Hillary Rodham Clinton

Hillary Rodham was born on October 26, 1947, in Chicago, Illinois. She was an excellent student and graduated valedictorian of her class at Wellesley College in 1969 with a degree in political science. She then went to Yale Law School and graduated in 1973. She and Clinton met at Yale Law School, and they both ended up teaching there while they were dating. They married on October 11, 1975. Together, the Clintons have one daughter, Chelsea.

Powerful First Lady

Hillary Clinton was an extremely powerful first lady and was heavily involved in directing policy during her husband's time in office. She was appointed in 1993 to head the Task Force on National Health Care Reform. However, the goal for nationalized health insurance never became reality as it met heavy resistance in Congress.

Throughout her time as first lady, she spoke out on women's and children's issues both at home and on the world stage. She was a driving force for important legislation like the Adoption and Safe Families Act, which dealt with the adoption of foster children. She was also responsible for hosting numerous events and refurbishing the Blue Room at the White House.

Senator Clinton

After Clinton retired from the presidency, Hillary decided to go into politics on her own merits. She successfully campaigned for and won a U.S. Senate seat, becoming the junior senator from New York. She has been very active in the Senate and has announced her intent to run for the presidency in 2008.

Early Career

In 1974, while Clinton was a first-year law professor at the University of Arkansas, he ran for the House of Representatives. He was defeated but remained undaunted. In 1976, he ran unopposed for attorney general of Arkansas. By 1978 he had become the youngest governor of Arkansas ever elected. He lost the governor's seat in the 1980 election but returned to office in 1982. Throughout the 1980s he was able to establish himself as a New Democrat who could appeal to both Republicans and Democrats.

Nomination and Elections

In 1992, William Jefferson Clinton was nominated by the Democratic party to run for president. President Bush seemed invincible with the successful completion of the First Persian Gulf War. However, the country was headed into a recession and as Clinton's top political strategist James Carville kept pointing out to staffers and the press, "It's the Economy, Stupid." Clinton ran on a campaign that emphasized job creation and played to the idea that he was more in touch with the common people than his opponent, the incumbent George H. W. Bush. His bid for the presidency was helped by the strong showing for third party candidate Ross Perot who was able to win 18.9 percent of the vote, mostly from the conservative and moderate base. Bill Clinton ended up winning 43 percent of the popular vote and 370 out of 538 electoral votes.

In 1996, when Clinton won reelection, he became the first Democrat to have done so since Franklin Roosevelt. He ran against Republican Bob Dole and Reform party candidate Ross Perot. Dole had heavy competition in the primary season from other Republicans and therefore got a late start campaigning against Clinton. Further, the economy was doing well and Clinton's popularity numbers were high. Clinton ended up winning 49.2 percent of the vote against Dole's 40.7 percent. Clinton received 379 out of 538 electoral votes.

Presidential Administration

Healthcare was an important issue from the time Clinton took office. One of his first significant actions was the passage of the Family and Medical Leave Act in 1993. This piece of legislation required large employers to give employees time off for illnesses or pregnancy. However, a huge defeat for Clinton was the failure of his and Hillary Clinton's plan for a nationalized health insurance program that would provide universal coverage. Many groups came out against the plan including the American Medical Association. In the end, the plan was soundly defeated in Congress.

SCANDALS & GOSSIP

A public relations nightmare during Clinton's first administration was the famous $200 haircut on the tarmac at the Los Angeles Airport that supposedly caused major delays for arriving and departing planes. However, this story was not exactly correct—while Clinton did receive a haircut on Air Force One, the stories about hours of delays proved to be unfounded.

Economically, Bill Clinton's time in office was marked by a unique period of prosperity. The stock market rose dramatically. Further, the federal government was able to balance the budget during his presidency by raising taxes and by cutting government spending. This economic prosperity helped add to Clinton's popularity as president.

NAFTA and the WTO

Clinton was a strong believer in promoting free trade, which was counter to the platforms of many members of his party, including labor unions. In 1993, he strongly supported the North American Free Trade Agreement (NAFTA) that would eventually allow for unrestricted trade between Canada, the United States, and Mexico.

Also ratified during Clinton's first term in office was a trade agreement that created the World Trade Organization (WTO). The WTO creates rules and standards for global trading and settles disputes between members of which there are currently 149. However, there are many who complain that the WTO, which espouses free trade, only benefits the wealthy. When the organization meets it draws a great deal of protest.

Terrorist Attacks: The World Trade Center and Oklahoma City

On February 26, 1993, a bomb exploded in the parking garage of the World Trade Center's north tower. The bomb killed six people and injured more than 1,000 others. Ramzi Yousef was the mastermind behind the bombing. He hoped that it would bring down both towers and predicted that they would be brought down at some point in the future. In the end, he was sentenced to life in prison without the possibility of parole. Nine other militant Islamic conspirators were convicted and sentenced to jail terms.

On April 19, 1995, a truck loaded with 5,000 pounds of explosives blew up outside of the Alfred P. Murrah federal building in Oklahoma City. The bomb killed 168 people including nineteen children at an on-site childcare facility. More than 800 people were injured and more than 300 buildings in the area were damaged or destroyed.

IN THEIR OWN WORDS...

Excerpt from Clinton's Oklahoma City Bombing memorial address: "Let us teach our children that the God of comfort is also the God of righteousness. . . . Justice will prevail. Let us let our own children know that we will stand against the forces of fear. When there is talk of hatred, let us stand up and talk against it."

Timothy McVeigh and Terry Nichols were convicted of the terrorist act. McVeigh was sentenced to death and executed in 2001. Nichols was sentenced to life in prison. Both men belonged to or sympathized with antigovernment militia groups.

Monica Lewinsky and Impeachment

Clinton's second term in office was marked by controversy. The ongoing Whitewater investigation, headed by Kenneth Starr, was looking into possible improprieties related to a land deal in which the Clintons profited while he was governor of Arkansas. The actual focus of the investigation was unable to prove any wrongdoing related to Whitewater, but it did lead to the uncovering of the relationship he had with White House staffer Monica Lewinsky. Clinton was sued while in office by Paula Jones who claimed that he had sexually harassed her while he was governor of Arkansas. While giving a deposition in the case, Clinton was asked about and denied having had sexual relations with Monica Lewinsky. However, he later recanted when it was revealed that she had evidence of their relationship. He admitted to an "improper physical relationship" with her. In the end, he had to pay a fine and was disbarred temporarily in the state of Arkansas. More importantly, however, the House of Representatives voted to impeach Clinton in 1998 based on perjury under oath and obstruction of justice. The voting took place largely along party lines and Clinton joined Andrew Johnson as the only other president to be impeached. The Senate, however, did not vote to remove him from office.

Foreign Affairs

Clinton attempted to carve out the future focus of U.S. Foreign policy during his two terms in office. The United States, as the only remaining superpower after the fall of the Soviet Union, needed to determine its role in resolving conflicts around the world. One example of America finding its place occurred when Bosnia declared independence from Yugoslavia and a civil war erupted. Bosnian Serbs wanted to remain part of Yugoslavia and attacked cities with large populations of Bosnian Muslims and Croats. Clinton at first wanted to help in the fight against the Serbs but eventually helped forge the peace between the two groups.

However, in 1998 the Serbs moved into Kosovo, which was mostly Muslim and ethnic Albanian. There were many claims of ethnic cleansing by the Serbs that resulted in the U.S.-led NATO troops bombing key Serbian targets. The attacks ended when the Serbs surrendered. The United States, under the direction of Clinton, emerged onto the world stage as interested in peacekeeping around the world, even if U.S. interests were not directly threatened.

Life After the Presidency

Upon leaving office, President Clinton entered the public speaking circuit, including delivering addresses to international audiences where he discusses contemporary politics.

SCANDALS & GOSSIP

Hours before leaving office, Clinton pardoned 140 people. Of these, three of the more controversial pardons were: fugitive Marc Rich, wanted for tax evasion and whose former wife was a Clinton family friend and campaign contributor; Roger Clinton, the president's half-brother, who had served time for drug charges; and Susan McDougal, who had served her sentence but refused to testify about Clinton's role in the Whitewater scandal.

He wrote his autobiography, *My Life*, in 2004. Clinton has developed a friendship with former rival President George H. W. Bush that has led to their collaboration on several humanitarian endeavors. Most visibly, the pair has led national campaigns to raise money for victims of the 2004 tsunami in Indonesia and for Hurricane Katrina, which devastated the Gulf Coast in 2005.

George W. Bush: Dubya

Born:	July 6, 1946
First Lady:	Laura Welch Bush
Political Party:	Republican
Presidential Term:	January 20, 2001 to the present
Famous Quote:	"Our Nation's founding commitment is still our deepest commitment: In our world, and here at home, we will extend the frontiers of freedom."

Timeline

1968 . . . . Graduated from Yale University
1968–1974 . . . . . . Served in the Texas Air National Guard
1975 . . . . Graduated from Harvard Business School
1977 . . . . Married Laura Welch
1995–2000 . . . . . . Governor of Texas
2001– . . . . Forty-third president of the United States

Childhood and Education

George W. Bush was born on July 6, 1946, in New Haven, Connecticut. He was the oldest of six children born to George H. W. Bush and Barbara Pierce Bush. Bush grew up in Texas from the age of two. His family was quite prestigious and wealthy and had a tradition of politics. His grandfather, Prescott Bush, had been a U.S. senator from Connecticut and his father served as the nation's forty-first president. Bush's brother John Ellis "Jeb" Bush is also involved in politics and served as governor of Florida from 1999 until 2007.

Bush attended Phillips Academy in Massachusetts and then went on to Yale University. An average student, he graduated with a degree in history in 1968. After serving in the National Guard, he went to Harvard Business School and earned his MBA in 1975.

First Lady: Laura Welch Bush

Laura Welch was born on November 4, 1946, in Midland, Texas. She was the only child of Harold Bruce Welch and Jenna Louise Hawkins. She became an elementary school teacher before earning a master's in library sciences in 1973 and then was a librarian until 1977. Laura met George W. Bush at a picnic in 1977. They had a very short courtship that led to their marriage on November 5, 1977. Together they have twin daughters, Jenna and Barbara.

Laura has spent her time as first lady championing education issues. Like her mother-in-law, Barbara Bush, she has placed literacy efforts at the cornerstone of her educational agenda. She has taken a less visible role in terms of affecting policy. However, she was the first president's wife to give the weekly president's address when she spoke about women in Afghanistan.

Early Career

After graduating from Yale University, Bush served in the Texas Air National Guard. He asked to be discharged six months early from his six-year tour of duty to go to Harvard Business School.

Bush has been criticized, especially during the 2004 campaign, for his service in the Texas Air National Guard. Critics charge that he received special consideration to get into the guard, thereby avoiding the draft during the Vietnam War. Further, there are some questions concerning his irregular attendance without any repercussions.

After getting his MBA, he moved back to Texas and began working in the oil industry there. He helped his father campaign for the presidency in 1988. Then, in 1989, he purchased part of the Texas Rangers baseball team and served as managing general partner.

From 1995 until 2000, Bush served as the governor of Texas. As governor he was known for education reform and implementing a huge statewide tax cut. He also gave government support to faith-based organizations that provided social programs throughout the state.

Nomination and Elections

The 2000 election was marked by a great deal of controversy. Bush overwhelmingly won the Republican nomination for president and chose Dick Cheney as his running mate. He ran against the outgoing vice president, Al Gore. The popular vote was won by Gore by 543,816 votes. However, the electoral vote was won by Bush-Cheney by five votes. The last time the president had won the electoral vote without winning the popular vote was in 1888.

Recount in Florida

The outcome of the vote centered on the state of Florida. On election night, several media outlets declared Gore the winner of Florida based upon exit polling. However, as the tallies continued to come in it appeared Bush won the state by a little more than 1,000 votes. In fact, he would go on to squeak out a win by only 537 votes. The tightness of the race forced a manual recount and many legal battles in the state. Eventually, the Supreme Court of the United States heard the case *Bush v. Gore* and ruled in favor of the election night results thereby halting the recounting efforts. The court decided that inconsistent vote-counting standards and the lack of a single judicial figure overseeing the process created an inequitable process which violated the Equal Protection Clause of the U.S. Constitution. The resolution of this election left many Democrats quite bitter about the outcome and they vowed to run a more vigorous campaign in 2004.

2004 Election

The Republican party nominated Bush for reelection against the Democratic challenger Senator John Kerry. The election centered on how each would deal with terrorism and the war in Iraq. Each candidate's military record was brought into question. George Bush's service in the National Guard was brought up again, but this time the issue was actually two-fold. First, there was the question of whether he gained preferential treatment to enter the National Guard, thus avoiding the draft and the Vietnam War. Also, there were questions as to whether he was given preferential treatment in fulfilling his service commitment to the guard. He had irregular attendance at the end with no apparent punishment and a six-month early dismissal to attend Harvard. John Kerry's military service was questioned because of his actions upon returning from Vietnam, when he became an outspoken critic of the war. In the end, Bush won a little more than 50 percent of the popular vote and 286 out of 538 electoral votes.

Presidential Administration

Bush took office in March 2001. His first months in office have often been characterized as lacking in direction, but this all changed on September 11, 2001. The Bush presidency gained a focus that before was lacking—the fight against terrorism. The whole world was focused on New York City and the Pentagon with the attacks by al-Qaeda operatives that resulted in the deaths of more than 2,900 people. This event changed Bush's presidency forever. His popularity skyrocketed after the tragedy. He ordered the invasion of Afghanistan and the overthrow of the Taliban, which had been harboring al-Qaeda training camps.

As part of the fight against terrorism, Bush created a new cabinet position and department: the Department of Homeland Security. The first secretary of homeland security was Tom Ridge. The department has three primary missions according to its own Web site: "Prevent terrorist attacks within the United States, reduce America's vulnerability to terrorism, and minimize the damage from potential attacks and natural disasters."

War in Iraq

Bush then moved to declare war on Saddam Hussein and Iraq on the premise that they were hiding weapons of mass destruction. When it was obvious that the UN would not agree to a combined effort against Iraq, America went to war with a coalition of twenty countries to enforce UN disarmament resolutions.

Bush in his 2002 State of the Union Address: "Iraq continues to flaunt its hostility toward America and to support terror. The Iraqi regime has plotted to develop anthrax, and nerve gas, and nuclear weapons for over a decade. . . . States like these, and their terrorist allies, constitute an axis of evil, arming to threaten the peace of the world."

It was later determined that, although Hussein was planning to purchase weapons of mass destruction after UN sanctions were lifted, he was not stockpiling them within the country. The lack of weapons of mass destruction has taken a toll on Bush's popularity. However, the initial military campaign in Iraq was quite successful. By implementing the strategy of "shock and awe," U.S. forces took Baghdad and occupied Iraq in a very short period of time. Hussein was captured in 2003. He was tried and convicted in November 2006 by Iraq's High Tribunal for crimes against humanity. He was executed by hanging on December 30, 2006. While in 2005 a referendum was held to approve a new Iraqi constitution and there was a huge voter turnout, fighting in Iraq has escalated and there is concern that the country is already in a state of civil war.

No Child Left Behind

One of Bush's major policy concerns first as governor of Texas and then as president has been education. In 2001, Bush joined forces with Democrat Ted Kennedy to create the No Child Left Behind Act, which was meant to improve public schools.

Its main goals are to make schools more accountable and create more choices for parents.

PRESIDENTIAL TRIVIA

President Bush is an avid baseball fan, as evidenced by his part-ownership of the Texas Rangers. In fact, Bush was the first president to hold a Little League game at the White House. In 2001, thirty-two little leaguers played one inning on the south lawn. He was also the first president to attend a Little League playoff game.

Space Race

On January 14, 2004, the Space Shuttle Columbia exploded, killing all on board. After this, Bush announced a new vision for NASA. The focus would move from the space shuttle to returning to the moon by 2018 and creating a new manned space vehicle. The point of returning to the moon is to enable deeper exploration into space.

As a sitting president, it is hard to assess Bush's future significance. Certainly, actions taken after September 11, along with America's involvement with the war in Iraq, will be scrutinized for years to come. Only time will tell how future historians will rank Bush as president.

Appendix A

Additional Resources

About.com American History

✐ *americanhistory.about.com*

This site, run by author Martin Kelly, provides extensive information on each of the presidents and on American history in general.

White House

✐ *www.whitehouse.gov*

The official White House Web site has biographical sketches of each of the presidents and first ladies.

AmericanPresident.org

✐ *www.americanpresident.org*

AmericanPresident.org is a comprehensive resource on the history of the presidency, created by the Miller Center of Public Affairs at the University of Virginia.

Ackerman, Kenneth D. *Dark Horse: The Surprise Election and Political Murder of President James A. Garfield.* New York: Carroll & Graf, 2003.

Ambrose, Stephen E. *Eisenhower.* New York: Touchstone, 1990.

Ammon, Harry. *James Monroe: The Quest for National Identity.* New York: McGraw-Hill, 1971.

Bauer, K. Jack. *Zachary Taylor: Soldier, Planter, Statesman of the Old Southwest.* Baton Rouge: Louisiana State University Press, 1985.

Black, Conrad. *Franklin Delano Roosevelt: Champion of Freedom.* New York: PublicAffairs, 2003.

Boller, Paul F. *Presidential Anecdotes.* New York: Oxford University Press, 1996.

———. *Presidential Wives: An Anecdotal History.* New York: Oxford University Press, 1998.

Bourne, Peter G. *Jimmy Carter: A Comprehensive Biography from Plains to Post-Presidency.* New York: Scribner, 1997.

Brodsky, Alyn. *Grover Cleveland: A Study in Character.* New York: St. Martin's, 2000.

Bush, George. *All the Best, George Bush: My Life in Letters and Other Writings.* New York: Scribner, 1999.

Calhoun, Charles W., and Arthur M. Schlesinger. *Benjamin Harrison.* New York: Times Books, 2005.

Campbell, Colin, and Bert A. Rockman. *The George W. Bush Presidency: Appraisals and Prospects.* Washington, D.C.: CQ Press, 2003.

Cannon, James. *Time and Chance: Gerald Ford's Appointment with History.* Ann Arbor: University of Michigan Press, 1998.

Clements, Kendrick A. *Woodrow Wilson: World Statesman.* Chicago: Ivan R. Dee, 1999.

Clinton, Bill. *My Life.* New York: Knopf, 2004.

Crapol, Edward P. *John Tyler: The Accidental President.* Chapel Hill: University of North Carolina Press, 2006.

Dallek, Robert. *An Unfinished Life: John F. Kennedy, 1917–1963.* New York: Little, Brown, 2003.

———. *Lyndon B. Johnson: Portrait of a President.* New York: Oxford University Press, 2004.

Degrario, William A. *The Complete Book of U.S. Presidents.* New York: Barricade Books, 2001.

Donald, David H. *Lincoln.* New York: Touchstone, 1995.

D'Souza, Dinesh. *Ronald Reagan: How an Ordinary Man Became an Extraordinary Leader.* New York: Touchstone, 1997.

Haynes, Sam W. *James K. Polk and the Expansionist Impulse.* White Plains, N.Y.: Longman, 2001.

Hoogenboom, Ari. *Rutherford B. Hayes: Warrior and President.* Lawrence: University Press of Kansas, 1995.

Johnson, Paul. *George Washington: The Founding Father.* New York: HarperCollins, 2005.

Klein, Philip S. *President James Buchanan: A Biography.* Newtown, Conn.: American Political Biography Press, 1995.

Loewen, James W. *Lies My Teacher Told Me: Everything Your American History Textbook Got Wrong.* New York: Touchstone, 1995.

McCullough, David. *Truman.* New York: Simon & Schuster, 1992.

———. *John Adams.* New York: Touchstone, 2001.

Morgan, H. Wayne. *William McKinley and His America.* Kent, Ohio: Kent State University Press, 2004.

Morris, Edmund. *Theodore Rex.* New York: Modern Library, 2002.

Nagel, Paul C. *John Quincy Adams: A Public Life, a Private Life.* Cambridge, Mass.: Harvard University Press, 1999.

Nash, George H. *The Life of Herbert Hoover, Vols. 1 and 2.* New York: W. W. Norton, 1983.

Niven, John, and Katherine Speirs. *Martin Van Buren: The Romantic Age of American Politics.* Newtown, Conn.: American Political Biography Press, 2000.

Peterson, Merrill D. *Thomas Jefferson and the New Nation: A Biography.* New York: Oxford University Press, 1970.

Peterson, Norma Lois. *Presidencies of William Henry Harrison and John Tyler.* Lawrence: University Press of Kansas, 1989.

Rakove, Jack. *James Madison and the Creation of the American Republic*. White Plains, N.Y.: Longman, 2006.

Rayback, Robert J. *Millard Fillmore: Biography of a President*. Newtown, Conn.: American Political Biography Press, 1998.

Reeves, Richard. *President Nixon: Alone in the White House*. New York: Simon & Schuster, 2002.

Reeves, Thomas C. *Gentleman Boss: The Life of Chester Alan Arthur*. Newtown, Conn.: American Political Biography Press, 1991.

Remini, Robert V. *The Life of Andrew Jackson*. New York: Perennial Classics, 2001.

Russell, Francis. *The Shadow of Blooming Grove: Warren G. Harding in His Times*. New York: McGraw-Hill, 1968.

Severn, William. *William Howard Taft, the President Who Became Chief Justice*. New York: Random House, 1970.

Smith, Jean Edward. *Grant*. New York: Touchstone, 2001.

Sobel, Robert. *Coolidge: An American Enigma*. Washington, D.C.: Regnery, 2000.

Trefousse, Hans L. *Andrew Johnson: A Biography*. New York: W. W. Norton, 1989.

Truman, Margaret. *First Ladies: An Intimate Group Portrait of White House Wives*. New York: Ballantine Books, 1995.

Wallner, Peter A. *Franklin Pierce: New Hampshire's Favorite Son*. Concord, N.H.: Plaidswede, 2004.

Wead, Doug. *All the Presidents' Children: Triumph and Tragedy in the Lives of America's First Families*. New York: Atria Books, 2003.

———. *The Raising of a President: The Mothers and Fathers of Our Nation's Leaders*. New York: Atria Books, 2005.

Appendix B

Presidents and Vice Presidents of the United States

President	Vice President	Political Party	Term
George Washington	John Adams	No Party Designation	1789–1797
John Adams	Thomas Jefferson	Federalist	1797–1801
Thomas Jefferson	Aaron Burr	Democratic-Republican	1801–1805
Thomas Jefferson	George Clinton	Democratic-Republican	1805–1809
James Madison	George Clinton	Democratic-Republican	1809–1813
James Madison	Elbridge Gerry	Democratic-Republican	1813–1817
James Monroe	Daniel B. Tompkins	Democratic-Republican	1817–1825
John Quincy Adams	John C. Calhoun	Democratic-Republican	1825–1829
Andrew Jackson	John C. Calhoun	Democrat	1829–1833
Andrew Jackson	Martin Van Buren	Democrat	1833–1837
Martin Van Buren	Richard M. Johnson	Democrat	1837–1841
William Henry Harrison	John Tyler	Whig	1841
John Tyler	None	Whig	1841–1845
James K. Polk	George M. Dallas	Democrat	1845–1849
Zachary Taylor	Millard Fillmore	Whig	1849–1850
Millard Fillmore	None	Whig	1850–1853
Franklin Pierce	William R. King	Democrat	1853–1857
James Buchanan	John C. Breckinridge	Democrat	1857–1861
Abraham Lincoln	Hannibal Hamlin	Republican	1861–1865
Abraham Lincoln	Andrew Johnson	National Union	1865
Andrew Johnson	None	National Union	1865–1869
Ulysses S. Grant	Schuyler Colfax	Republican	1869–1873
Ulysses S. Grant	Henry Wilson	Republican	1873–1877
Rutherford B. Hayes	William A. Wheeler	Republican	1877–1881
James A. Garfield	Chester A. Arthur	Republican	1881
Chester A. Arthur	None	Republican	1881–1885
Grover Cleveland	Thomas Hendricks	Democrat	1885–1889
Benjamin Harrison	Levi Morton	Republican	1889–1893

President	Vice President	Political Party	Term
Grover Cleveland	Adlai Stevenson	Republican	1893–1897
William McKinley	Garret A. Hobart	Republican	1897–1901
Theodore Roosevelt	None	Republican	1901–1905
Theodore Roosevelt	Charles Fairbanks	Republican	1905–1909
William Howard Taft	James S. Sherman	Republican	1909–1913
Woodrow Wilson	Thomas R. Marshall	Democrat	1913–1921
Warren G. Harding	Calvin Coolidge	Republican	1921–1923
Calvin Coolidge	None	Republican	1923–1925
Calvin Coolidge	Charles G. Dawes	Republican	1925–1929
Herbert Hoover	Charles Curtis	Republican	1929–1933
Franklin D. Roosevelt	John Nance Garner	Democrat	1933–1941
Franklin D. Roosevelt	Henry Wallace	Democrat	1941–1945
Franklin D. Roosevelt	Harry S. Truman	Democrat	1945
Harry S. Truman	None	Democrat	1945–1949
Harry S. Truman	Alben Barkley	Democrat	1949–1953
Dwight D. Eisenhower	Richard Nixon	Republican	1953–1961
John F. Kennedy	Lyndon B. Johnson	Democrat	1961–1963
Lyndon B. Johnson	None	Democrat	1963–1965
Lyndon B. Johnson	Hubert Humphrey	Democrat	1965–1969
Richard Nixon	Spiro Agnew	Republican	1969–1973
Richard Nixon	Gerald Ford	Republican	1973–1974
Gerald Ford	Nelson Rockefeller	Republican	1974–1977
James Earl Carter	Walter Mondale	Democrat	1977–1981
Ronald Reagan	George H. W. Bush	Republican	1981–1989
George H. W. Bush	J. Danforth Quayle	Republican	1989–1993
William Clinton	Albert Gore Jr.	Democrat	1993–2001
George W. Bush	Richard Cheney	Republican	2001–

Index

Note: Page references in **bold** indicate fact summaries and timelines.

The EVERYTHING Series!

BUSINESS & PERSONAL FINANCE

Everything® Accounting Book
Everything® Budgeting Book
Everything® Business Planning Book
Everything® Coaching and Mentoring Book
Everything® Fundraising Book
Everything® Get Out of Debt Book
Everything® Grant Writing Book
Everything® Guide to Personal Finance for Single Mothers
Everything® Home-Based Business Book, 2nd Ed.
Everything® Homebuying Book, 2nd Ed.
Everything® Homeselling Book, 2nd Ed.
Everything® Improve Your Credit Book
Everything® Investing Book, 2nd Ed.
Everything® Landlording Book
Everything® Leadership Book
Everything® Managing People Book, 2nd Ed.
Everything® Negotiating Book
Everything® Online Auctions Book
Everything® Online Business Book
Everything® Personal Finance Book
Everything® Personal Finance in Your 20s and 30s Book
Everything® Project Management Book
Everything® Real Estate Investing Book
Everything® Retirement Planning Book
Everything® Robert's Rules Book, $7.95
Everything® Selling Book
Everything® Start Your Own Business Book, 2nd Ed.
Everything® Wills & Estate Planning Book

COOKING

Everything® Barbecue Cookbook
Everything® Bartender's Book, $9.95
Everything® Cheese Book
Everything® Chinese Cookbook
Everything® Classic Recipes Book
Everything® Cocktail Parties and Drinks Book
Everything® College Cookbook
Everything® Cooking for Baby and Toddler Book
Everything® Cooking for Two Cookbook
Everything® Diabetes Cookbook
Everything® Easy Gourmet Cookbook
Everything® Fondue Cookbook
Everything® Fondue Party Book
Everything® Gluten-Free Cookbook
Everything® Glycemic Index Cookbook
Everything® Grilling Cookbook

Everything® Healthy Meals in Minutes Cookbook
Everything® Holiday Cookbook
Everything® Indian Cookbook
Everything® Italian Cookbook
Everything® Low-Carb Cookbook
Everything® Low-Fat High-Flavor Cookbook
Everything® Low-Salt Cookbook
Everything® Meals for a Month Cookbook
Everything® Mediterranean Cookbook
Everything® Mexican Cookbook
Everything® No Trans Fat Cookbook
Everything® One-Pot Cookbook
Everything® Pizza Cookbook
Everything® Quick and Easy 30-Minute, 5-Ingredient Cookbook
Everything® Quick Meals Cookbook
Everything® Slow Cooker Cookbook
Everything® Slow Cooking for a Crowd Cookbook
Everything® Soup Cookbook
Everything® Stir-Fry Cookbook
Everything® Tex-Mex Cookbook
Everything® Thai Cookbook
Everything® Vegetarian Cookbook
Everything® Wild Game Cookbook
Everything® Wine Book, 2nd Ed.

GAMES

Everything® 15-Minute Sudoku Book, $9.95
Everything® 30-Minute Sudoku Book, $9.95
Everything® Blackjack Strategy Book
Everything® Brain Strain Book, $9.95
Everything® Bridge Book
Everything® Card Games Book
Everything® Card Tricks Book, $9.95
Everything® Casino Gambling Book, 2nd Ed.
Everything® Chess Basics Book
Everything® Craps Strategy Book
Everything® Crossword and Puzzle Book
Everything® Crossword Challenge Book
Everything® Crosswords for the Beach Book, $9.95
Everything® Cryptograms Book, $9.95
Everything® Easy Crosswords Book
Everything® Easy Kakuro Book, $9.95
Everything® Easy Large Print Crosswords Book
Everything® Games Book, 2nd Ed.
Everything® Giant Sudoku Book, $9.95
Everything® Kakuro Challenge Book, $9.95
Everything® Large-Print Crossword Challenge Book

Everything® Large-Print Crosswords Book
Everything® Lateral Thinking Puzzles Book, $9.95
Everything® Mazes Book
Everything® Movie Crosswords Book, $9.95
Everything® Online Poker Book, $12.95
Everything® Pencil Puzzles Book, $9.95
Everything® Poker Strategy Book
Everything® Pool & Billiards Book
Everything® Sports Crosswords Book, $9.95
Everything® Test Your IQ Book, $9.95
Everything® Texas Hold 'Em Book, $9.95
Everything® Travel Crosswords Book, $9.95
Everything® Word Games Challenge Book
Everything® Word Scramble Book
Everything® Word Search Book

HEALTH

Everything® Alzheimer's Book
Everything® Diabetes Book
Everything® Health Guide to Adult Bipolar Disorder
Everything® Health Guide to Controlling Anxiety
Everything® Health Guide to Fibromyalgia
Everything® Health Guide to Postpartum Care
Everything® Health Guide to Thyroid Disease
Everything® Hypnosis Book
Everything® Low Cholesterol Book
Everything® Massage Book
Everything® Menopause Book
Everything® Nutrition Book
Everything® Reflexology Book
Everything® Stress Management Book

HISTORY

Everything® American Government Book
Everything® American History Book, 2nd Ed.
Everything® Civil War Book
Everything® Freemasons Book
Everything® Irish History & Heritage Book
Everything® Middle East Book

HOBBIES

Everything® Candlemaking Book
Everything® Cartooning Book
Everything® Coin Collecting Book
Everything® Drawing Book
Everything® Family Tree Book, 2nd Ed.
Everything® Knitting Book
Everything® Knots Book
Everything® Photography Book

Everything® Quilting Book
Everything® Scrapbooking Book
Everything® Sewing Book
Everything® Soapmaking Book, 2nd Ed.
Everything® Woodworking Book

HOME IMPROVEMENT

Everything® Feng Shui Book
Everything® Feng Shui Decluttering Book, $9.95
Everything® Fix-It Book
Everything® Home Decorating Book
Everything® Home Storage Solutions Book
Everything® Homebuilding Book
Everything® Organize Your Home Book

KIDS' BOOKS

All titles are $7.95
Everything® Kids' Animal Puzzle & Activity Book
Everything® Kids' Baseball Book, 4th Ed.
Everything® Kids' Bible Trivia Book
Everything® Kids' Bugs Book
Everything® Kids' Cars and Trucks Puzzle
  & Activity Book
Everything® Kids' Christmas Puzzle
  & Activity Book
Everything® Kids' Cookbook
Everything® Kids' Crazy Puzzles Book
Everything® Kids' Dinosaurs Book
Everything® Kids' First Spanish Puzzle and
  Activity Book
Everything® Kids' Gross Cookbook
Everything® Kids' Gross Hidden Pictures Book
Everything® Kids' Gross Jokes Book
Everything® Kids' Gross Mazes Book
Everything® Kids' Gross Puzzle and
  Activity Book
Everything® Kids' Halloween Puzzle
  & Activity Book
Everything® Kids' Hidden Pictures Book
Everything® Kids' Horses Book
Everything® Kids' Joke Book
Everything® Kids' Knock Knock Book
Everything® Kids' Learning Spanish Book
Everything® Kids' Math Puzzles Book
Everything® Kids' Mazes Book
Everything® Kids' Money Book
Everything® Kids' Nature Book
Everything® Kids' Pirates Puzzle and Activity Book
Everything® Kids' Presidents Book
Everything® Kids' Princess Puzzle and Activity Book
Everything® Kids' Puzzle Book
Everything® Kids' Riddles & Brain Teasers Book
Everything® Kids' Science Experiments Book
Everything® Kids' Sharks Book
Everything® Kids' Soccer Book
Everything® Kids' States Book
Everything® Kids' Travel Activity Book

KIDS' STORY BOOKS

Everything® Fairy Tales Book

LANGUAGE

Everything® Conversational Japanese Book with
  CD, $19.95
Everything® French Grammar Book
Everything® French Phrase Book, $9.95
Everything® French Verb Book, $9.95
Everything® German Practice Book with CD,
  $19.95
Everything® Inglés Book
**Everything® Intermediate Spanish Book with
  CD, $19.95**
**Everything® Learning Brazilian Portuguese
  Book with CD, $19.95**
Everything® Learning French Book
Everything® Learning German Book
Everything® Learning Italian Book
Everything® Learning Latin Book
**Everything® Learning Spanish Book with
  CD, 2nd Edition, $19.95**
Everything® Russian Practice Book with CD, $19.95
Everything® Sign Language Book
Everything® Spanish Grammar Book
Everything® Spanish Phrase Book, $9.95
Everything® Spanish Practice Book
  with CD, $19.95
Everything® Spanish Verb Book, $9.95
Everything® Speaking Mandarin Chinese Book
  with CD, $19.95

MUSIC

Everything® Drums Book with CD, $19.95
**Everything® Guitar Book with CD, 2nd
  Edition, $19.95**
Everything® Guitar Chords Book with CD, $19.95
Everything® Home Recording Book
Everything® Music Theory Book with CD, $19.95
Everything® Reading Music Book with CD, $19.95
Everything® Rock & Blues Guitar Book
  with CD, $19.95
**Everything® Rock and Blues Piano Book
  with CD, $19.95**
Everything® Songwriting Book

NEW AGE

Everything® Astrology Book, 2nd Ed.
Everything® Birthday Personology Book
Everything® Dreams Book, 2nd Ed.
Everything® Love Signs Book, $9.95
Everything® Numerology Book
Everything® Paganism Book
Everything® Palmistry Book
Everything® Psychic Book
Everything® Reiki Book

Everything® Sex Signs Book, $9.95
Everything® Tarot Book, 2nd Ed.
Everything® Toltec Wisdom Book
Everything® Wicca and Witchcraft Book

PARENTING

Everything® Baby Names Book, 2nd Ed.
Everything® Baby Shower Book
Everything® Baby's First Year Book
Everything® Birthing Book
Everything® Breastfeeding Book
Everything® Father-to-Be Book
Everything® Father's First Year Book
Everything® Get Ready for Baby Book
Everything® Get Your Baby to Sleep Book, $9.95
Everything® Getting Pregnant Book
Everything® Guide to Raising a One-Year-Old
Everything® Guide to Raising a Two-Year-Old
Everything® Homeschooling Book
Everything® Mother's First Year Book
**Everything® Parent's Guide to Childhood
  Illnesses**
Everything® Parent's Guide to Children
  and Divorce
Everything® Parent's Guide to Children
  with ADD/ADHD
Everything® Parent's Guide to Children
  with Asperger's Syndrome
Everything® Parent's Guide to Children
  with Autism
Everything® Parent's Guide to Children with
  Bipolar Disorder
**Everything® Parent's Guide to Children with
  Depression**
Everything® Parent's Guide to Children
  with Dyslexia
**Everything® Parent's Guide to Children with
  Juvenile Diabetes**
Everything® Parent's Guide to Positive Discipline
Everything® Parent's Guide to Raising a
  Successful Child
Everything® Parent's Guide to Raising Boys
Everything® Parent's Guide to Raising Girls
Everything® Parent's Guide to Raising Siblings
Everything® Parent's Guide to Sensory
  Integration Disorder
Everything® Parent's Guide to Tantrums
Everything® Parent's Guide to the Strong-Willed
  Child
Everything® Parenting a Teenager Book
Everything® Potty Training Book, $9.95
Everything® Pregnancy Book, 3rd Ed.
Everything® Pregnancy Fitness Book
Everything® Pregnancy Nutrition Book
Everything® Pregnancy Organizer, 2nd Ed., $16.95
Everything® Toddler Activities Book
Everything® Toddler Book

Everything® Tween Book
Everything® Twins, Triplets, and More Book

PETS

Everything® Aquarium Book
Everything® Boxer Book
Everything® Cat Book, 2nd Ed.
Everything® Chihuahua Book
Everything® Dachshund Book
Everything® Dog Book
Everything® Dog Health Book
Everything® Dog Obedience Book
Everything® Dog Owner's Organizer, $16.95
Everything® Dog Training and Tricks Book
Everything® German Shepherd Book
Everything® Golden Retriever Book
Everything® Horse Book
Everything® Horse Care Book
Everything® Horseback Riding Book
Everything® Labrador Retriever Book
Everything® Poodle Book
Everything® Pug Book
Everything® Puppy Book
Everything® Rottweiler Book
Everything® Small Dogs Book
Everything® Tropical Fish Book
Everything® Yorkshire Terrier Book

REFERENCE

Everything® American Presidents Book
Everything® Blogging Book
Everything® Build Your Vocabulary Book
Everything® Car Care Book
Everything® Classical Mythology Book
Everything® Da Vinci Book
Everything® Divorce Book
Everything® Einstein Book
Everything® Enneagram Book
Everything® Etiquette Book, 2nd Ed.
Everything® Inventions and Patents Book
Everything® Mafia Book
Everything® Philosophy Book
Everything® Pirates Book
Everything® Psychology Book

RELIGION

Everything® Angels Book
Everything® Bible Book
Everything® Buddhism Book
Everything® Catholicism Book
Everything® Christianity Book
Everything® Gnostic Gospels Book
Everything® History of the Bible Book
Everything® Jesus Book

Everything® Jewish History & Heritage Book
Everything® Judaism Book
Everything® Kabbalah Book
Everything® Koran Book
Everything® Mary Book
Everything® Mary Magdalene Book
Everything® Prayer Book
Everything® Saints Book, 2nd Ed.
Everything® Torah Book
Everything® Understanding Islam Book
Everything® World's Religions Book
Everything® Zen Book

SCHOOL & CAREERS

Everything® Alternative Careers Book
Everything® Career Tests Book
Everything® College Major Test Book
Everything® College Survival Book, 2nd Ed.
Everything® Cover Letter Book, 2nd Ed.
Everything® Filmmaking Book
Everything® Get-a-Job Book, 2nd Ed.
Everything® Guide to Being a Paralegal
Everything® Guide to Being a Personal Trainer
Everything® Guide to Being a Real Estate Agent
Everything® Guide to Being a Sales Rep
Everything® Guide to Careers in Health Care
Everything® Guide to Careers in Law Enforcement
Everything® Guide to Government Jobs
Everything® Guide to Starting and Running a Restaurant
Everything® Job Interview Book
Everything® New Nurse Book
Everything® New Teacher Book
Everything® Paying for College Book
Everything® Practice Interview Book
Everything® Resume Book, 2nd Ed.
Everything® Study Book

SELF-HELP

Everything® Dating Book, 2nd Ed.
Everything® Great Sex Book
Everything® Self-Esteem Book
Everything® Tantric Sex Book

SPORTS & FITNESS

Everything® Easy Fitness Book
Everything® Running Book
Everything® Weight Training Book

TRAVEL

Everything® Family Guide to Cruise Vacations
Everything® Family Guide to Hawaii
Everything® Family Guide to Las Vegas, 2nd Ed.
Everything® Family Guide to Mexico
Everything® Family Guide to New York City, 2nd Ed.
Everything® Family Guide to RV Travel & Campgrounds
Everything® Family Guide to the Caribbean
Everything® Family Guide to the Walt Disney World Resort®, Universal Studios®, and Greater Orlando, 4th Ed.
Everything® Family Guide to Timeshares
Everything® Family Guide to Washington D.C., 2nd Ed.

WEDDINGS

Everything® Bachelorette Party Book, $9.95
Everything® Bridesmaid Book, $9.95
Everything® Destination Wedding Book
Everything® Elopement Book, $9.95
Everything® Father of the Bride Book, $9.95
Everything® Groom Book, $9.95
Everything® Mother of the Bride Book, $9.95
Everything® Outdoor Wedding Book
Everything® Wedding Book, 3rd Ed.
Everything® Wedding Checklist, $9.95
Everything® Wedding Etiquette Book, $9.95
Everything® Wedding Organizer, 2nd Ed., $16.95
Everything® Wedding Shower Book, $9.95
Everything® Wedding Vows Book, $9.95
Everything® Wedding Workout Book
Everything® Weddings on a Budget Book, $9.95

WRITING

Everything® Creative Writing Book
Everything® Get Published Book, 2nd Ed.
Everything® Grammar and Style Book
Everything® Guide to Magazine Writing
Everything® Guide to Writing a Book Proposal
Everything® Guide to Writing a Novel
Everything® Guide to Writing Children's Books
Everything® Guide to Writing Copy
Everything® Guide to Writing Research Papers
Everything® Screenwriting Book
Everything® Writing Poetry Book
Everything® Writing Well Book